FACES OF
LATIN
AMERICA

Latin America
Bureau

FACES
OF LATIN AMERICA

Duncan Green

For Catherine and Calum

980
G795

Latin America
Bureau

First published in 1991 by the Latin America Bureau (Research and Action) Ltd, 1 Amwell Street, London EC1R 1UL

© Duncan Green

A CIP catalogue record for this book is available from the British Library

ISBN 0 906156 59 9 PBK
ISBN 0 906156 61 0 HBK

Written by Duncan Green
Edited by James Ferguson
Additional research by Emma Gawne-Cain

Cover photographs: main picture, Alain Keler/Sygma; soldiers, Randy Taylor/Sygma; Kayapo child, Susan Cunningham; Guatemalan women, Mike Goldwater/Network; Diego Maradona, David Cannon/Allsport

Cover and book design by Andy Dark

Typeset, printed and bound by Russell Press, Nottingham NG7 3HN
Trade distribution in UK by Central Books, 99 Wallis Road, London E9 5LN
Distribution in North America by Monthly Review Press, 122 West 27th Street, New York, NY 10001

Printed on environmentally friendly paper.

Contents

List of tables and figures

Acronyms and Glossary
of Spanish and Portuguese words

AD	*Acción Democrática* Democratic Action (Venezuela)
APRA	*Partido Aprista Peruano* Popular Revolutionary Alliance (Peru)
ARENA	*Aliança Renovadora Nacional* National Renovating Alliance (Brazil)
ARENA	*Alianza Republicana Nacionalista* Nationalist Republican Alliance (El Salvador)
CEB	*Comunidad Eclesial de Base* Base Christian Community
CLAI	Latin America Council of Churches
COPEI	*Comité de Organización Política Electoral Independiente* Organising Committee for Independent Electoral Policy (Venezuela)
EGP	*Ejército Guerrillero de los Pobres* Guerrilla Army of the Poor (Guatemala)
ELN	*Ejército de Liberación Nacional* National Liberation Army (Colombia)
EPL	*Ejército Popular de Liberación* People's Liberation Army (Colombia)
ERP	*Ejército Revolucionario del Pueblo* People's Revolutionary Army (El Salvador)
ESG	*Escola Superior de Guerra* Higher War School
FAR	*Fuerzas Armadas Rebeldes* Rebel Armed Forces (Guatemala)
FARC	*Fuerzas Armadas Revolucionarias de Colombia* Revolutionary Armed Forces of Colombia
FMLN	*Frente Farabundo Martí para la Liberación Nacional* Farabundo Martí National Liberation Front (El Salvador)
FPL	*Fuerzas Populares de Liberación — Farabundo Martí* Popular Liberation Forces (El Salvador)
FSLN	*Frente Sandinista de Liberación Nacional* Sandinista National Liberation Front
IMF	International Monetary Fund
M-19	*Movimiento 19 de Abril* 19 April Movement (Colombia)
MDB	*Movimento Democrático Brasileiro* Brazilian Democratic Movement
MIR	*Movimiento de la Izquierda Revolucionaria* Movement of the Revolutionary Left (Bolivia)
MNR	*Movimiento Nacionalista Revolucionario* Revolutionary Nationalist Movement (Bolivia)

MRTA	*Movimiento Revolucionario Túpac Amaru*
	Túpac Amaru Revolutionary Movement (Peru)
MST	*Movimento dos Trabalhadores Rurais Sem Terra*
	Landless Workers' Movement (Brazil)
OPEC	Organisation of Petroleum Exporting Countries
ORPA	*Organización del Pueblo en Armas*
	Organisation of the People in Arms (Guatemala)
PCN	*Partido de Conciliación Nacional*
	National Conciliation Party (El Salvador)
PCS	*Partido Comunista Salvadoreño*
	Salvadorean Communist Party
PDVSA	*Petróleos de Venezuela S.A.*
	Venezuelan state oil company
PGT	*Partido Guatemalteco del Trabajo*
	Guatemalan Labour Party
PJ	*Partido Justicialista*
	Justicialista Party — (Peronists, Argentina)
PLN	*Partido de Liberación Nacional*
	National Liberation Party (Costa Rica)
PRD	*Partido Revolucionario Democrático*
	Democratic Revolutionary Party (Panama)
PRI	*Partido Revolucionario Institucional*
	Institutional Revolutionary Party (Mexico)
PRN	*Partido de Reconstrução Nacional*
	National Reconstruction Party (Brazil)
PRTC	*Partido Revolucionario de Trabajadores Centroamericanos*
	Revolutionary Party of Central American Workers (El Salvador)
PT	*Partido dos Trabalhadores*
	Workers' Party (Brazil)
RN	*Resistencia Nacional*
	(National Resistance) El Salvador
Sendero Luminoso (Shining Path)	*Partido Comunista del Peru — por el Sendero Luminoso de José Carlos Mariátegui*
	Communist Party of Peru — for the Shining Path of José Carlos Mariátegui
URNG	*Unidad Revolucionaria Nacional Guatemalteca*
	Guatemalan National Revolutionary Unity
WBT	Wycliffe Bible translators, also known as the Summer School of Linguistics (US)

altiplano	high plateau region, Bolivia
babaçu	type of palm tree
candomblé	religion of African origin
campesino	peasant
capoiera	traditional Brazilian slave dance combining both dance and ritualised martial arts
caudillo	leader, political boss
chicha	corn beer

comedores	communal kitchens
compañeros	comrades
conscientización	education and organisation to counteract injustice
Contras	Nicaraguan counter-revolutionary
criollo	Latin-American born descendant of Spanish settlers
descamisados	the 'shirtless ones', the dispossessed of Argentina
ejidos	communally-owned Indian lands
empate	confrontation
encomenderos	landowners and beneficiaries of the encomienda
encomienda	forced labour system
favela	shanty town
foco	small nucleus of guerrilla fighters
foquismo	theory of guerrilla warfare based on focos
garimpeiros	gold-prospectors
gaucho	Argentine cowboy
gringo	uncomplimentary name for North American/ European
hacienda	large traditional farms
huaynu	traditional Andean musical form
justicialismo	Peronism
ladinos	Spanish-speaking people of mixed Indian and Spanish descent
macho	male, masculine, tough
malocas	communal houses
maquila	manufacturing assembly industry
maquiladora	maquila factory
marianismo	female equivalent of machismo
mestizo	people of mixed Spanish and Indian descent
mita	forced labour system
nahual	animist spirit
pampas	Argentine grasslands
tamales	maize cakes, El Salvador
telenovela	soap opera
tío	'uncle', god of the underworld, Bolivia
toma	land invasion
tortillas	maize pancakes

SIERRA MADRE

MEXICO

ATLANTIC OCEAN

Havana
CUBA
DOMINICAN REPUBLIC
Mexico City •
JAMAICA
Santo Domingo
BELIZE
Kingston
PUERTO RICO
Belmopan
CARIBBEAN SEA
HONDURAS
GUATEMALA
Guatemala City
Tegucigalpa
EL SALVADOR
San Salvador
TRINIDAD & TOBAGO
Managua
Port of Spain
NICARAGUA
Caracas
San José
COSTA RICA
Panama
City
GUYANA
PANAMA
VENEZUELA
Georgetown
Paramaribo
SURINAME
Cayenne
FRENCH GUIANA

Bogotá
COLOMBIA

Quito
ECUADOR

Amazon

CORDILLERA

PERU
BRAZIL
MATO GROSSO

Lima •
Brasilia •

• La Paz
BOLIVIA

PACIFIC OCEAN

PARAGUAY
Rio de Janeiro
São Paulo

Asunçion

DE

LOS

Paraná

CHILE
ANDES
URUGUAY
Santiago •
Montevideo
Buenos Aires
ARGENTINA

**Latin America
and the Caribbean**

Peters Projection

Latin America in Figures

Country	1	2	3	4	5
Argentina	32.3	2,685	70.6	32.2	4.7
Belize	0.2	-	-	-	-
Bolivia	7.2	763	58.8	97.1	22.5
Brazil	150.4	2,280	64.9	63.2	18.9
Chile	13.2	2,454	71.5	18.1	6.6
Colombia	33.0	1,432	68.2	39.7	13.3
Costa Rica	3.0	1,659	74.7	19.4	7.2
Cuba	10.6	-	75.2	15.2	6.0
Dominican Republic	7.2	777	65.9	65.0	16.7
Ecuador	10.6	1,272	65.4	63.4	14.2
El Salvador	5.3	1,074	62.2	57.4	27.0
Guatemala	9.2	888	62.0	58.7	44.9
Guyana	0.8	568	63.2	56.0	3.6
Honduras	5.1	913	64.0	68.4	26.9
Mexico	88.6	1,954	68.9	42.6	12.7
Nicaragua	3.9	694	62.3	61.7	13.0
Panama	2.4	1,890	72.1	22.7	11.9
Paraguay	4.3	1,493	68.9	48.9	9.9
Peru	22.3	1,343	61.4	88.2	14.9
Suriname	0.4	3,460	68.8	33.0	5.1
Uruguay	3.1	2,908	72.0	24.4	3.8
Venezuela	19.7	3,035	69.7	35.9	11.9
Latin America	432.7	1,936			

Figures are for mainland South and Central America and the Spanish-speaking Caribbean

Columns and sources:
1. Population, millions, 1990; *UN Statistical Yearbook for Latin America and the Caribbean*, 1990
2. Gross Domestic Product per capita, 1989, 1988 US dollars; *Economic and Social Progress in Latin America*, 1990, Inter-American Development Bank
3. Life Expectancy at birth, 1985-90; *UN Statistical Yearbook for Latin America and the Caribbean*, 1990
4. Infant mortality per thousand live births, 1985-90; *UN Statistical Yearbook for Latin America and the Caribbean*, 1990
5. Illiteracy as percentage of population over 15, 1990, UNESCO estimates, (Nicaragua figure for 1985); *UN Statistical Yearbook for Latin America and the Caribbean*, 1990

Introduction

Carnival in Rio; Maradona on a cocaine charge; sleek, best-selling novelists on the TV; cholera in Peru; Inca ruins and condors; death squads and disappearances; lambada and salsa; snapshots of a continent which fail to add up to a sense of place and people.

Latin America has been portrayed to the outside world through stereotype and myth since *El Dorado*, the mirage of a golden king in a golden city, first excited the Spanish conquistadores' greed. Back in Europe, idealised accounts of the Inca and Mayan civilizations inspired Thomas More's *Utopia*. The West has both plundered and been dazzled by Latin America ever since. Today the new heroes are Latin American writers such as Mario Vargas Llosa or Gabriel García Márquez who have, in the words of one critic 'become the equivalent of the Amazon rainforest, providing oxygen for the stale literary lungs of the developed world.'

This book tries to fill in some of the missing pieces, to make sense of the jumbled images that pour from television, newspaper, novel and tourist brochure. It is about Latin Americans, not just generals and presidents, but the millions of faces of the shanty towns, small farms, mountains and rainforests, factories and plantations. It explores the processes which have shaped their lives, the jobs they do, where they live, and how they see the world. Through the lives of its inhabitants, the book attempts to capture the everyday ebullience and dynamism of Latin America, a world away from the cynicism and corruption of much of its formal political life.

Far from being the passive victims of circumstance, ordinary Latin Americans possess depths of courage and creativity, enabling them to confront with humour and grace a seemingly endless array of problems: how to feed and educate their families, find a home, improve their neighbourhood. In recent years, many such attempts at self-help have been led by women, struggling to free themselves from the stifling values of *machismo*. The indigenous peoples of Latin America have also belied their reputation for passivity by fighting vigorously to defend their ways of life.

They face a dispiriting number of obstacles. Internationally, Latin America is a region in decline, still largely dependent on the export of its raw materials, with an ever-diminishing slice of world trade. The debt crisis of the 1980s persists, sucking out the region's wealth as interest payments to western banks and governments. At home, the rural poor must struggle for a plot of land on which to feed their families in an environment devastated by deforestation, soil erosion, and unregulated mining and industrial development. Landless peasants flock to the shanty towns that encircle the region's cities, where they must improvise both a house and a means of earning a living if they are to survive. Although currently content to remain in their barracks, the military, who have rarely proved friends of the poor, have yet to relinquish their enormous power.

Faces of Latin America is published in the run-up to the 500th anniversary of Christopher Columbus' first voyage to the Americas. The quincentenary has aroused great passion on both sides of the Atlantic. Although the Spanish and many Latin American governments have insisted on commemorating the 'discovery' and the birth of empire, many Latin Americans have protested at the celebration of conquest. They point to the near extermination of the indigenous population by the conquerors, part of a system of colonial exploitation which persists, albeit in new forms, to this day. Instead, writers and indigenous groups have called on Europeans, North Americans and Latin Americans to reflect on the unequal relationship between new and old worlds, and to set about creating a new, free Latin America for the first time since Columbus first set foot on a Caribbean beach.

Once the Columbus media circus moves on, Latin America could once again fade from public consciousness in the West. If this book has one principal purpose, it is to celebrate the vigour, hope and inspiration that the region offers, and to urge its readers not to turn their backs on Latin America's people.

Duncan Green, August 1991

Indian woman examines tin ore, looking for higher grade deposits, Potosí, Bolivia.

Chronology

1493	Columbus introduces sugar-cane in Hispaniola
1545	Silver discovered in Cerro Rico, Potosí
1690s	Brazilian gold rush begins in Minas Gerais
1808-26	Latin American independence: Britain takes over from Spain as the major trade partner and foreign power
1913	Royal Dutch Shell begins drilling for oil in Venezuela
1930s	Great Depression — collapse of commodity prices
1938	Nationalisation of Mexican oil industry
Early 80s	Beginning of cocaine boom
1989	Collapse of International Coffee Agreement
1989	New deposits of silver discovered in Potosí

The Curse of Wealth

The Commodity Trade

1

'The Indians have suffered, and continue to suffer, the curse of their own wealth. That is the drama of all Latin America.'
Galeano 1973

Fourteen thousand feet up on the Bolivian plateau, Cerro Rico ('Rich Hill') looms high over the bleak mining town of Potosí. A giant rust-red spoil heap, it tells the story of Bolivia's cruel past and impoverished present. For two centuries after the Spanish conquistadores marched into the Andes and defeated the Inca empire, a stream of silver ore flowed down the slopes of Cerro Rico, through the furnaces and mints of Potosí and over the sea to Spain. Hundreds of thousands of press-ganged Indian labourers died bringing out the ore.

The silver rush made 17th-century Potosí into the largest city in the Hispanic world and earned Cerro Rico a place on the Bolivian national flag, but today only some fine colonial churches recall the days when the streets were literally paved with silver. For the Corpus Christi procession of 1658 the authorities ordered that the cobbles be removed in the centre of the city and be replaced with solid silver bars.

Boomtown Potosí was a chaotic, brawling city of 160,000 people, including, according to a census in 1601, 800 professional gamblers and 120 prostitutes. Today some Latin Americans still describe immense wealth with the phrase 'worth a Potosí', first coined by Cervantes in *Don Quixote*. But behind the splendour of the churches and the antics of the Spaniards lay the grim reality of the *mita*, the Spanish-imposed system by which each Indian community had to send a portion of its able-bodied men to work in the mines, working shifts of up to 36 hours, only to be swindled of what little wages they were due.

Cerro Rico is now an anthill of 5,000 tunnels, where self-employed miners scratch a perilous living from what the Spanish left behind. 'In the old days the veins were a yard thick. Now they're half an inch', says Marco Mamani, a young Indian miner. 'It's like a tree — the Spaniards took the trunk and left us the little branches'. For many years, Potosí has been the poorest region of the poorest country in South America.

Potosí's path from poverty to riches and back to even greater poverty is an extreme example of the process which has dominated Latin American development, the commodity trade. Although the exact definition varies, commodities are the raw materials which drive the world's economy. They include natural resources, such as oil and copper, and agricultural products like wheat or coffee. Europe's insatiable appetite for commodities was the driving force behind the centuries of colonial expansion which left the largest part of what is now called the Third World under the rule of competing European powers.

Ever since the Conquest, Latin America has produced commodities for export — coffee, tin, oil, sugar, and used the proceeds to import manufactured products from industrialised nations in Europe, and later from the US and Japan. The richer nations used their power to keep commodity prices low, playing one desperate producer country off against another and when necessary using their military and technological might to reinforce their supremacy. In human terms the unequal struggle between commodity producers and industrialised

TABLE 1: MAJOR WORLD COMMODITIES

Commodity	Latin America and Caribbean's share of world production %	Value of annual world trade
Oil (1989)	10.9	$165bn
Cocaine (mid 1980s)	100	$20bn
Coffee (1988)	23.9	$10.5bn
Cane Sugar (1988)	48.6	$8.0bn
Cotton (1988)	10.8	$7.6bn
Soybeans (1988)	32.2	$6.9bn
Bananas (1988)	42.5	$2.0bn
Copper (1986)	23.9	$2.0bn

Sources: FAO Production Yearbook 1989; FAO Trade Yearbook 1988; OPEC 1989 Annual Statistical Bulletin; World Metal Statistics Yearbook 1988; South America, Central America and the Caribbean 1991, Europa, London, 1990

Sean Sprague/Panos

Migrant cotton pickers, Bolivia.

powers has condemned millions of the Third World's people to lives of suffering and want. Only in the 20th century have the larger countries like Brazil and Mexico developed large-scale industry, and even then much of it has been under foreign control (see chapter 5).

Within Latin America commodities have chiefly enriched those engaged in exporting them abroad. Export crops such as cotton or sugar are more profitable when grown on large plantations, so the expansion of cash crops led to a concentration of land ownership and wealth in the hands of a few very powerful individuals. Mining interests were historically controlled by entrepreneurs like Simón Patiño, Bolivia's greatest tin baron, who rose from poverty to become one of the ten wealthiest men on earth. From the luxury of his European home, Patiño could make or break Bolivia's governments, acting as an absentee landlord towards an entire country.

The fabulous wealth of a few commodity exporters failed to 'trickle down' to the poor majority, since it was either invested abroad or used to import luxury goods. Farmers could make more money growing crops for export than by growing food to sell at home. The commodity barons felt no need to create a domestic market by redistributing wealth more evenly, since this would have meant giving up some of their privileges. The source of their wealth and power lay overseas; all they required at home was cheap and docile labour. When the workforce in their mines or plantations demanded better wages or living conditions, the commodity magnates were quite prepared to use the most extreme violence to prevent them winning. In El Salvador the heads of the coffee-growing families are still believed to run the death squads that have killed tens of thousands of peasant activists and trade unionists over the last 15 years.

White Gold

The European colonists pursued different commodities depending on the soil, climate, mineral deposits and accessibility of each region. On his second voyage to the Americas in 1493, Christopher Columbus brought sugar-cane to Hispaniola (now the Dominican Republic) and it flourished. Sugar subsequently fuelled Brazil's first and greatest commodity boom. Per acre the 'white gold' produces four times the food energy of potatoes and ten times that of wheat, and sugar was in great demand to feed Europe's new industrial working class. Brazil's sugar boom was centred in the North East, around Salvador de Bahia.

Sugar is a capital-intensive crop, requiring substantial investment to part-process the cane immediately after cutting, before it can be shipped off to foreign refineries. In Brazil, the Dutch West Indies Company initially financed the sugar industry. The monotonous cane fields rapidly spread across the North East, squeezing out food crops such as beans and maize, so that even in the best years of the sugar boom, there was chronic malnutrition. Today in the North East little has changed: on the ten metre strip of ground between the road and the barbed wire fences of the sugar estates, landless peasants hack at the soil with handtools, planting food crops. The verges belong to the state and therefore are the only places which the peasants can squat

and farm, safe from the depredations of the sugar barons. Every few miles, behind the fences, the opulent whitewashed house of a sugar grower shines among the green cane-fields.

An elusive El Dorado. Poor miners haul gold-rich soil at the open-cast gold mine, Serra Pelada, Brazil.

The Dutch later expanded into the Caribbean, which was nearer to the European market. In Brazil, the soil was already losing its fertility through overuse. By the end of the 17th century, the Caribbean had completely eclipsed north-east Brazil: production rose, prices fell, and the North East became one of the most deprived areas of the continent. Refugees fled its famine and drought-stricken lands and headed for the next commodity boom — the gold-rush in the south in the 18th century.

Sugar also left its mark on Brazil's racial composition. The plantations were worked by African slaves, victims of a deadly but lucrative trade dominated by British slavers. Today the people are largely a blend of black African and white European immigrant stock, and there is an unmistakeable, 'pigmentocracy'. Although the Brazilian government denies claims of racism, most black people are poor, most rich people are white.

In the last 15 years Brazilian sugar has had a revival as the government has struggled to overcome its dependence on imported oil by replacing petrol with 'gasohol' — sugar-based alcohol. The sugar plantations resumed their march across the North East, driving out new generations of peasant farmers and forcing them to take jobs as poorly paid plantation labourers. However, the days of the gasohol boom appear numbered. Brazil's own petroleum discoveries offer the prospect of self-sufficiency in oil, while the government has recently cut subsidies to cane growers.

THE CURSE OF WEALTH **9**

Hides drying ready for
export, Argentina.
Exports of wool, hides
and beef made Argentina
into a major world power
by the early 20th century.

Boom and Bust

Gold was discovered in the Brazilian state of Minas Gerais in the 1690s,
and came on stream just as Portugal signed a trade agreement with
Britain. Brazil's gold underwrote British industrialisation, and the
accumulated gold reserves later paid for Britain's war against
Napoleon.

Although Brazil's boom-bust cycles have been the most spectacular,
they have occurred at regular intervals all over the continent right up
to the present day. In El Salvador the indigo industry collapsed
following the discovery of synthetic dyes in 19th-century Germany.
In the northern deserts of Chile, the nitrate fields which had provided
fertilisers for Europe's agriculture, and over which Chile had fought a
war with Peru and Bolivia, became worthless overnight in 1909 when
a German chemist discovered how to make artificial fertilisers. In the
1980s, the bottom fell out of the Caribbean's sugar market as US
manufacturers switched to maize-based sweeteners and the Europeans
increased their production of sugar beet.

Some commodities have produced better long term results than
others. In Argentina, the cattle and grain trades laid the basis for
significant economic development which made Argentina perhaps the
tenth largest world power in 1914. In Brazil, the coffee boom which
gave the country 50-70 per cent of the world market between 1850
and 1950 made São Paulo into the economic boilerhouse of the most
powerful nation in Latin America.

The commodity trade has shaped both European and Latin American
history. The flow of gold and silver through Spain and Portugal to the
manufacturing nations of Holland, France and Britain fuelled the early

'Take his whole equipment — examine everything about him — and what is there not of raw hide that is not British? If his wife has a gown, ten to one it is made in Manchester; the camp-kettle in which he cooks his food, the earthenware he eats from, the knife, his poncho, spurs, bit, are all imported from England'

Description of *pampas gaucho* (cowboy) by British consul in La Plata. Sir Woodbine Parish, *Buenos Ayres and the Provinces of the Rio de la Plata*, London, 1839

'In all of Brazil's haciendas the master and his slaves dress in the products of free labour, and nine-tenths of them are British. Britain supplies all the capital needed for the internal improvements in Brazil and manufactures all the utensils in common use, from the spade on up, and nearly all the luxury and practical items from the pin to the costliest clothing...Great Britain supplies Brazil with its steam and sailing ships, and paves and repairs its streets, lights its cities with gas, builds its railways, exploits its mines, is its banker, puts up its telegraph wires, carries its mail, builds its furniture, motors, wagons...'

James Watson Webb, US Ambassador in Rio, c.1840

stages of their development as world industrial powers. After most Latin American nations won their independence in the early 19th century, Britain rapidly became the dominant economic influence. In 1824 the British Foreign Minister, George Canning, wrote to a friend, 'the deed is done, the nail is driven, Spanish America is free; and if we do not mismanage our affairs sadly, she is English.'

When necessary, the British government used its political clout to give its businesses a helping hand. In 1879 when Chile embarked on the War of the Pacific against Peru and Bolivia, the then US Secretary of State, James Blaine, commented, 'one shouldn't speak of a Chilean/Peruvian war, but rather of an English war against Peru with Chile as an instrument'. Britain's reward lay in the hostile deserts which Chile seized from Peru, where British capital bought up the world's greatest deposits of nitrates, used as fertilisers in agriculture.

By the early 20th century, Britain had been overtaken by the US as the major continental power, and most recently Japan and West Germany have risen to become major economic influences, although they do not yet dispute US political dominance in the region.

Rise of the Multinationals

Up to the late 19th century, European and US businesses used their capital and control over transport, processing and marketing to ensure they obtained a low price from local growers of agricultural commodities. However, by the end of the century increasingly powerful US companies had decided to take over production as well in order to achieve 'vertical integration' — control over each stage of production, transport and marketing in their chosen product. The pioneers were the banana companies like United Fruit and Standard Fruit which acquired so much power over domestic politics in countries like Honduras, that these countries became perjoratively known as 'banana republics'. In the 1920s, one banana baron boasted of his company's political might, observing that 'in Honduras a mule costs more than a deputy'. Since then the multinational companies have steadily extended their grip to most key areas of Latin America's economy, including virtually all mineral extraction and many agricultural commodities.

In today's agriculture, multinationals increasingly prefer to concentrate on the transport and marketing of a product, which are the most profitable areas. For example, just 37 per cent of the final retail value of a jar of coffee finds its way back to the producing countries.

Unilever is one of the largest food manufacturers in the world, and is a giant among multinational companies. Its annual turnover in 1990 was £22.3 billion, giving this one company an economy comparable in size to that of Colombia, the fifth largest in Latin America. Founded in the early years of the century by an amalgamation of British and Dutch companies, its operations now span the globe, employing some 300,000 people worldwide.

Like many of the largest multinationals, Unilever is less well known than the brand names of some of its products, including Flora margarine, Birds Eye and Walls frozen foods, Liptons teas, Persil washing powder and Calvin Klein perfumes. It operates throughout Latin America, from soap factories in Brazil to salmon farms in the south of Chile.

Multinational companies such as General Foods (coffee), Amstar (sugar) and Cargill (grain) make up an informal coalition with western banks and commodity brokers which exerts a powerful grip on the world market in each product. Their sheer size also places them in a strong bargaining position with third world governments who are competing for sources of jobs and investment.

Black Gold

Petroleum is the greatest commodity of all. As a fuel and source of plastics and chemicals, it drives world industry. Latin America contains major world oil exporters, such as Mexico and Venezuela, and many other less fortunate countries condemned to dependence on oil imports. Over the last 70 years, control over oil has become a politically explosive issue. In 1938, Mexico became the first Latin American country to nationalise its oil industry, and in the decades that followed other countries followed suit, weakening the grip of the seven great US and European-owned oil multinationals, known as the 'seven sisters'. Such was the importance of oil that governments were willing to incur US displeasure in the process, as when General Velasco's military government in Peru seized the installations of the International Petroleum Corporation in 1968.

In 1960 Venezuela joined Saudi Arabia and five smaller producers to found the Organisation of Petroleum Exporting Countries, OPEC, which became the king of commodity cartels. Mexico refused to join for fear of US trade sanctions, but both countries cashed in when OPEC shocked the industrialised world with large price rises in 1973/4 and 1978/9, taking oil from $2.70 to $40 a barrel. The oil producers

TABLE 2: OIL PRODUCTION AND RESERVES, top ten producers, 1989		
Country	Production (bn barrels/year)	Reserves (bn barrels)
USSR	4.6	58.4
USA	3.4	34.1
Saudi Arabia*	2.0	257.6
Mexico	1.1	58.4
Iran*	1.1	92.9
Iraq*	1.0	100.0
China	1.0	24.0
United Arab Emirates*	0.8	98.1
Venezuela*	0.7	58.5
UK	0.7	3.8

* OPEC member

Source: Statistical Review of World Energy, BP, 1989

Susan Cunningham

paid the price for their defiance, as recession cut demand for oil and consumer countries responded to higher prices by investing in alternative sources of energy and energy conservation. In 1986 the ensuing price collapse took the price back down to $10 a barrel.

State oil companies such as Petrobras in Brazil, Pemex in Mexico, and Venezuela's PDVSA became giants, wielding great economic power and channelling large amounts of cash back into exploration and development of new oil reserves. Oil transformed Venezuela from a rural backwater to one of Latin America's wealthiest nations, although the poor did not always share in the bonanza. The price of success was pollution and debt, as Venezuela borrowed heavily on the strength of its oil reserves. In Mexico, Pemex ran up a debt of $15 billion by the early 1980s.

State companies ensured national control over a vital resource and were able to use profits to benefit their countries. By investing in exploration, they managed to quadruple Latin America's known reserves between 1974-88, as countries such as Colombia and Brazil became significant new oil producers. Yet they were also plagued by problems; a shortage of qualified managers was aggravated as governments made political appointments within the bureacracy. Corruption and inefficiency reduced economic benefits, while nationalisation risked closing the door to the oil multinationals' modern technology.

Even in the late 1980s, as the tide turned against statism and governments promised the wholesale privatisation of state assets, they were reluctant to sell off state oil companies. Oil's enormous political significance, and the likely domestic opposition to such a move, meant that such companies were likely to be the last to go under the hammer, long after state airlines, telecommunications networks or factories had been sold off.

'Today, Caracas is a supersonic, deafening, air-conditioned nightmare, a centre of oil culture that might pass as the capital of Texas. Caracas chews gum and loves synthetic products and canned foods; it never walks, and poisons the clean air of the valley with the fumes of its motorisation; its fever to buy, consume, obtain, spend, use, get hold of everything leaves it no time to sleep. From the surrounding hillside hovels made of garbage, half a million forgotten people observe the sybaritic scene....

[Lake Maracaibo] is a forest of towers. Within these iron structures the endlessly bobbing pumps have for half a century pumped up all the opulence and all the poverty of Venezuela. Alongside, flames lick skyward, burning the natural gas in a carefree gift to the atmosphere. There are pumps even in houses and on street corners of towns that spouted up, like the oil, along the lakeside — towns where clothing, food and walls are stained black with oil, and where even whores are known by oil nicknames, such as "the Pipeline", "The Four Valves", "The Derrick", "The Hoist".'

Galeano 1973

Commodities and Development

Over the 500 years since the arrival of the Spanish, the commodity trade has exacted enormous social costs. In the mines the Spanish forced Indian labourers to work in inhuman conditions until hundreds of thousands died from the dust, poor food and disease. Today in Bolivia

TABLE 3: EXAMPLES OF COMMODITY DEPENDENCE, figures for 1988

Country	Principal commodities	% of Total exports
Argentina	Oilseeds/oils	38.5
Bolivia	Natural gas	36.2
Brazil	Soya	6.0
	Coffee	5.9
Colombia	Coffee	30.4
Chile	Copper	48.4
El Salvador	Coffee	58.3
Honduras	Bananas	40.8
	Coffee	21.31
Mexico	Crude petroleum	28.5
Nicaragua	Coffee	39.9
	Cotton	24.9
Paraguay	Cotton	41.0
	Soya beans	30.2
Peru	Copper	22.6
	Fish meal	13.5
Uruguay	Hides and leather	15.0
Venezuela	Petroleum	81.1

Source: *Economic Survey of Latin America and the Caribbean*, UN, 1988.

miners still die young, their lungs destroyed by dust and poisonous fumes which could have been removed by simple ventilation equipment.

In the countryside the introduction of each new export crop has led to more land coming under the control of big landowners and more peasants being expelled. The onward march of export agriculture has been largely responsible for the tide of displaced peasants who have poured into the continent's cities over the last 50 years, creating the sprawling shanty towns which surround the continent's small 'first world' city centres. By allowing peasant farmers, who generally grow food crops like maize and beans, to be driven out to make way for export crops, many countries have lost their self-sufficiency in food production — Mexico, where maize was first cultivated, now has to import it.

On a national level the commodity trade has proved an unreliable basis for Latin America's development. In the long term, commodities are liable to follow a boom-bust cycle, rather than steady growth, for a variety of reasons:

★ Substitution: the discovery of a cheaper or better-quality substitute, as in the case of indigo in El Salvador.

★ Exhaustion: either the exhaustion of mineral deposits, as occurred with Bolivian silver, or impoverishment of the soil, as befell the sugar plantations of north-east Brazil.

★ Development of cheaper production methods: the British smuggled out rubber seeds from Brazil and started a more cost-effective rubber industry in Malaysia; improved technology has allowed US tin can manufacturers to use less tin per can, thereby undermining demand for Bolivia's tin.

★ Changes in patterns of demand: in recent years the taste for better coffee in Europe and the US has increased demand for high-quality beans from Central America and Colombia, and reduced demand for lower-quality Brazilian beans.

Even while the market lasts, the price fluctuations common to commodities make planning extremely difficult and can lead to disaster. For example, in 1980, when sugar earned 17 cents a pound on the world market, the Nicaraguan government decided to build the Timal sugar mill, capable of producing sugar at 12 cents a pound. By the time the mill was ready in 1985, sugar's world price had dropped to four cents, invalidating the whole project.

To make matters worse, countries are often extremely dependent on one or two commodities, exacerbating their vulnerability to any sudden fluctuations.

In an attempt to avoid the problems of price fluctuations and trade wars between producer nations, many third world countries have joined forces in setting up price stabilisation agreements. But even when they have succeeded in guaranteeing more stable prices, these agreements have often merely encouraged producer nations to increase production, eventually leading to oversupply, a price war and the collapse of the agreement. In 1989, following the collapse of the International Coffee Agreement, the market price fell from $1.40/lb to

$0.70/lb in only 4 months. This was an enormous blow for a country like Colombia, where coffee made up nearly a third of all exports in 1988.

Many Latin American governments have recognised the pitfalls of commodity dependence and tried to avoid them. One obvious path was to develop local industry which would replace dependence on foreign imports. In doing so governments have had to challenge both the industrial powers abroad who benefit from the system and their local allies, the commodity exporters and importers of manufactured goods.

'Import substitution' has faced many problems. In order to protect fledgling local industries, governments had to prevent them being undercut by cheap foreign goods. This meant either an outright ban, or taxing imports to make them more expensive than locally-made products (tariff barriers). Any attempt to impose tariffs challenged the colonial, and later British or American, doctrine of free trade and left the country open to all kinds of sanctions. As one Argentine Minister explained in the early 19th century: 'We are not in a position to take measures against foreign trade, particularly British, because we are bound to that nation by large debts and would expose ourselves to a rupture that would cause much harm'. However, one nation in the Americas did successfully defy the British — the United States of America. In a prophetic speech the US President Ulysses S. Grant (1869-77) said:

> For centuries England has relied on protection, has carried it to extremes and has obtained satisfactory results from it. There is no doubt that it is to this system that it owes its present strength. After two centuries, England has found it convenient to adopt free trade because it thinks that protection can no longer offer it anything. Very well then, gentlemen, my knowledge of our country leads me to believe that within 200 years, when America has gotten out of protection all that it can offer, it too will adopt free trade.

President Grant apparently underestimated the speed of history — the US became the world's foremost economic power and its most determined advocate of free trade within 70 years of his death.

The world depression of the 1930s destroyed the market for Latin America's commodities and brought home the vulnerability of its economies. In response, many Latin American governments tried to follow the US example and opt for protection and industrialisation. In doing so, they came up against the problem of the unequal distribution of wealth in most Latin American countries. Because most people were poor, very few were able to buy manufactured products, whether imported or locally produced. This problem of a restricted domestic market meant industries could not develop mass production, and Latin America's elites were not willing to consider redistributing their wealth, through measures like agrarian or tax reforms, to create bigger markets for industry. The rush for industry is discussed in chapter 5.

The chewing of coca leaves, the raw material for cocaine, is traditional in the Andes. Coca is legal and sold in street markets. Bolivia.

Coca — The Latest Boom-Bust?

'Were it not for the drug's effect abroad, coca would be lauded as an ideal export crop' *Financial Times*, 15 February 1990

The recent surge in the production of coca, the raw material for cocaine, is in many ways just Latin America's latest commodity boom, and is already showing signs of being followed by the usual bust.

In the Andean countries of Peru and Bolivia, thousands of peasant farmers depend on the scrubby coca bushes for their livelihoods. They usually semi-process the leaves by treading them in pits filled with kerosene. The resulting coca paste is then shipped out to clandestine laboratories in Colombia, where it is turned into refined cocaine powder before being smuggled into the US and Europe. In 1988, there were an estimated eight million consumers of cocaine in the US, and the value of the world trade in the drug came to at least $20 billion, making it the second most valuable commodity in the world after oil.

The cocaine boom began in the early 1980s, even though the drug had been known for over a hundred years and was used by such illustrious figures as Sigmund Freud and Queen Victoria. The trade differs from the normal pattern for commodities in that Latin Americans control the profitable stages of its journey to market. Colombian cartels have come to control 80 per cent of processing, shipment and distribution, and take the lion's share of the profits.

In Peru, the major producer nation, income from cocaine is believed to equal 20 per cent of legal exports. In Bolivia, it brings in more dollars than all the country's legal exports combined. However, most of the huge profits generated by the trade never return to Latin America — they circulate in Caribbean, US and European bank accounts. By one estimate, only $1 billion of the annual $20-25 billion trade finds its way back to Colombia.

During the boom years, coca production did, however, offer a lifeline to poor peasants in Peru and Bolivia, thousands of whom made their way to the coca-growing regions and began cultivating the crop. Now, as with so many other commodity booms in the past, the coca growers are in crisis. By May 1990, in the Bolivian region of Chapare, which produces a third of the world's cocaine, prices had dropped to $10 for a 100lb sack of leaves, compared to ten times that amount in the mid-1980s. Desperate farmers were queueing up to destroy their coca bushes in return for government compensation.

The reason generally given for the collapse in the market price for coca leaves is the drug war between the Colombian government and the Medellín cartel, triggered by the cartel's assassination of Luis Carlos Galán, the Liberal Party's presidential candidate, in August 1989. Yet even before the drug war took off, the market was already beginning to collapse due to overproduction. Street prices in the US had halved between 1983 and 1988, and US government sources claimed that annual world production was running at twice consumption. The market was glutted.

In Colombia, the cartels, like the coffee barons before them, are trying to convert their economic power into political strength which will guarantee their long-term security. The drug war can be seen as a power struggle between the traditional establishment and a new generation of 'narco-capitalists', men like Pablo Escobar, a small-time car thief turned drugs billionaire and chief of the Medellín cartel. Significantly, the war has exclusively involved Escobar's group, while the much lower-profile Calí cartel, made up of traditional businessmen who are already part of the elite, has quietly carried on its business as usual, expanding into areas previously dominated by Medellín. In June 1991 Escobar gave himself up to the Colombian authorities in exchange for a commitment not to extradite him to the US. He faced a maximum eight-year sentence in a specially-constructed luxury jail, complete with a private football pitch and satellite telephone links which would enable him to run his multi-billion dollar cocaine business from behind bars. His period in jail could clear the way for Escobar to join Colombia's official elite as its richest member.

Cocaine's illegality has made it different from traditional commodity trades. Its production has remained in the hands of those peasant farmers desperate enough to run the risk of growing it, rather than being taken over by large-scale farmers. It has not produced any tax income for either producer or consumer countries, and there is no regulation over supply or quality. Finally, its illegality has diverted vast profits into the hands of organised crime, leading to enormous social disruption in both Colombia and the US. Many observers compare this to the era of prohibition in the US, when gangsters like Al Capone controlled the illegal alcohol trade.

On the basis of this analysis, a surprising range of organisations and individuals, from the *Financial Times* to former President Carter's drugs adviser, Peter Bourne, have argued for some level of legalisation of the cocaine trade. According to the US Surgeon General, cocaine killed 2,000 US citizens in 1988, compared to 390,000 tobacco-related deaths, and critics like Bourne believe that the real danger is not to the nation's health, but stems from the violence and criminality created by the drug's illegal status.

Given US domestic opinion, it is hard to see how legalisation could come about, but it is worth considering what effect it would have on the cocaine trade. Coca would become a normal commodity like tobacco; big farmers could move in and take over production from the peasant producers who currently grow the bushes, and the Colombian cartels would suddenly be faced by a trade war with major multinational companies. Although it might bring an end to violence on the streets of the US, legalisation would not necessarily benefit ordinary Latin Americans!

Epilogue

In 1989 a United Nations survey added a new twist to Potosí's tale. It showed that, far from being exhausted, twice as much silver is still in Cerro Rico as was ever taken out by the Spanish. Yet, rather than causing general rejoicing, the news provoked suspicion from local people. The problem with the new finds, estimated at $8 billion of silver ore, is that Bolivia has neither the technology, nor the capital to extract them. The only solution is to invite in multinational mining companies, a move which would touch raw nerves left by centuries of foreign plunder. As a final indignity, mining experts say the only way to extract the new finds, which lie in the top 1,000 feet of the Cerro Rico, is by using open-cast pits, requiring the beheading of the hill, Bolivia's national symbol.

Joe Fish

Shanty town resident shows the remains of squatters' shacks after they were burned down by police in an eviction. Cali, Colombia.

Chronology

1519-35   Spanish conquest: colonisers introduce new animals and crops
           and take back to Europe novelties such as tomatoes, maize,
           tobacco and potatoes; Spanish hand out land and forced labour
           to their officers through the *encomienda* system

1538   First slaves brought from Africa to work Latin America's sugar
           plantations

1881   Communal land-ownership by Indian peasants banned in El
           Salvador, enabling coffee plantations to expand onto Indian
           lands

1899   United Fruit establishes a monopoly over Central American
           banana production

1917   Beginning of Mexican land reform — the greatest in Latin
           American history

1950s on   Expansion of commercial agriculture throughout Latin America

1952   Bolivian revolution redistributes land and ends the near-feudal
           status of Indian 'serfs'

1959   Cuban revolution: state farms take over sugar production

1964   Military coup in Brazil: new government promotes agro-
           exports and the colonisation of the Amazon basin

1979   Nicaraguan revolution: half of the country's farming land is
           included in a land reform

Promised Land

2

Land Ownership, Power and Conflict

The priest was holding an open-air mass for the Indian coffee pickers. Women in their bright traditional costumes listened on rough benches under the hot sun, the men sat on the ground, hats in hands. Round about were their tents, made of transparent plastic sheets stretched over sticks. Maize grinders, essential for the staple food, *tortillas*, were mounted on branches stuck into the earth. A few possessions were hung from other branches, clear of the pigs.

In Guatemala such scenes are reenacted every December, as the coffee harvest starts and Indians are trucked down from their tiny plots of land in the highlands of Chimaltenango to live rough and pick coffee for several months. The wages are $3 to $4 a day, the food is worm-ridden and insufficient, but they come every year because they have no choice. Their land does not grow enough food to keep them going all year round, so they must pick coffee.

As the priest said mass, the owner of the coffee plantation, Loren, opened a beer on the verandah of his estate house. He had driven out in his jeep from his town house in Guatemala City, to visit his farm, a crumbling but still beautiful building with whitewashed walls, palm trees and a stagnant swimming pool full of tadpoles. Green fields of coffee bushes cloaked the hillsides.

Loren is white, owns a great deal of land, speaks French, English and Spanish, and is very rich. Back in Guatemala City, he plays the international coffee market by computer. 'His' Indians inhabit a different world; they own minute plots of land, are mostly illiterate, speak Kekchi and broken Spanish, and will probably never see either a computer or Guatemala City. Loren makes his excuses: 'I can't give them meat and vegetables on top of everything else or I'd go bankrupt. Anyway, those people are not used to it — they don't want it'. Outside, the priest exhorts the coffee pickers to 'work hard and be humble'.

In the mid-1980s, a third of Latin America's people lived in the countryside. Of those 127 million, just over 71 million lived in extreme poverty. The continent has vast underused areas of cultivable land, climates and soils to suit every crop, and good water resources, yet 15 per cent of its children are highly or severely malnourished. The roots of this hunger amid plenty lie in the patterns of unequal land ownership established from the first days of the Spanish Conquest.

Before the conquistadores came, most land was communally owned and largely used for arable crops. The most advanced civilisation, the Incas in Peru, had large scale irrigation systems, crop terracing whose remnants can still be seen today, and a storage and distribution system which ensured that everyone ate.

'I saw many horrific punishments in slavery. That's why I hated that life. In the boilerhouse were the stocks, which were the most cruel. There were stocks which made you lie down, and others which kept you on your feet. They were made from wide boards with holes where they forced the slaves to put their feet, hands and head. They kept them stuck like that for two or three months, for any unimportant misdemeanour. They used to whip pregnant women as well, but lying face down with a hole in the earth to protect their bellies. They used to really give them a good beating! They took care not to damage the child because they wanted them unharmed'.

'The rowdiest days on the plantations were the Sundays. I don't know how the slaves had so much energy. That's when slavery's biggest fiestas took place. On some plantations the drums started at midday. The hubbub started as soon as the sun rose, and the kids started to run around and get underfoot. The slave quarters was throbbing from early on, it felt like the end of the world! And to think that after all that work, people woke up happy.'

Miguel Barnet, *Biografía de un Cimarrón*, Havana, 1980, author's translation

The Spanish brought in cows, sheep, horses, wheat and sugar-cane to add to traditional crops like maize, beans, tobacco and potatoes. The Spanish Crown rewarded its troops with grants of land and Indian slaves. Under the *encomienda* system (a predecessor of the *mita*) in the Andean areas, conquistadores had the right to exact forced labour from specified Indian communities. In return they had to send a percentage of the proceeds to Madrid and convert the Indians to Catholicism.

From these massive land grants, three main forms of land ownership became established during the colonial period:

Plantations: these were large farms geared to exports, often using foreign capital and slave labour (the first slaves were brought from Africa in 1538). They were mainly in areas where the indigenous population was less advanced and soon wiped out by the European conquerors. The first great plantation crop was sugar in north-east Brazil, coastal Peru, parts of Colombia, and the Caribbean. On the plantations African slaves worked in gangs, often in the most brutal conditions, watched over by armed guards. An average plantation had between 80-100 slaves. Plantation owners were businessmen, motivated by profit, and their farms were usually both efficient and inhumane.

Haciendas: these produced for the domestic market, rather than export. They grew food crops for pack animals and raised cattle to feed the Spanish armies and mine workers. The haciendas were mainly in regions with advanced Indian civilisations at the time of the Conquest, such as Peru, Ecuador and Mexico. Hacienda owners valued

On the haciendas of Bolivia, prior to the revolution of 1952, *pongos* were peasant farmers who did three of four days of unpaid work for the owner in exchange for the right to farm a small piece of often substandard land.

'The *pongo* must bring his own food, even though he has a right to the leftovers from the master's table. So when he goes to fulfil his obligation, he takes with him an earthenware or copper cooking pot, quite covered in soot, a faggot of kindling wood and a sack of llama turds for fuel, and some supplies of food.

The *pongo* is given a spot in the great house for his quarters, some alleyway near the mangers and pigsties, and here he builds a fire to prepare his soup, boil up his corn-grits or toast his corn. But like a watch-dog he must sleep in the lobby ready to open the door for the master's children and for the master himself if he is a night-bird and likes to spend his time at the club or in a tavern.

His work occupies him from dawn until far into the night, amongst his labours are the following: to help in the kitchen, to look after the harness and mind the poultry. He must sweep out the rooms, the courtyards, clean the stables and pigsties and do the garden. The traditional colonial estate house is a little world, a kind of Noah's ark with every kind of animal in it. The *pongo* is builder, messenger, nanny and brewer of *chicha* (corn beer). He fills in the gaps in the phalanx of servants during the day. And at night he has other tasks to complete the dark rosary of his obligations: spinning, weaving, husking corn, *mukeo* (chewing corn for *chicha*, fermented with saliva) and of course, minding the doorway'.

Rafael Reyéros, *El Pongueaje*, La Paz, 1949

the power and status conferred by land ownership rather than profits; they more closely resembled aristocrats than businessmen and their farms were frequently underused and inefficient. The workers on the hacienda had a feudal relationship with the landlord, renting land in return either for a share of their crop (sharecropping), or for cash, or more often paying by working on the landowners' estate for a certain number of days a year. Hacienda owners controlled every aspect of their lives — some even ran their own local police and jails. The hacienda was a closed world where the owner was the main channel for contact with the outside.

Smallholder Communities: residual Indian communities in inaccessible areas tried to carry on as before despite the heavy tribute and labour payments exacted by the colonial authorities. These peasant farmers retained many pre-Columbian practices, such as communal ownership of land, a strong spiritual bond with the soil, and the use of simple technology such as hoes and digging sticks.

A typical peasant family today still lives in a one or two room shack made of wood or adobe. They own a few animals and handtools, and plough by hand or rented oxen from a better off local family. Families are large, sons helping from an early age in the fields, while daughters

Sean Sprague/Panos

Small-scale farming, peasant farmers harvesting potatoes, a staple food crop, Bolivia.

work both in the home and on the land. They usually grow traditional food crops such as beans, maize, or potatoes.

Unbridgeable Gulf

The legacy of the colonial system has been an extreme and growing concentration of land, wealth and power in the hands of a tiny minority of big landowners, while the vast majority of rural people have insufficient or no land, are poor, hungry and excluded from the political system. In Mexico at the turn of the century one per cent of farmers owned an extraordinary 97 per cent of the land, while as recently as 1962 one per cent of Peruvian farmers owned 80 per cent of the land. These dry statistics hide a system akin to apartheid in much of the continent, where an almost unbridgeable cultural and economic gulf divides the rich elites from peasant farmers.

After independence in the early decades of the 19th century, Latin America became increasingly bound in to the world economy. Foreign investment from the new industrial powers such as Britain and the US started to arrive, turning the old plantation system into the new capitalist farm. Waged labour replaced slavery, which was abolished everywhere in Latin America by the end of the 19th century, and farmers began to invest more capital in machinery and fertilisers. This model proved extremely profitable, and soon began to grow at the expense of the traditional, but inefficient hacienda system. As each new crop was introduced, the plantation system and the power of the plantation owners grew.

At the end of the 19th century, US companies started to buy up land themselves, rather than work through local farmers. The pioneers were the multinational banana companies, like United Fruit, which set

In the black community of Vertente, in the Brazilian North East, 60 families live crowded onto 5 hectares of drought-stricken land. It is April, and six months since the last rain fell. The only water supply is a trickle of a stream, where it can take four hours to fill a bucket. Dusk is falling and a shining green humming bird hovers in front of an enormous purple bud on one of the few banana trees that keep the community going. As it grows dark, sounds seem louder: children's voices, birdsong, the rustle of banana leaves. 'The banana trees are falling, because they only have one leg', says one old man, 'A man has two legs to support him, but now we too are falling.' The pot-bellied children gather round to dance, as the adults talk of their endless struggle for farms big enough to feed their families. At the moment they are sharecropping, meaning a large portion of whatever pitiful crop they harvest must go to the landlord. There is good soil lying idle nearby, but they dare not farm it for fear of reprisals. A greater proportion of Vertente's children die than anywhere else in north-eastern Brazil.

up banana enclaves in Central America and the Caribbean. On these enclaves workers lived in barracks, and were permanently in debt to the company store, while the multinational built its own railroads to take the bananas to ports and its waiting ships. The system brought scant benefit to the host country, which usually received very little tax income from the banana trade.

The concentration of land in very few hands, which grew as capitalist agriculture expanded, made Latin America the most unequal continent in the world. Big farmers, whether local or foreign, became rich and used their influence to ensure government policies favoured their own interests. Governments duly encouraged exports, kept taxes low on the luxury imports the elites desired, and made sure that the big farmers received the lion's share of state spending through bank loans, investment in roads and railways, and training and technical advice for their administrators. As they grew richer, the big farmers bought more land, whereas the peasant farmers were deprived of state help, credit and social services like health care and education. The gap between rich and poor grew ever wider. In her autobiography *I, Rigoberta Menchú*, the Guatemalan Indian leader Rigoberta Menchú recalls how her parents lost their land to incoming *ladinos* (Spanish-speaking Guatemalans of mixed race):

They weren't exactly evicted but the *ladinos* just gradually took over. My parents spent everything they earned and they incurred so many debts with these people that they had to leave the house to pay them. The rich are always like that. When people owe them some money they take a bit of land or some of their belongings and slowly end up with everything.

As the rural population grew, families had to subdivide their land between their children. Broken up, their small plots proved unable to sustain a family and both adults and children were forced to seek

A GREEN PRISON

'In the midst of a dense undergrowth of brambles, reeds and tall grasses that choked the abandoned banana fields, the clearers made their machetes whistle through the air as, bent double and breathing noisily like cattle, they hacked their way through the tangle. Clouds of thistledown flew up and settled again, sticking into their reddened, sweaty skin as they plodded along like sleepwalkers, heavy with weariness and enervation.

And, amidst all this confusion of labourers and banana trees, sun and pestilence, sweat and machines, creeks and malaria, rang out the cocky shouts of the foremen, the whistling of the overseers, and the arrogant, all-powerful gringo slang.

So it went on all day long. The peasants' exhausting toil stretched out until nightfall when, their legs buckling under them with weariness, they quit the green prison of the banana plantations only to be engulfed in the dispiriting prison of their soulless, barrack-like quarters.'

Ramón Amaya Amador, *Prisión Verde*, Mexico, 1950, translated by Nick Caistor

work on the plantations at harvest time. Millions more abandoned the countryside for the shanty towns that were springing up around the major cities. The combination of peasant farming and seasonal labour, known as semi-proletarianisation, has become the norm in much of the countryside. In Central America 70 per cent of the rural population are seasonal migrants, joining the coffee pickers of Guatemala in their annual trek to the plantations at harvest time. For the plantation owners, this system provides a cheap labour force at harvest time, with no need to pay year-round wages to regular employees.

Factory Farms

After the Second World War many economists saw further modernisation as the solution to Latin America's inadequate agricultural system. This meant increasing productivity and making Latin America's farms more like the capital-intensive farms of the United States and Canada. Since the 1960s, a new wave of state and foreign investment has transformed Latin American agriculture. In Colombia, state spending on agriculture increased 50-fold between 1950 and 1972. Most of the money went on grandiose schemes favouring large-scale export agriculture; for example, the Mexican government irrigated the arid north-west of the country which subsequently became a major producer of fruit and vegetables for the US market.

Driving through the rich Cauca valley of Colombia, for example, one passes through mile after mile of lush new sugar and sorghum fields, punctuated by billboards advertising the latest in tractors and pesticides. In Mexico's northwest the fast-growing fruit and vegetable industry has transformed the fertile river

Sean Sprague/Panos

Migrant cotton pickers move into their dormitory on a cotton estate, Bolivia.

valleys into a vast patchwork of irrigated fields and packing sheds resembling those of California's Imperial Valley. In southern Brazil, more than a dozen multi-million dollar soybean processing plants owned by US multinationals are scattered through the region, surrounded by large-scale mechanized soybean farms, none of which existed two decades ago. While a few countries such as Brazil, Colombia, Mexico and Argentina, are clearly in the forefront of the agricultural revolution, no part of the countryside has been left untouched by capitalist development.
Burbach and Flynn 1980

Following the military coup of 1964, Brazil provided the most dramatic example of government involvement in boosting agro-exports. Through lending, tax concessions, state investment and a guaranteed minimum price for farmers growing export crops like soybeans, southern Brazil has been transformed into one of the most modern agricultural regions in the hemisphere. Although a few Brazilian families have grown very rich in the process, they remain heavily dependent on foreign banks and multinationals to finance and buy their crops. For the mass of the population, the new crops have meant yet another round of land concentration, increasing inequality of wealth, and an increase in malnutrition as food crops are once again squeezed out by commodity exports. Rather than abolishing hunger in the countryside, modernisation has often made it worse.

In some cases foreign investment has taken the form of direct control: one US multi-millionaire, Daniel Ludwig, bought up over one million hectares (about half the size of Wales) in the Amazon basin in the late 1960s. Today his Jari agribusiness includes cattle ranches, rice farms and mills, forestry operations and a kaolin plant. However, in

'When Del Monte first sent its technicians to look at the Bajío [valley in Mexico] in 1959, they found a region ill-suited to the needs of the world's largest canner of fruits and vegetables. Grain production predominated, with corn and beans serving as the mainstays of the local diet. In Del Monte's own words, "vegetable production was small and limited to a few crops grown exclusively for the local fresh market."

The Bajío's land tenure system was also incompatible with Del Monte's needs. Due to the valley's population density, and the breakup of the large landed estates under Mexico's agrarian reform laws, the average land holding was small, ranging from 10 to 20 acres. Some of the land was held in ejidos, large state-owned farms that are subdivided into many small plots and worked by peasants. Mexican law prohibited the sale of these lands, and it also placed restrictions on land ownership by foreign corporations. For a company used to owning plantations and working with US growers who own hundreds or even thousands of acres, the conditions in the Bajío did not appear auspicious.

But Del Monte found the perfect tool for changing the valley's agriculture — contract farming. Under the contract system, the farmer or grower agrees to plant a set number of acres of a particular crop, and the company in return provides financial assistance which usually includes seeds and special machinery, as well as cash outlays for purchasing fertilizers and hiring farm labor. All these costs are discounted from the farmer's income when the crop is delivered to the cannery.

In a country like Mexico, where agricultural credit is limited or non-existent, contract farming is a powerful instrument. Del Monte revealed just how influential its crop financing was when it noted that 'in the early 1960s Productos Del Monte was practically the only source that many of its growers could turn to for short term crop loans.' By skilfully using its financial leverage, Del Monte affected the valley in several ways: it introduced crops that had never been grown there, favored the development of the larger growers at the expense of the smaller more marginal producers, and gained operating control over large tracts of land.'

'Canned Imperialism', *Report on the Americas*, New York, September 1976

recent years transnational companies have largely drawn back from the direct control which made them so unpopular in the past, leading to extensive nationalisation of their operations in the 1960s and 1970s. Instead, they prefer to sign contracts with local farmers, under which the companies provide credit and agricultural inputs such as fertilisers and equipment in return for buying the farmer's crops at a guaranteed price. This leaves the transnational in control of the profitable processing and marketing of a product, while the local farmers must deal with the local labour force and run the risk of a failed harvest. The transnationals lose little through this arrangement: one study in the early 1970s showed that of each dollar earned by bananas in the marketplace, only 11 cents finds its way back to the producer country.

In today's Latin America, high-tec farms resemble islands of modern capitalism in a sea of traditional peasant agriculture. The two worlds are intimately connected — peasant farms provide seasonal labour and often sell their produce to local agribusinesses. But power lies firmly in the hands of the big farms, with their near-monopoly on capital, credit, state support and access to world markets.

Fighting For Land

The three forms of land ownership — haciendas, plantations and peasant farms — have competed for land, and the expansion of one at the expense of the others has generated conflict, land seizures, political unrest and even war.

As commercial agriculture spread onto lands traditionally farmed by peasant families, the big landowners forced them out through a combination of money, legal trickery (for example, over the deeds to the land) and brute force. In the Brazilian Amazon, landowners commonly hire gunmen to expel peasant farmers from land they want to turn over to cattle. Peasants have responded by seizing land left idle by the landowners and organising political movements to demand agrarian reform and access to social services. Peasant movements are discussed in chapter 8.

On the plantations disputes have been over wages and conditions, rather than demands for land and credit. Since plantation owners are determined to keep wages as low as possible, these disputes have frequently been bloody, often involving the army and police on the side of the owners. According to Amnesty International, in 1987 alone there were 200 political killings in Colombia's banana-growing Urabá region. Most of the victims were trade unionists and plantation workers.

> A typical incident was the arrest by members of the [local army] battalion of 19 banana plantation workers in the municipality of Apartadó in March 1989. They were taken to the battalion headquarters in Carepa and twelve were later released. Four others were released after several days during which they were tortured, and three needed hospital treatment for their injuries. The bodies, or rather the remains, of two other workers were found on 4 April. They had been killed by having charges of dynamite attached to their bodies and exploded.
> Jenny Pearce, *Colombia: Inside the Labyrinth*, London, 1990

In many cases when local disputes were met with repression, they have escalated into national political protest movements. In El Salvador in the 1970s frustrated peasant activists decided they could not improve conditions in the countryside without a radical change of government. As a result, many joined new guerrilla movements, fighting in a bloody civil war in which over 70,000 people have died, mostly at the hands of the army and their associated death squads.

Over the last 50 years governments have tried to alleviate pressure on the land through colonisation programmes. These have consisted largely of irrigation projects which have reclaimed arid land in countries such as Mexico and Peru, and the deforestation and occupation of the Amazon basin in Brazil and the neighbouring Andean nations of Bolivia, Peru, Ecuador and Colombia. Governments have often seen these programmes as an alternative to agrarian reform, since they can ease pressure on the land by sending landless peasants off to colonise new areas. Unfortunately, the lands being colonised in the rainforest have often been unsuitable for sustained agriculture, and have been in remote areas, making it expensive or impossible for small farmers to get their produce to market. Colonisation programmes have often been chaotic and violent, as in Brazil where large landowners have moved in to throw peasants off the land, once they have cleared it for farming. In her autobiography, *Mi Despertar*, (My Awakening), Ana María Condori, a Bolivian Indian woman describes the colonisation programme of the 1950s:

> My father went there because our farm at home was all divided up and wasn't producing enough for all the children. Going on the colonisation seemed like a solution to him, because the government at that time promised people heaven and earth. They gave out publicity at the fairs in the Altiplano [high plateau region of the Andes where most Bolivians live] trying to get people to sign up — leaflets, posters, adverts on the radio offering ready-made houses, a hectare of land already cleared, schools, hospitals, paved roads, technical assistance and credit for the farm. But once people got to the colonisation zone, they found nothing of all that; the government handed out food to make sure people didn't actually starve to death, but apart from that they were left to their fate.

The conflicts generated by growing inequality in the countryside have made agrarian reform one of the hottest issues in Latin American politics. For both rich and poor, land is literally a matter of life and death.

The first, and greatest Latin American agrarian reform followed the Mexican revolution of 1910-17. Over the ensuing decades, especially during the radical presidency of Lázaro Cárdenas (1934-40), Mexico's vast haciendas were broken up and given out to 1.5 million families in the form of *ejidos* — communally owned land administered by Indian communities along traditional lines. However, the Mexican government failed to back up the programme with a reform of credit and investment to benefit the peasants. Credit is the essential oxygen supply for all farmers because of the cyclical nature of agriculture. Every year a farmer has to borrow cash to buy seeds and fertiliser, pay employees, and hire or buy equipment before the harvest brings in a lump sum which must pay off debts and maintain the farmer's family until the next harvest. Even after the agrarian reform in Mexico, big farmers have continued to receive most of the credit, and government spending on roads and irrigation has benefited their farms most. Agrarian reform has provided the security that goes with owning a piece of land, but has done little to improve the living standards of Mexico's peasantry.

The Bolivian revolution of 1952 also led to a radical reform of its almost feudal rural society. Large estates were divided up among the

sharecroppers who had previously been forced to give the landowner a large proportion of their crop in exchange for farming the land. Titles were established for Indian communities and the worst forms of labour exploitation were made illegal. In Guatemala a similarly radical land reform after 1952 came to an abrupt end when the Arbenz government was overthrown by a US-backed military coup.

Agrarian reform on a continental level took off in the 1960s. Following the Cuban revolution in 1959, the US government decided it had to end social unrest in the countryside of Latin America if it was to preempt further revolutions. In 1961 President Kennedy launched the Alliance for Progress, a joint Latin American-US initiative under which the US gave money and advice for agrarian reform programmes throughout the region, in countries such as Chile, Colombia and Venezuela.

However, agrarian reform as understood by Washington had two often incompatible aims: it sought to increase productivity by modernising agriculture along capitalist lines, and at the same time to redistribute land and wealth to the rural poor. In practice, modernisation came first, often causing further land expulsions and impoverishment for the peasantry. Landlords successfully resisted US pressure to reduce their influence, and instead benefited from the drive for modernisation.

In the 1980s two land reform programmes in Central America exemplified the gap between rhetoric and reality. The Sandinista government in Nicaragua and the Christian Democrat government in El Salvador both instituted agrarian reform programmes at about the same time, but with very different results. The Salvadorean reform fizzled out in the face of opposition from the coffee-growing elite and lack of credit and training, while the Nicaraguan reform succeeded in

'Now we too have land!' Peruvian peasant farmers celebrate after receiving land titles through the agrarian reform.

radically redistributing land and wealth in the countryside, breaking up much of the old landowning system and affecting about half of the country's farming land. After an initial emphasis on state farms proved unpopular, the Sandinistas rewrote the reform to first benefit peasants grouped into cooperatives, and then to hand out land to individual families. Although the Sandinistas' ideological conversion from statism to individualism took only five years, thousands of Nicaragua's more conservative peasants had already been outraged by the government's initial opposition to the peasants' age-old hunger for their own piece of land. Many ended up supporting or joining the US-backed Contra rebels who fought to overthrow the Sandinista government.

Where agrarian reforms have worked to the advantage of the rural poor, they have generally been associated either with revolution (Mexico, Bolivia 1952, Cuba 1959, Nicaragua 1979) or with the election of left-wing governments (Chile 1970-73, Guatemala 1950-54). In both Chile and Guatemala, the governments were overthrown by military coups, in part because of the hostility of the landed elite to their agrarian reforms. In Peru one of Latin America's few radical military governments, the regime of General Velasco (1968-75) also transformed the country's semi-feudal land system with a radical reform.

Some writers now believe that agrarian reform has declined in importance as a political issue. They claim that the growing urbanisation of the continent has reduced the relevance of rural questions, and that governments' growing police and military strength has allowed them to contain peasant protest. Nevertheless, a third of the region's people still live in the countryside, where they suffer the consequences of unequal land distribution and a system which invariably favours the rich farmers over the peasants. The modernisation of agriculture seems only to exacerbate the situation, while half-hearted colonisation programmes and agrarian reforms have done little to change the system, and in some cases, (see chapter 9) may have made matters worse. Experience shows that government initiatives like agrarian reform can only work when they are carried out democratically, in consultation with their supposed beneficiaries, and are willing to challenge the power of the big landowners. Only if such reforms take place, is there hope that a more just society can grow in rural Latin America, one which does not perpetuate poverty, hunger, sickness and an endless flight to the cities.

Unregulated industry in Latin America pollutes air, land and waterways. Chemical works, Colombia.

Chronology

1930s	Industrialisation leads to explosion of shanty towns and environmental deterioration in cities
1966	Brazil's new military government unveils 'Operation Amazonia' to colonise and industrially develop the rainforest
1980	Brazilian government decrees tax incentives for enterprises taking part in the Grande Carajas development programme
1984	Opening of giant Itaipú dam between Brazil, Argentina and Paraguay
1985	US Congress forces World Bank to temporarily suspend road-building loans due to their environmental impact and include environmental criteria in its project assessments
1988	Five million hectares of rainforest burned in the Amazon, bringing total proportion burned to one tenth
1988	Chico Mendes, leader of Amazon rubber-tappers, assassinated by landowners
late 1980s	45,000 gold prospectors pour into traditional lands of the Yanomami Indians, bringing disease and destruction
1990	Chilean government declares first ever 'environmental state of emergency' in Santiago.
1990	Incoming Brazilian president Fernando Collor de Mello appoints prominent environmentalist José Lutzenberger as new Secretary for the Environment

A Land in Flames

The Environment

3

The burning season starts in June in the Brazilian Amazon. The sky turns a dirty ochre, as a pall of smoke closes local airports and cuts off whole towns from the outside world. Each year the flames engulf a vast and irreplaceable area of virgin rainforest — in 1988, a region over twice the size of Wales was deforested.

Although many people in the industrialised nations see environmental questions in Latin America as synonymous with the Amazon rainforest, the damage stretches to every corner of the continent, blighting cities and countryside alike.

✭ In May 1990 the Chilean government declared its first ever Environmental State of Emergency in the capital, Santiago. The authorities ordered car drivers to stay off the streets and industries to cut their toxic emissions, while children and pregnant women were told to keep clear of the city centre, where air pollution had reached unprecedented levels.

✭ On the Pacific Coast of Central America, fishermen must watch as their catch is poisoned twice a year: when the rains start in May they wash accumulated pesticides from the cotton fields into the sea, killing marine life for miles around. When the rains end, and crop-spraying begins, a new dose of chemicals flows into bays and estuaries.

✭ In Mexico, acid rain from oil refineries is threatening to obliterate the region's history: it is eating away the stone inscriptions at the Mayan temple of Palenque, while at the great ruined city of Chichén-Itzá walls have been covered in a black soot left by the polluted rains.

The assault on Latin America's environment began with the Conquest. The subsistence economies of the great Indian civilisations were replaced by a colonial gold-rush mentality which aimed to plunder Latin America's resources, whether mineral or agricultural, as quickly as possible and send them abroad. When one resource was exhausted, another was found, with no attempt to build long-term sustainability. The philosophy was even applied to people: when Indian labourers began to die out on Brazil's sugar plantations, the plantation owners chose to ship in Africans to do the job, rather than try and reduce the death rate among the indigenous population. In this century, the urban environmental crisis took off with the wave of industrialisation in the 1930s and 1940s. Cities sprang up, sucking the rural poor into shanty-towns with few facilities. Unregulated industry poured effluents into the air and the water and millions of dilapidated cars choked the cities with carbon monoxide.

In both cases environmental abuse stems from a model of

development which has proved unsuccessful and deeply destructive to the very fabric of the continent. The greed and short-sightedness of both local and foreign interests have changed little since the Conquest — they still mistakenly treat the New World and its people as an inexhaustible and indestructible source of riches. Recent developments such as the debt crisis have merely accelerated the process, forcing entire nations to mortgage their environmental future to keep up with their interest payments to western banks. The voices crying out for a long-term solution involving sustainable, rather than destructive, development are growing louder, but remain scattered and weak.

Fight for the Forest

Deforestation has galvanised the green movement outside Latin America. Public opinion has been horrified at the spectacle of vast tracts of rainforest falling under the chainsaw, and the possible (though often exaggerated) implications for the global climate. Latin America contains 62 per cent of the world's remaining tropical rainforest, chiefly in the Amazon basin countries of Brazil, Peru, Colombia, Venezuela and the Guyanas. There are also smaller areas in Mexico and Central America, where the process of deforestation is both more rapid and much more advanced.

Accurate figures are hard to come by, but between 8 and 12 per cent of the Amazon rainforest had been destroyed by 1988 — some 40 million hectares. According to the UN Food and Agriculture Organisation, the rate of tropical forest destruction worldwide doubled during the 1980s.

In the Amazon forests are burned in order to turn the land over to pasture for cattle. The huge, inefficient cattle ranches have been encouraged by the Brazilian government with a variety of tax concessions and other incentives as part of its scheme for colonising the Amazon. One study in the 1970s showed that each ton of beef received $4,000 in subsidies, yet earned only $1,000 on the international market. Although the farms made little commercial sense, they were seen as an inflation-proof investment by companies or individuals living in the industrialised south.

The forest is also hacked down by poor peasant colonisers using 'slash and burn' methods. The precise division of blame between peasants and cattle barons is controversial. Up until 1980, cattle ranching accounted for 72 per cent of the deforestation. Since then, however, hundreds of thousands of peasants have marched in along the new roads like an army of leaf-cutter ants, while some of the tax incentives for cattle ranching have been removed in response to international pressure. Many of the peasant colonisers are themselves environmental refugees from soil erosion elsewhere or have lost their land to the onward march of soybean and other agribusiness in the south. Frequently they migrate following government advice to seek their fortunes as pioneers in the Amazon. What the government fails to tell them is that rainforest soil is unsuitable for sustained agriculture. Stripped of its trees, the fragile ecosystem rapidly collapses, nutrients

are washed out of the soil, and within two or three years declining fertility forces the peasant farmer to move on and cut down more forest.

Soil erosion turns rich farmlands into barren wastes, Oaxaca, Mexico.

In Central America, the hamburger, epitome of US consumerism, is the driving force behind the breakneck pace of deforestation. Unlike their Brazilian counterparts, whose meat is destined largely for domestic consumption, cattle ranches in countries like Costa Rica are commercial ventures aimed at the US fast food market. As in the Amazon, peasant farmers enter the forests and do the work of clearing the land for agriculture, but are soon squeezed out by declining fertility and pressure from cattle ranchers coming in behind them. Under cattle, the soil deteriorates further over 7-10 years, leaving an increasingly barren scrubland supporting fewer and fewer animals per hectare. By one calculation, Costa Rica loses 2.5 tonnes of topsoil for every kilogramme of beef exported. Even though beef production has boomed, squeezing out other food crops like beans and maize, domestic meat consumption has actually fallen as more and more of Central America's beef heads north. The average US cat now eats more beef than a typical Central American.

The costs of deforestation are enormous:

★ Deforested land is quickly eroded, and tons of topsoil are washed into the watercourses, silting up streams and rivers, clogging hydroelectric installations and disrupting marine ecosystems along the coast.

★ Deforestation disrupts the local climate, since the trees regulate the storage and release of rain water. By returning water vapour to the atmosphere, trees also encourage further rainfall. The loss of forests therefore makes both drought and flooding as well as mudslides more likely. In Panama, deforestation has reduced the rainfall needed to replenish the Panama Canal's lock system, endangering the Canal's future as a major trade route.

★ Many of Latin America's poor rely on firewood for fuel. As the forests become depleted, they must travel farther afield to scavenge for supplies, and in the towns the price rises to reflect wood's increasing scarcity.

★ Indigenous peoples who live in harmony with the forest have little hope of surviving sustained contact with incoming settlers, although some Indian groups are now fighting to survive and even benefit from the environmental onslaught (see chapter 10).

★ The rainforest is a repository of plant and animal species which, besides their intrinsic value, are a vital source of new genetic material — a quarter of all pharmaceutical products are derived from rainforest products, even though only one per cent of all Amazon plants have been intensively investigated for their medicinal properties. Tropical forest plants have provided treatments for leukaemia, Hodgkin's disease, breast, cervical and testicular cancer and are currently being used in AIDS research.

★ A number of investigations show that the commercial potential of the forest is far greater than that of the pasture which replaces it. In addition the forest can be farmed in a sustainable way, yielding rubber, brazil nuts and many kinds of fruit.

★ Most western attention has centred on the issue of global warming. The burning itself releases greenhouse gases (especially carbon dioxide which accounts for half the global warming effect) into the atmosphere, and the forests are no longer there to convert carbon dioxide to oxygen through photosynthesis. However, developing countries point out that 75 per cent of the world's carbon dioxide emissions come from the factories and cars of the industrialised nations, who long ago destroyed their own forest environments. They say the North has not yet put its own house in order, and therefore has little moral authority to tell Latin America what to do with its rainforest.

G. Foley/Panos

Sustaining Development

In devising ways to end the destruction of the forests, western environmentalists tend to fall into two camps, arguing either for straightforward conservation, or for 'sustainable development'. Conservationists want to preserve the forest from further contact with the outside world, turning it into something akin to a giant national park. The supporters of sustainable development argue that this ignores the numerous colonists and traditional inhabitants already living in the forests, and that what matters is to find a form of development which does not destroy the very forest on which these people depend.

A key proponent of sustainable development was Chico Mendes, the leader of the Brazilian rubber tappers who was assassinated by a landowner in 1988.

The martyrdom of Chico Mendes may prove a turning point for the Amazon rainforest. His death was widely publicised by the international environmental movement, and drew new attention to the problem within Brazil. In response to international pressure, the government of Fernando Collor de Mello, which took office in March 1990, appointed José Lutzenberger, one of Brazil's foremost environmentalists, as Secretary for the Environment. Several new extractive reserves have been created, including one named after Mendes, and Lutzenberger claims that the exponential increase in the rate of deforestation has been halted. From a peak of about five million hectares in 1987 and 88, only 2.6 million were destroyed in 1989 and initial figures for 1990 suggest a further sharp decline. Yet euphoria may be premature: 1987 and 1988 were exceptional years, with long dry seasons ideal for burning. These two years also saw a rush to clear

Devouring the forest. Twenty-four-hour burning, wood-fired gasifiers for lime kilns, São Paulo state, Brazil.

CHICO MENDES

'We realised that in order to guarantee the future of the Amazon we had to find a way to preserve the forest while at the same time developing the region's economy.

So what were our thoughts originally? We accepted that the Amazon could not be turned into some kind of sanctuary that nobody could touch. On the other hand, we knew it was important to stop the deforestation that is threatening the Amazon and all human life on the planet. We felt our alternative should involve preserving the forest, but it should also include a plan to develop the economy. So we came up with the idea of extractive reserves.

What do we mean by an extractive reserve? We mean the land is under public ownership but the rubber tappers and other workers that live on that land should have the right to live and work there. I say "other workers" because there are not only rubber tappers in the forest. In our area, rubber tappers also harvest brazil nuts, but in other parts of the Amazon there are people who earn a living solely from harvesting nuts, while there are others who harvest babaçu and jute.'

Cachoeira ("rapids") was the name of the rubber estate in the forest outside Xapuri where Chico Mendes was brought up and started life as a rubber tapper. He worked on the Cachoeira estate from the age of ten until his early thirties, when he began devoting most of his time to the rural workers' union.

In 1987 Cachoeira was bought by Darli Alves da Silva. Using a mixture of inducements and threats, he tried to drive out the 60 families of rubber tappers who had lived and worked on the estate for generations. Chico Mendes invested a great deal of effort and all his powers of persuasion and leadership to convince the rubber tappers of Cachoeira to stay where they were, and Darli issued death threats against him. In the second half of 1988, following the shooting of two youths during the *empate* [confrontation] at the Ecuador rubber estate in May and the assassination of Ivair Higino in June, the federal government sought to defuse the situation by signing expropriation orders for three extractive reserves. One of these was Cachoeira, where 15,000 acres were allocated to the rubber tappers.

This victory for the rubber tappers was also the death sentence for Chico, as the family of Darli Alves sought to avenge their defeat. The attempts on his life became systematic and on 22 December 1988 he was murdered.

Chico Mendes, *Fight for the Forest*, London, 1989

land before the government reduced its tax incentives for ranchers. In contrast, the dry seasons in 1989 and 1990 were shorter and wetter, so many trees were felled but left lying on the ground to await a dryer year. Since the satellites used to estimate the rate of burning only detect fires, unburned trees would not register in the figures.

More importantly, the long term structural reasons for deforestation remain. The vested interests of industrialists, energy producers, loggers, gold prospectors and ranchers still generate huge profits in

Crop-spraying on the outskirts of Lima, Peru.

the Amazon. Furthermore, as a large landowner himself, Collor has shown little interest in the kind of agrarian reform which would end the flood of land-hungry peasants from the south. More time and research is needed to show whether Chico Mendes' fight for the forest has doused the flames of destruction engulfing the Amazon.

It is not just deforested soil that becomes eroded. In Central America 40 per cent of all lands suffer a degree of erosion which undermines their productivity. The worst case is El Salvador, where an estimated 77 per cent of arable land is eroded. This war-torn nation is the most densely populated in Latin America and has an extremely unequal system of land distribution. In the Salvadorean countryside peasant farmers hand-tend tiny plots of maize and beans on steep hillsides, while down below on the fertile valley floor the rich landowners' tractors prepare the land for cotton or sugar. When the rains come, they wash the soil off the hillsides by the ton, yields decrease and the poor peasant becomes even poorer.

Downstream the silt, often laden with pesticides, devastates the marine environment. Siltation, pollution and wood-cutting have reduced El Salvador's 300,000 acres of mangrove estuary to a pitiful 6,800 acres. The loss is also an economic one: mangroves provide a rich breeding ground for marine life, and one square kilometre of mangrove estuary is worth $100,000 a year in fish and shellfish. Siltation has also greatly reduced the lifespan of a number of hydro-electric dams in the region, (themselves often damaging to the environment) by clogging up the lakes which feed the generators.

Despite efforts to show poor farmers the virtues of terracing, crop rotation and tree-planting, hard-pressed families are likely to continue to plough up hillsides or cut down trees unless a serious land reform gives them better lands elsewhere. In Nicaragua, one of the Sandinista government's main contributions to the environment was their land reform programme, which eased pressure on the country's remaining Etropical forests by giving peasants land.

Pesticide Poisons

An early morning bus ride through the cotton-growing area of Central America provides a stinging glimpse of everyday reality. As the bus passes plantations, its windows film over. Most of the passengers, knowing what to expect, close their eyes, slow their breathing, and cover their nose and mouth with a scarf. Those riders caught unaware feel their eyes begin to smart, their lungs involuntarily contract, and a bitter chemical smell starts to clog their noses.

Visitors to the area will likely rush off the bus to change clothes and to wash their stinging skin with soap and water. The local population is not so fortunate; their exposure to agricultural chemicals for the day has only begun. They will toil long hours in the fields, drenched with chemicals that crop dusters sprayed earlier that morning. Three out of four farm workers have no running water in their homes to wash off the day's accumulation of pesticides. Many bathe in irrigation canals or streams contaminated with still more agrochemicals, or try to wash off with water stored in a discarded pesticide drum.

Barry 1987

All over rural Latin America glossy roadside billboards peddle the wares of the big agrochemical multinationals. Names like Bayer, Ceiba-Geigy, Shell, Monsanto and Du Pont adorn adverts promising farmers prosperity if they administer just one more dose of chemicals to their crops. In jeeps and village bars, the plantation owners sport brand names such as Tordon or Gramoxone on their T-shirts and baseball caps. The pesticide companies claim to sell their wares in philanthropic pursuit of an end to world hunger, and that, in the words of one Bayer annual report, 'emotional attacks against conscientious agrochemicals research are attacks against humanity'.

In fact, nearly all pesticides are used on export crops, not food for local people, and the cotton and banana plantations of Central America provide some of the worst examples of pesticide abuse in the world. In the 1970s Central America consumed 40 per cent of all US pesticide exports. Chemicals like DDT which were illegal in the US were routinely exported and sold in the region, where about 75 per cent of the pesticides used are either banned, restricted or unregistered in the US. In mid-1990 the US Congress finally took action and passed laws preventing the 'dumping' of banned pesticides on third world markets.

There are several thousand cases of pesticide poisoning every year. In the children's hospital in El Salvador, 50 children die from pesticide poisoning every year. A number of factors exacerbate the damage:

✴ Cotton spraying is mainly done by light aircraft. Over half the sprayed chemicals miss the cotton fields altogether, drifting over neighbouring villages, streams and crops. Most workers on cotton farms live near the fields, and therefore suffer almost constant exposure to toxic chemicals during the spraying season.

★ Chemicals for hand-spraying frequently carry instructions in English, but even those in Spanish mean nothing to illiterate farmworkers. Governments and companies typically provide no education for plantation workers on the risks of pesticide poisoning and how to avoid them.

★ Safety gear such as masks and gloves is either not provided, or is designed for temperate climates and is unbearable in the sun-baked fields of Central America.

★ Farm managements are often extremely irresponsible towards their workforce. In the words of one United Brands foreman in Panama, quoted in *Roots of Rebellion*, 'If you get careless and forget to rotate [the workers], the next thing you know the damn Indian's bleeding at the nose all the time and you gotta pay for his sick care for the next couple of weeks.'

★ Saturation spraying often leads to pests increasing their resistance, meaning ever heavier spraying. Applications of pesticide on some farms have risen from eight to 40 times a year in the last 20 years.

★ Any protective legislation is almost entirely ignored and rarely enforced.

From the plantations, the pesticides enter the food chains of animals and humans alike. Milk in some Guatemalan cotton regions has registered 90 times the highest level of DDT permitted in the US, while Central American beef exports are increasingly refused entry to the US market because of pesticide contamination. They are sent home to be eaten by Central Americans.

In the early 1980s, the Sandinista government in Nicaragua won praise from environmentalists for challenging the multinationals and big agribusiness interests. It prohibited pesticides that were banned in their country of origin, began an education campaign among rural workers on the dangers of pesticides, and insisted that all instructions be in Spanish and colour-coded for the illiterate. It also revived a previous pilot programme of integrated pest management (IPM). IPM involves finding alternatives to chemical overdoses as a means of controlling pests. The programme used natural predators, particularly viruses and bacteria, to prey on the pests, with the advantage that once the predators have eaten all the pests, they themselves then die out. Another technique is that of 'trap rows' — planting a strip of the crop earlier than the rest, which then attracts all the local pests. An application of pesticide to that smaller area can then greatly reduce the total number of pests.

Big is Beautiful

Governments and international lenders have added to the damage done to Latin America's environment through their prediliction for 'pharaonic' projects. Especially attractive to military governments, giant dams, huge road building programmes, nuclear power, and vast mining complexes have wrought enormous human and environmental damage to the continent in the last 30 years.

Roads are the kiss of death for the rainforest. Seen from the air,

Susan Cunningham

Megaprojects;
megadestruction. The
Grande Carajas iron ore
mine, Brazil.

Amazonian roads are bordered by a corridor of deforested land, spanning roughly a day's walk either side for the peasant farmers who move in as soon as a road is built and start hacking back the forest.

Dams were originally hailed as a clean and renewable energy source — every environmentalist's dream. Small-scale dam projects, such as those of Costa Rica, which relies on hydro-schemes for 99 per cent of its energy, are indeed environment-friendly. They affect a small area, and do not create the social, economic or environmental disruption caused by the great dams. Elsewhere, notably in Brazil and Argentina, governments have built gigantic constructions, flooding vast areas of the countryside, displacing indigenous peoples and local farmers, and causing unpredictable climatic change.

On the border between Brazil and Paraguay, the Itaipú dam has been described as 'a monument built of raw superlatives'. For five years Brazilian construction companies poured enough concrete every day to build a 350 storey building. The construction contract alone weighed 220lb. The dam began operation in 1984, straddling the giant Paraná river which flows out to the sea as the River Plate between Argentina and Uruguay. It produces as much electricity as ten average nuclear power stations.

Dams on this scale carry costs not associated with smaller projects. The initial investment adds enormously to the country's debt burden — Itaipú cost Brazil $20 billion, roughly 20 per cent of its entire foreign debt at that time. Dams are usually accompanied by other developments, such as industries using cheap energy. Since they are often built in relatively untouched parts of the country, this can cause great environmental damage. A prime example is the Grande Carajas project (see below), for which Brazil is building the Tucurui dam, 50 per cent bigger than Itaipú. Furthermore, flooding leads to a massive loss of forest, and kills wildlife. The Tucurui dam flooded 216,000 hectares in 1984, killing 2.8 million trees which were first sprayed with chemical defoliants. In populated areas the valleys flooded by dam projects are often the most fertile farm land. In some regions, the sudden increase in standing water has led to epidemics of parasitic diseases such as malaria, and can even substantially alter the local climate. Finally, deforestation upstream can increase siltation rates, shortening the dam's lifespan and turning it into a huge loss-maker, even before environmental costs are included in the balance sheet.

The generals' fascination for giant projects has been shared by many western governments and multilateral lenders like the World Bank. In 1981 the World Bank signed a $330 million agreement with Brazil to fund a highway and feeder roads linking the industrialised south with the forested areas of Rondônia and Mato Grosso. At the time the loan was made, David Price, a consultant anthropologist to the Bank, warned in a report:

> If [the project] is carried out, land values will rise vertiginously, there will be an influx of settlers, and the pressures on the native population will be redoubled. More than 8,000 Indians in Mato Grosso and Rondônia will be affected. To entrust their welfare to [the government Indian agency] as it is now constituted would be criminal.

According to Price, officials prevented the report from being distributed within the Bank. Other World Bank staff pointed out that the road could provoke uncontrollable colonisation and that the soils which would be deforested would be unsuitable for agriculture. Despite these warnings the project went ahead and the road was inaugurated in 1984. Six days after the road's inauguration, the US Congress began hearings on the environmental devastation caused by the project, leading it in 1985 to pressure the World Bank into temporarily suspending payments on the loan. It was too late for Rondônia. By the following year the state's governor was lamenting, 'Rondônia is being trampled down by a migration of 180,000 people a year'.

International lenders and multinational companies have also been involved in some grandiose but destructive mining projects. The most spectacular is the Grande Carajas project in Brazil, which will cost an estimated $62 billion, and occupy an area the size of Britain and France put together. The EEC has contributed $600m to the project, while the World Bank is also a major funder.

The project is intended to open up the eastern Amazonia to industry and commercial agriculture. Its centrepiece is the giant Serra dos Carajas open-cast iron ore mine, which will have iron and steel foundries located nearby. Other projects include a mine producing eight million tons of bauxite a year, an enormous aluminium smelter producing for the Japanese market, and the Tucurui dam.

The environmental impact of the project takes several forms. The smelters will be fuelled by charcoal, requiring deforestation which it is estimated will double the government's official deforestation rate for the whole of Brazil. The smelters and foundries have no pollution controls, and emphysema, bronchitis and other respiratory diseases

'Uniformed men with pistols and clubs patrol the dusty road that cuts deep into the Jamari National Forest in Brazil — 500,000 acres of supposedly protected Amazonian rainforest...Inside the security cordon verdant Amazonian rainforest is rapidly being transformed into a moonscape of cratered, open-cast mines. Signs of dying forest are everywhere, some trees felled, others shrivelling under thick coatings of dust...The Brazilian foresty service...calculates that up to 240,000 acres have been damaged.

There is a cruel irony about what is happening to Jamari: the devastation is being wrought in the name of a British company which, 6,000 miles away in its London headquarters has embarked on a multi-million pound publicity and advertising campaign to convince its Western customers that conservation is its creed. That company's name is BP.

Barclays owns half of BCN Barclays Banco de Investimento SA, which, in partnership with Banco de Credito Nacional of Brazil and one of Brazil's wealthiest families, the Condes, owns two huge cattle ranching operations, Codeara and Agropastoril.

Since the late 1960s Codeara and Agropastoril have expanded to cover enormous amounts of rainforest. About half that land — an area the size of Warwickshire, has already been turned to rough pasture by chopping and burning trees.

Hundreds of miles northeast of the ranches, in the state of Para, the Anglo-Dutch company, Shell's.... Billiton subsidiary has invested in a $1.25 billion aluminium smelter...The obvious benefits to the community, however, have resulted in damage to a large area of ecologically important mangrove swamps. To build the smelter, about 50 acres of swampy mangrove forest were destroyed and 1,700 acres of forest, depleted before Shell took over, were razed. Biologists at the local university also claim a further 3,700 acres of mangrove were lost ..to provide fuel for the smelter.

BAT (formerly British American Tobacco) has an important stake in a paper and pulp manufacturing operation which is destroying Atlantic rain forest in the east Brazilian state of Espírito Santo.'

'The Ravaged Rain Forest', *Sunday Times*, 18 June 1989

are already on the increase. The men working in the furnaces have already started coughing up black phlegm. As in Potosí four centuries ago, the poor lose their lungs to enrich the vested interests.

In the late 1980s 45,000 impoverished gold prospectors (*garimpeiros*) poured in to lands occupied by the Yanomami Indians on Brazil's northern border. The Yanomami were previously one of the largest and most isolated of Brazil's indigenous groups. The miners brought guns, diseases and mercury, which they used in a crude process to separate gold dust from mud. According to Survival International, 1,500 of the 9,000 Yanomami died over a two year period, while in settlements near the mining camps there were almost no children under the age of two. At that rate, Survival predicts that

A poor gold prospector toils in the mud, pursuing a dream of sudden riches. Mercury used by the prospectors is poisoning Amazonia's waterways.

the Yanomami will be extinct by the end of the century.

In Amazonia as a whole there are an estimated 300,000 *garimpeiros* sifting through the region's alluvial silt for gold dust. Since 1980, they have poured over 2,000 tons of mercury, one of the most toxic of all metals, into the region's streams and rivers. By early 1989 its effects were showing: at the village of Gorutire on the Amazon tributary of Rio Fresco, a Kayapo Indian woman gave birth to a monstrously deformed baby. The Kayapo had never known anything like it, and the baby was swiftly killed.

Pressure from environmental groups has forced organisations like the World Bank to reassess the impact of their lending on the environment. US Congressional legislation in 1985/6 obliged the Bank's officials to include environmental criteria in their project assessments. However, western governments have done little to ease the pressure exerted by the debt crisis on Latin American economies (see chapter 5). The debt burden has forced governments to give top priority to exports, in order to earn the hard currency needed to pay the interest on their debts. Environmental concerns have therefore taken second place to the need for quick returns. Not only did much of the initial lending go to environmentally damaging projects, such as dams, but now further damage must be done to pay the debt back!

Some governments and western environmentalists have proposed so-called 'debt for nature swaps' as a means of easing the debt crisis while helping safeguard the environment. Under the swaps, an environmental group buys part of a country's debt from a creditor at a discount, then uses it to finance environmental projects in the country concerned. Such swaps have already taken place in Costa Rica, Bolivia and Ecuador, and Brazil's President Fernando Collor de Mello has also expressed interest. Debt for nature swaps have been criticised on a number of grounds, principally that they lead to only a minute reduction to the total foreign debt, and therefore do not represent a solution to the debt crisis. On a political level, they have been attacked for effectively selling off large areas of land to foreign interests, albeit ecologically conscious ones, which tend to look on the land as an uninhabited nature park and ignore local people.

Lax anti-pollution laws have made Latin America into a dumping ground for millions of tons of toxic waste from Europe and the US, releasing poisons into the environment which could endanger lives for decades. The waste spans everything from household rubbish to radioactive materials. Local environmentalists claim that US and European companies use bribes to circumvent what few regulations exist, misinforming Latin American authorities on the content and dangers of the waste. In 1978 dioxanes and benzene produced by foreign multinationals were buried near the Brazilian city of Cubatão. Several years later, housing was built on the dumping site and dozens of residents have since suffered blood disorders such as sickle cell anaemia and leukemia, according to a report by São Paulo state health officials. Some companies have made crude attempts to turn the region's poverty into a bargaining chip — in 1988 a New York company offered to build schools, hospitals and roads in San Clemente, Peru in return for the right to dispose of incinerator ash near the city. A public outcry forced Peruvian officials to turn the offer down. 'We are being forced to choose between poverty and poison', commented one dumping opponent.

Lost Volcanoes

The cities of Latin America are losing their volcanoes. In Santiago, Chile, people recall the days when the snow-capped Andes loomed over the city. Now they rarely break through a dense blanket of smog. The Chilean government has even proposed blasting a hole through the mountain chain to allow the wind through to clear away the murk.

'They think it's easier to move mountains than to control the bus drivers', explained a resident.

In Mexico, the two great volcanoes of the Aztecs, Popocatepetl and Ixtaccihuatl have similarly been lost to sight. Average visibility has dropped from 12km to just 3km in 40 years. Air pollution exceeds internationally acceptable levels in São Paulo, Buenos Aires, Santiago, Caracas and Mexico City. Mexico is probably the worst, as any visitor will agree who has had the misfortune to be there on one of the 225 days a year when a thermal inversion prevents the city's filth from escaping. Pedestrians weep as they walk through the streets in air that does as much damage as smoking 40 cigarettes a day. Mexico is uniquely damned by geography — it lies in a natural bowl where pollution collects, and at its high altitude of 7,400 feet car engines produce twice their sea-level amount of carbon monoxide. For the inhabitants of such cities, air pollution is far more than an irritant. The daily dose of poisoned air kills an estimated 100,000 Mexicans a year, and 70 per cent of all babies are born with unacceptable levels of lead in their bloodstreams.

Following the Great Depression, all of the larger Latin American nations embarked on a programme of industrialisation aimed at reducing their dependence on commodity exports and manufactured imports (see chapter 5). The consequence was a sudden surge in unchecked industrial growth and a chaotic exodus of impoverished farmers from the countryside to the cities. Latin America's cities rapidly became some of the biggest in the world — Mexico City and São Paulo both had about 15 million inhabitants by 1985. Even if population growth slows, Mexico City is expected to have a population of about 30 million by the year 2000, compared to just one million in 1930. A thousand migrants a day currently flood into the city, whose total population rises by 700,000 a year.

Protesters supporting Kayapo Indians in a campaign against the great hydro-electric project at Altamira, Brazil.

Three-quarters of Mexico City's pollution comes from its three million cars and its huge and filthy industrial complex. 'If the [US] Environmental Protection Agency standards were applied to this country', comments one US embassy official, 'Mexico would surpass the highest tolerable levels for sulphur dioxide, cadmium, lead, zinc, copper and particulate matter'. What he omits to mention is that many US and other multinational companies have been quick to relocate some of their dirtiest factories to Latin American countries precisely to avoid those EPA standards, and the increased costs they imply.

The growth of the cities seems inexorable, but could be slowed if governments undertook serious agrarian reform in the countryside and used regional planning to decentralise the economy. In the towns, the environmental damage could be reduced if factories and vehicles were regulated. However, such changes would need governments willing to stand up to vested interests both at home and abroad, who currently see no reason to stop the destruction.

City of contrasts. Rich city centre and poor shanty towns, La Paz, Bolivia.

Chronology

1920	First shanty towns recorded in Rio de Janeiro
1930s	Start of industrialisation leads to mass migration to the cities
1950	41.2% of Latin Americans live in towns
1960	500 people invade land in Lima to found the Cuevas settlement
1970	Population of Cuevas settlement reaches 12,000
1978	Argentine military government bulldozes shanty towns in clean up campaign before World Cup
1979	Informal sector now accounts for over half Colombia's jobs
1980	64.7% of Latin Americans live in towns
1985	Mexico City earthquake, thousands made homeless
1990	25 million Hispanics now constitute 10% of the US population

Mean Streets

4

Migration and Life in the City

The tourist hotels along Ipanema beach in Rio de Janeiro are some of the most expensive real estate in the world. Luxury tower blocks, their balconies bursting with foliage, overlook beaches strewn with perfect brown bodies sporting skimpy swimsuits known locally as 'dental floss'. Far above the beach, dozens of hang-gliders circle lazily down from one of Rio's extraordinary bare-rock mountains, to which clings the Rocinha *favela*, a shanty town which is home to 350,000 of Rio's poor. Shimmering in the heat haze, Rocinha looks down on the beaches like a bad conscience.

Shanty towns surround most Latin American cities, bulging with migrants from the countryside or the city's youth, fleeing the overcrowded tenements of the inner city in search of a house of their own. In Peru the poor have built their settlements on the barren desert around Lima. In Ecuador, 60 per cent of Guayaquil's population have built shacks over the muddy and polluted water of the swamps, their

---

TABLE 4: PERCENTAGE OF POPULATION LIVING IN URBAN AREAS 1965-88

Country	Urban population as % of total population		Per capita GNP (£, 1988)
Most Urbanised	**1965**	**1988**	
Argentina	76	86	1482
Uruguay	81	85	1453
Chile	72	85	888
Venezuela	70	83	1912
Intermediate			
Brazil	50	75	1271
Mexico	55	71	1035
Peru	52	69	756
Colombia	54	69	694
Least Urbanised			
Paraguay	36	46	694
El Salvador	39	44	553
Honduras	26	42	506
Guatemala	34	33	529

Source: *World Development Report*, World Bank, 1990

houses suspended on stilts. Some homes are a 40 minute walk along rickety boardwalks to dry land.

Between 1950-80, 27 million people left their farms and villages and joined the great trek to the cities. The driving forces behind this great human tide include war, famine, the shortage of land and the often illusory glitter of the city, with its promise of jobs, education and excitement. If present trends continue, Latin America will be more urbanised than Europe or the US by the early 21st century. Already the majority of people live in towns and cities in all but five Latin American nations — Honduras, El Salvador, Guatemala, Paraguay and Guyana (see table).

Contrary to the common image of poor, desperate peasants trailing into the cities, most migrants are literate young adults, frustrated with the lack of opportunity in the countryside. In Latin America, unlike Asia and Africa, women migrants outnumber men, reflecting women's lesser role in agriculture compared to the other continents. However, catastrophes like war and famine change the pattern, as people of all ages and educational backgrounds flee to the cities en masse.

Often migrants arrive in the main city by stages — first, they go to live in their local town, and from there board trucks and buses to the capital or other major city. As rural transport and communications improve, travel to the city becomes easier. Today, most rural communities already have sons and daughters in the city, who come home on holidays, bringing information about conditions and job opportunities, stimulating further migration if conditions are right. In Bolivia one Aymara Indian woman recalls:

> At that time I was nine years old, and was already seeing the older girls coming back from working as servants saying: 'I'm happy in the city. Life is great there'. To me they seemed physically happier; they talked beautifully, they had lovely clothes with embroidered shawls, with luxurious skirts. Pretty Indian girls, they looked. So I said 'Ah! I'm going too'.
> Ana María Condori, *Mi Despertar*, La Paz, 1988 (author's translation)

Unless driven by war or natural disaster, migration is usually a carefully planned operation; for example, a family will send an eldest daughter on ahead to find work and establish a base before the rest of the family follows. Few families who have experienced the precariousness of life in the countryside will take lightly such a leap into the unknown. Since they are mainly young people, migrants then have their children in the city, further boosting urban population growth.

The growth of the cities is a consequence of Latin America's drive for industrialisation (see chapter 5). As industry grew from the 1930s onwards, the prospect of jobs pulled in the rural population. In addition, as commercial agriculture spread further into the countryside, peasants were forced off the land and left with the choice of seasonal labour on the plantations or moving to the city in search of a better life. Although many migrants never found regular employment, they still lived better in urban squalor than in rural poverty. Their children were more likely to get some schooling, and there was more chance of

Julio Etchart/Panos

winnning eventual access to basic services like water and electricity. At a national level, wealth in Latin American countries is disproportionately concentrated in the urban areas, especially the capital. This enduring inequality is the driving force behind the continued drift to the cities.

Indian woman selling chewing gum at the traffic lights, Mexico City.

The same lopsided division of wealth between urban and rural areas takes place between countries. Table 4 shows that those countries which remain predominantly rural, such as Honduras and Paraguay, are among the poorest in the continent, while the more urbanised countries are among the best off.

Urbanisation is a serious headache for Latin America's planners, swamping existing services, and stretching such resources as water and food dangerously thin. In recent years pollution and congestion have added to their problems. Governments' attempts to check urban growth have had little impact, however, since they have failed to question the logic of the development model which was fuelling migration. The only exception has been Cuba, where the Castro government used its central planning of jobs, housing and food-distribution to dissuade would-be migrants to Havana, while investing in other, smaller cities and rural improvements. As a result, it managed to reverse Havana's growing share of the population. In some of the giant cities like Buenos Aires, congestion and pollution have started to make life so difficult that some companies are relocating to nearby cities.

Crossing the Border

Many migrants, especially those from Mexico, Central America and Colombia, decide to leave their country altogether. Their usual destination is 'El Norte', the promised land of the US, where they work

TABLE 5: POPULATION OF LATIN AMERICA'S LARGEST CITIES

City	Population (thousands)	Year
Mexico City, Mexico	13,879	1980
São Paulo, Brazil	12,184	1980
Buenos Aires, Argentina	9,968	1980
Rio de Janeiro, Brazil	5,615	1985
Lima-Callao, Peru	5,044	1981
Bogotá, Colombia	4,208	1985
Santiago, Chile	4,132	1983
Caracas, Venezuela	2,944	1981
Belo Horizonte, Brazil	2,461	1980
Guadalajara, Mexico	2,265	1980
Recife, Brazil	2,132	1980
Medellín, Colombia	2,069	1985
Monterrey, Mexico	2,001	1980

Source: J Wilkie et al, *Statistical Abstract for Latin America*, 1988

illegally in factories, on farms, or in restaurants in the hope of one day acquiring the coveted green card, or work permit. The route to the US is uncertain and dangerous, and involves running the gauntlet of unscrupulous 'coyotes' or guides, as well as US Immigration Service patrols. Migrants caught at the border are swiftly returned to their home country, often to begin another attempt to head north and find safety in the anonymity of the Hispanic quarters of major US cities.

In percentage terms, El Salvador is probably the leading Latin American exporter of people; 20 per cent of its five million population have left the country, half of them to the US. So many Salvadoreans now live in Los Angeles, that it is known as the second city of El Salvador. When they return home, their years of second-class citizenship in the US become transformed into wealth and status:

> In Reno, I was a busboy and later a waiter. When I went, I was 16 years old; I went illegally. I just decided to go. I dreamed all the time I'd live in the United States, since I was a little boy. I tried to get a visa, but they denied me; I was very poor. I never got a green card, but I got permission to live in the United States and they gave me social security. After four years, I came back here and married my wife and took her back into the US, illegally, through Mexico. Both my mother and father I brought there illegally; now they have alien [resident] status. The whole family's there now; they're okay. I got a good record in the States. I never got arrested.
>
> I worked very hard to get my money and then I got my properties here. I got my first property five years ago and my next property a year ago. It was a couple of years ago I thought about coming back to enjoy my real life. I was working in the

MGM hotel in Reno and was making a hundred, hundred forty dollars a night in tips.

But I don't miss the money. I got my hammock here. I've got a very good 26-inch color with remote control. I got three stereos. I just sold my four-by-four truck — the guerrillas bothered me too much for it — and my 750 motorcycle. I decided to run for mayor.

Jon Lee Anderson and Scott Anderson, *War Zones*, New York, 1988

The exodus has also changed the US. By 1990 an estimated 10 per cent of the US population, some 25 million people, were 'Hispanics', over half of them hailing originally from Mexico. Hispanics are concentrated in a few states, notably California, where by 1991 they made up over a quarter of the population. Successive immigration amnesties have swelled the number who hold green cards to prove legal citizenship and the right to vote, although so far Hispanics have made little impact on national politics. Although Cuban emigrés dominate political life in Florida, the Hispanic community has not found national leaders to play Jesse Jackson's role in galvanising black voters; there are as yet no Hispanic senators, and only a handful of Hispanics in the House of Representatives.

Not all migrants head for the US; inequalities of wealth and opportunity between neighbouring countries often force Latin America's migrants over the nearest border. In Buenos Aires the people of Ciudad Oculta (Hidden City) are shorter and darker than the rich white inhabitants of the city centre. Indian features denote the thousands of Bolivians and Paraguayans who have come to Argentina in search of a decent living. City centre stores are full of the latest labour-saving gadgets, yet the women of Ciudad Oculta cook in mud ovens, and watch over scruffy, barefoot children. Infant mortality is four times higher than the national average — one child in ten never reaches its first birthday.

Builders and Squatters

Recently-arrived migrants in Latin America's cities frequently stay with friends and relatives until they get used to their new surroundings, and find some way of earning a living. With space at a premium, however, they soon come under pressure to find a place of their own. Choices are limited: renting a tiny room in an overcrowded inner city tenement, or joining the increasing number of squatters in the shanty towns.

Shanty towns have transformed Latin America's urban landscape. In Rio de Janeiro the first were recorded in 1920. Today they house over a third of the city's inhabitants. In Caracas that figure is nearer two-thirds. Each country has a different word for them — in Brazil they are called *favelas*, in Argentina the evocative term is *villas miserias* (towns of poverty), in Peru the progressive military regime which came to power in 1968 insisted they be called by the more dignified *pueblos jovenes*, (young towns). In Chile they are simply *callampas*, (mushrooms), springing up overnight on the outskirts of Santiago.

Liba Taylor/Panos

Helping yourselves.
Tapping into the
electricity supply, Mexico
City.

Shanty-town homes are built by their residents and are nearly always illegal, either because the squatters do not own the land, or because they have no planning permission to build. Many squatter settlements begin with a 'land invasion'; a group of the urban poor, often including recent migrants, invades a piece of ground at night and hastily raises temporary shacks. If they succeed in fending off initial attempts by the authorities or the landlord to evict them, the temporary homes stand a chance of becoming permanent.

As time goes by and the settlement's prospects improve, residents start the long process of improving their homes. The improvements take up much of their spare time and money. The first cardboard and plastic shacks are replaced by planks or corrugated iron. Over the years brick houses start to appear, some even acquiring a second storey. Eventually they come to resemble other parts of the city, and become absorbed into the city's economy as increasing numbers of the houses are sold or rented out by their original inhabitants.

Squatter settlements face enormous initial problems. Often the land they have occupied was empty precisely because it was unsuitable for building. In Rio the poor cling to sheer hillsides, risking landslides every time it rains. In El Salvador's capital, San Salvador, shanty towns are huddled into ravines, often side by side with the local rubbish tip, or along railway lines. In Lima the *pueblos jovenes* are built into the desert, leaving the new arrivals at the mercy of private water suppliers. Typically, the most urgent problems are water and sanitation. In São Paulo, over a third of the city's houses, mainly in the peripheral shanty towns, have no sewer connections or cesspools. People use open holes or dry latrines, which often contaminate the shallow wells which provide their only water supply.

The key to improving living standards is organisation, and squatter settlements have produced some of Latin America's best organised and

most vocal neighbourhood organisations. The list of demands is
dispiritingly long: roads, drinking water, sewers, electricity, schools,
rubbish collection, health clinics and bus routes. Another major
battlefield concerns their illegality, since without proper legal title to
the land, the inhabitants will never be secure in their homes. Once a
settlement is established it can grow rapidly. In Lima 500 people
organised a land invasion in 1960 and founded the Cuevas settlement.
By 1970, 12,000 people lived there.

The authorities may respond to land invasions with violent attempts
at eviction, but in the long term many recognise that illegal settlement
and self-build housing are the only solution to the shortage of
accommodation. In cities like Lima and Mexico, local politicians
support squatters in exchange for votes, while political parties
frequently try to co-opt the neighbourhood organisations' leaders. In
Argentina, on the other hand, the military government bulldozed the
villas miserias while cleaning up the city for the World Cup in 1978.
Bolivian and Paraguayan migrants were beaten up, then herded onto
trains and trucks for deportation. Often, however, the settlements'
successes produce a spirit of optimism and self-confidence which is
lacking in the gloomy tenements of the city centre.

> ### BUILDING A SELF-HELP HOME
>
> Alfonso and Isabel Rodriguez live with their three children in a low-income settlement in the south of Valencia, a Venezuelan city with around 800,000 inhabitants. The population has grown rapidly as manufacturing plants have moved to the city in preference to the crowded conditions found in Caracas. Alfonso works in the Ford plant. He was born in the mountain state of Mérida and arrived in Valencia in 1975 after an uncle told him that work was available. He stayed with his uncle for a while in a consolidated self-help house in the south of the city and then moved into rental accommodation nearer the centre. He met Isabel, who had been born in Valencia, six months later. They rented a new home together and stayed there for 18 months. Two years later, he managed to obtain a plot of land through an invasion. The invasion was organised by an employee of the local authority who was trying to win support for a councillor who was hoping to be re-elected that year. One hundred and twenty families established rudimentary shacks early one Sunday morning. Because of the protection given by the councillor there was little trouble with the police and the settlers soon began to improve their accommodation. Since Alfonso had a reasonably well-paid job, he could afford to buy cement and bricks with which to improve the house. In addition, he sold half of the 20 by 35 metre plot he had obtained to two other families; this was sufficient to buy the rest of the materials he needed. He could also employ, on an occasional basis, a friend who worked in the construction industry. Progress on the house was slow but steady. Since he had to work at his paid job during the week, he could do little except at weekends. Even then there were interruptions, family visits, the occasional fiesta, demands by the children to go out. Isabel helped with some of the lighter jobs when she could, but three rapid pregnancies and a miscarriage limited her participation in the actual building.
>
> By 1985, five years later, the house had three rooms. It was not pretty to look at but it was solidly built and the roof kept out the rain. It had electricity, stolen from the mains by a neighbour who worked for the electricity board. Water had been provided by the government during the last election campaign, but sewerage was still lacking. There was a school in the next settlement, and the eldest child would start to attend it in a couple of years' time.
>
> Gilbert 1990

The only alternative to uneasy coexistence between authorities and squatters is a serious urban land reform. There are many parallels between the rural land crisis and that in the cities. Like agrarian reform, an urban land reform requires far more than mere distribution of land if it is to succeed. Settlers also need access to credit to enable them to buy building materials, physical infrastructure such as roads and electricity, and technical advice on building. Just as in the countryside, the big urban landowners resist any attempt to challenge their control, and are usually successful in their efforts.

Visitors to Latin America may see little of life in the shanty towns

At the settlement Márquez del Callao, hundreds of children line up in front of the dining hall. They begin two hours before noon, every day, plate and spoon in hand. They beg and shout in hopes of getting a free portion from the mothers who organised this communal kitchen. Forty mothers cook 400 portions a day, half for member families and half for the hungry children.

These organisations depend on donations of oil, oatmeal and flour, and on their own purchases. In their search for better prices, the women will frequently contact the producers directly. This form of organising has proven so successful that, by 1986, 800 *comedores* (communal canteens) were represented by a National Commission of Comedores. Some are independent while others may be funded by the Church, the state, political parties or development agencies.

Rosario de Meléndez, recently laid off from a stocking factory, is a new member of the Glass of Milk committee of the neighbourhood of El Carcamo. When it is her turn, she gets up at five in the morning, turns on the stove and begins to heat a huge pot of milk, oatmeal, some sugar, cloves and cinnamon. She knows that at seven the children will begin lining up at the door of her house waiting for the hot milk. Each member of her committee contributes 200 *intis* (less than 10 cents) a week for the purchase of kerosene, cocoa and cloves.

By working together, these women come to see their oppression as a social ill and open up new horizons for themselves. The voice of the women, before silent, is making itself heard. Formerly taboo subjects are now discussed. The mere fact that they are no longer shut up in their houses cooking for their husbands transforms relationships within the home. The women like to talk about the time one leader arrived at a meeting barefoot because her husband had hidden her shoes to keep her from going.

Carolina Carlessi, 'The Reconquest', *Report on the Americas*, New York, November 1989

and tenements, since tourists' hotels and friends or contacts are usually in the wealthier areas, either pleasant suburbs or modern city centres. The level of crime in the shanty towns, while often exaggerated, is a further powerful disincentive to travelling into the poorer quarters. In the middle-class areas, families lead a relatively comfortable existence, aided by servants and access to household appliances.

As a proportion of the total population the middle class in Latin America is far smaller than in Europe or the US, and a vast gulf separates it from the poor masses of the slums. Along the main road north out of Recife, in Brazil, car drivers are even spared the sight of the long lines of cardboard and wooden shacks. A municipal billboard hundreds of yards long apologises for the 'inconvenience caused by temporary housing'. The billboard can hide the houses from view, but not the hot stench of the canal passing through the encampment. Scrawny children swim in the polluted waters. In places the canal banks are made up entirely of rubbish.

Lucio Quispe/Cusco/TAFOS

A community comes
together to build its own
street, Cusco, Peru.

Scraping a Living

New Year's Eve on the road to Mexico City's airport. When the cars
pull up at the traffic lights, a firebreather steps out in front of the
queue. A jet of flame lances across the night, lighting up a shiny face,
glazed eyes and a hand clutching a bottle of petrol. After the show, the
ragged performer goes up the line of car windows, hand outstretched.
On New Year's Eve the drivers are in a good mood and he does well.

Although many migrants come to the city looking for regular paid
jobs in industry, few find them. Despite Latin America's attempts at
industrialisation, most of the investment has been in capital-intensive
industry where machines do the work instead of people.
Consequently, manufacturing employment has failed to keep up with
the demand for jobs. In most Latin American nations, social security
provision only applies to those in regular employment for the state or
big companies — unemployment and maternity benefits or pensions
are not available to the majority. Without the safety net of a welfare
state, migrants unable to find a way of earning an income face
starvation, and most of the inhabitants of the shanty towns are forced
to find work in what has become known as the 'informal sector' of the
economy.

The informal sector is the umbrella term for a mass of different tasks
including street selling, domestic service, odd-jobs, casual building
labour, small-scale industry recycling tyres into sandals, picking
through garbage for tin cans and paper, or even firebreathing at traffic
lights.

Such work is in stark contrast to the formal sector of waged jobs
more familiar to those in the industrialised nations. Formal-sector jobs
are provided by large private and state-owned businesses, subsidiaries

of multinational companies, and the public sector. Often such jobs take place in the westernised centres of the cities, with their office blocks, government departments and shops, while economic life in the poor fringes of the city operates through the networks of the informal sector.

To the visitor, the street traders are the most striking members of the informal economy. In La Paz, the Avenida Buenos Aires and adjoining streets are the site of the capital's biggest street market. Young men dressed in denims sell the latest line in microwaves or stereos, smuggled in from Brazil, while one street along, Indian women sit patiently in their bowler hats and ponchos, selling dried llama foetuses which are buried under the foundations of most new houses in Bolivia to bring good luck. Herbal remedies, BMX bicycles, imported disposable nappies, toiletries and pots and pans — the list of available goods is endless.

As the numbers of the urban poor have grown, so has the informal sector. In Colombia it rose from employing 30 per cent of the economically active population in 1960 to 52 per cent in 1979. In the continent as a whole the service sector, which is largely made up of informal jobs, accounts for two-thirds of all employment.

The comparison between formal and informal sectors has led some economists to talk of two parallel circuits existing within the urban economy. The first circuit is a formal, western-style world of banks, factories and supermarkets, existing alongside a second circuit of street traders, money lenders and casual labourers. The two worlds are linked, however, since the informal sector provides low-cost services which often benefit the formal economy. The system resembles agriculture, where modern capital-intensive commercial agriculture exists alongside traditional labour-intensive peasant farming, which supplies it with cheap labour at harvest time.

In *The Other Path*, a ground-breaking book published in 1989, Peruvian economist Hernando de Soto took a new look at the role of the informal sector in Latin America's economic future. Following extensive research in Lima, de Soto argued that the informal sector is a potential source of entrepreneurs who could bring growth and prosperity to Peru. However, this nascent capitalist class is held back by the state's bureaucratic red tape. To demonstrate the obstructive role of the state, de Soto tried to register a fictitious textile factory by going through the proper legal channels. Along the way, he was asked for ten separate bribes (two of which he was compelled to pay) and took 289 days to complete eleven separate procedures for legal registration. At no point did the authorities realise that the factory did not exist.

De Soto argues that Peruvians join the informal sector because the red tape makes legality impossibly difficult, asphixiating aspiring entrepreneurs. The answer, he argues, is to remove the red tape and give the informal sector the recognition it deserves, at which point he believes it will become the engine for growth. Even operating illegally, the sector has already generated enormous wealth. He calculates that the value of the self-help housing built by Lima's poor over the past 40 years comes to more than $8 billion. 'This new business class is a

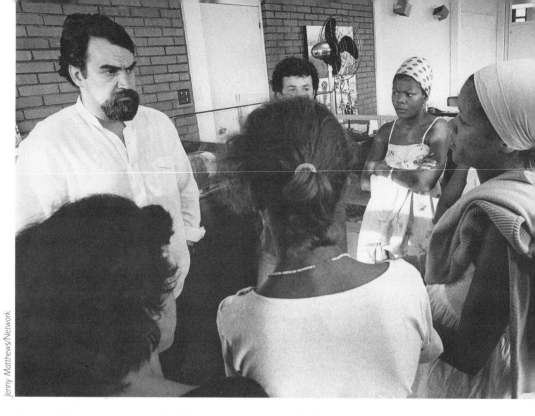

Angry faces. Women visit the water authority to demand more standpipes for their shanty town, Vila Prudente, São Paulo.

Jenny Matthews/Network

very valuable resource', he concludes, 'it is the human capital essential for economic takeoff'.

Although de Soto's work has made people look at the informal sector as something other than a dustbin for society's poor, it has been attacked both for flaws in its original research, and because it over-emphasises legal questions. Even if red tape were removed, small informal sector operators would still face problems analogous to those confronted by small farmers — the difficulty in raising bank loans, lack of technical assistance and government help, and a government which is far more influenced by the vested interests of big business than by street traders and small businesses. By analogy with Latin America's experience of agrarian reform, an urban reform which would truly benefit the informal sector can only be achieved by challenging the power of big businesses and involving the informal sector in planning and carrying through such a reform. This would be a revolutionary programme far removed from both the statism of countries like Cuba, and the ideas of thinkers like Hernando de Soto.

Instead, de Soto's suggested free market reforms in Peru resemble the agrarian reforms which sought to modernise agriculture at the expense of the old hacienda system. Just as the expansion of commercial agriculture harmed peasant farmers, de Soto's plans would flood the market with cheap manufactured imports and drive informal-sector producers out of business. The danger is that *The Other Path*, which has been publicly praised by President George Bush among others, will be used merely to justify governments abdicating responsibility for regulating commerce and industry, a process which works to the advantage of larger enterprises and can do far more harm than good to Latin America's poor.

The great divide. Cleaning car screens, Lima, Peru.

Chronology

1929	Wall Street Crash and ensuing depression in the US and Europe pushes Latin America into industrialisation
1958	Brazil becomes Latin America's leading industrial power
1973/4	First oil price rise leads to wave of loans to Latin America. Foreign debt soars.
1982	Mexico defaults on interest payments on its foreign debt
1985	Announcement of Baker Plan to try and increase lending to Latin America.
1985	Through debt interest payments, Latin America sends abroad $32.3 billion more than it receives
1989	Announcement of austerity package in Venezuela provokes riots in which at least 276 people die
1989	US Treasury Secretary Nicholas Brady announces plan to reduce overall debt, but with limited impact

Growing Pains

Industrialisation and the Debt Crisis

5

São Paulo is made of cheap concrete. Millions of tons, poured in a hurry, spewed forth to make houses, tower blocks, factories and flyovers. Within a few years rain and sun leave it stained and crumbling, but quantity matters more than quality, for dilapidated buildings can always be replaced by bigger and newer constructions, using yet more concrete. The flood of concrete that created the great megalopolis of São Paulo is part of Brazil's rush for industrialisation, a titanic effort which has turned a relatively primitive coffee-exporter into a great industrial power, the eighth largest economy in the non-communist world. However, like the concrete, Brazil's industry is flawed and vulnerable. In the main thoroughfares of São Paulo, the rush-hour is a stampede of the well-heeled, the manicured and beautiful beneficiaries of Brazil's growth. On the street corners the losers, the old and unemployed, earn a pittance by working as human billboards. Standing in bored clumps all day, they wear T-shirts saying 'I buy gold', with a phone number.

Since the Great Depression of the 1930s, many Latin Americans have seen industrialisation as the path to development. The satanic mills whose fumes now choke Caracas or Mexico City may seem unlikely saviours, but the region's planners point to the experience of the rich countries, like the UK, US or Japan, where the growth of industry has led to a rise both in political power and the standard of living. Industrialisation, they argue, offers Latin America a way out of its crippling dependence on commodity exports, and its humiliating reliance on foreign governments and multinational companies for aid and manufactured goods.

However, industrialisation in Latin America has not brought the predicted dividends. Although the nation as a whole became richer, Brazilian society has become more unequal, not less, since the factories began to spring up. Neither has Latin America shed its dependence; instead of buying its consumer goods from the industrialised world, it now has to buy the machinery for its factories, which in turn are often owned by foreign companies who take their profits out of the country. Capital-intensive western technology created far fewer jobs than anticipated. Latin American governments borrowed heavily abroad to finance the later stages of industrialisation, and the loans from foreign banks and governments finally rebounded in the debt crisis which broke in 1982, turning the 1980s into a 'lost decade' of development.

Latin America's industrial quest started late. During the colonial period, the Spanish and Portuguese governments did everything they could to prevent the growth of domestic industry, which they feared would disrupt the continent's dependence on commodity exports. In the late 18th century, the Portuguese even went to the extent of ordering Brazilian textile looms to be burnt. When independence arrived in the early 19th century, Britain's cheap manufactures soon undercut what little local industry had arisen as the colonial ties had weakened. Nevertheless, most countries managed to achieve a first stage of industrialisation; they semi-processed agricultural crops and minerals for export, and local industries produced simple goods like soap, clothing and bottled drinks. European immigrants set up many of the first local industries — in Argentina and Uruguay, British immigrants built slaughter-houses, freezer plants and tanneries to serve the beef export industry, while Germans set up Peru's beer industry and controlled 90 per cent of Brazil's textile production by 1916.

Despite these primitive local industries, Latin America remained a commodity exporter, dependent on manufactured imports, until the late 1920s. By then, the cattle and grain trade had made Argentina one of the richest countries in the world, and coffee had establised São Paulo as Brazil's economic powerhouse. In 1929 the Wall Street Crash and the ensuing depression in the industrialised world rudely awoke Latin American governments to the perils of commodity dependence. Brazil's exports fell by 60 per cent between 1929-32, and the country suddenly had no hard currency with which to import manufactured goods.

Latin America learned its lesson. As local entrepreneurs moved in to start producing simple manufactured goods to plug the gap left by the import collapse, several governments began looking at ways to encourage 'import substitution'. By the late 1930s they were taking the first steps to improve transport, electricity and water supplies for local factories. When the Second World War came, the dilemma of the Great Depression was reversed; the industrialised nations were now desperate for Latin America's exports, but had fewer manufactures to spare as factories were converted to war production. The largest Latin American economies accumulated great wealth during the war, and afterwards used it to begin import substitution in earnest.

Besides improving national infrastructure, countries such as Argentina, Brazil and Mexico set up state-owned companies in strategic industries such as iron and steel and raised taxes on imported manufactured goods. These tariff barriers were essential to protect fledgling local industries from being undercut by cheap imports. At the same time, governments encouraged multinational companies to set up factories on Latin American soil, arguing that this would create jobs, while providing the technology and capital that the region lacked. Volkswagen built its first factory in Brazil in 1949, with other car producers from the US, West Germany and Japan hot on its heels. By 1970, 80 per cent of the country's cars were assembled in Brazil itself.

The initial results of import substitution were impressive. From 1950-70 Latin America's Gross Domestic Product (a measure of all the goods and services produced by a country) tripled, and even in per capita terms it rose by two-thirds. By the early 1960s, domestic industry supplied 95 per cent of Mexico's and 98 per cent of Brazil's consumer goods. By this time, however, there were already clear signs that the

Liba Taylor/Panos

model was approaching exhaustion:

★ Although it had substituted imports of simple manufactured goods like televisions and fridges, the new factories depended on imported capital goods, such as heavy machinery, turbines and cranes which in some cases cost more than the original imports.

★ The factories used capital-intensive western technology, creating far fewer jobs than expected and ignoring the supplies of cheap labour available. Governments and companies failed to spend on research and development of appropriate technology to meet Latin American needs.

★ Where industries were protected from outside competition by tariff barriers, they often became monopolies. They had no incentive to improve efficiency and keep costs down, since these could always be passed on to the consumer. Quality also suffered, and local middle classes soon came to equate local manufacture with low standards. In Argentina, during a national spending spree in the early 1980s, the shops of Buenos Aires would plaster their windows with signs saying *todo importado*, 'everything imported', to attract customers. Furthermore, state-owned companies frequently made losses, secure in the knowledge that the government would bail them out rather than see them go bankrupt.

★ The local market for manufactured goods was limited because most people in Latin America were too poor to buy more than the most basic necessities. This prevented industry from growing and reducing costs through mass production. Even Brazil, the most populous country in the region, faced this problem, although among its 140 million people, there was at least a significant middle class to buy locally-produced goods, enabling Brazilian industry to outperform its Spanish American counterparts. The problem of a small domestic market could only be solved if wealth were redistributed to allow more people to buy goods, an option ruled out by the wealthy elite.

Initially, governments responded to the lack of an internal market by establishing a variety of free trade agreements with other Latin American nations. Organisations like the Latin American Free Trade Association and the Central American Common Market, both established in 1960, soon foundered, however, because the smaller countries opened their markets to the more industrialised nations in the agreement, but received little in return.

The Dance of the Millions

Many Latin American governments were forced to adopt austerity programmes to cope with the slowdown in growth. In Brazil and Argentina, military governments seized power in order to implement such unpopular policies. They used both the law and brute force to suppress trade unions and lower the living standards of the poor majority. The major economies then set off in pursuit of the elusive third stage of industrialisation, the move from import substitution to

---

TABLE 6: INDUSTRIALISATION IN LATIN AMERICA

Country	A	B	C
Brazil	94.9	28	24 (1986)
Mexico	46.9	27	19 (1980)
Argentina	20.9	24	21 (1980)
Venezuela	11.6	19	18 (1988)
Colombia	9.3	20	18 (1980)
Peru	8.7	29	13 (1982)
Chile	7.1	22	16 (1988)
Ecuador	2.8	21	11 (1986)
Uruguay	1.7	19	20 (1982)
Guatemala	1.2	15	14 (1985)
Paraguay	1.0	16	14 (1982)
Costa Rica	1.0	21	16 (1983)
El Salvador	0.9	17	14 (1985)
Bolivia	0.8	14	9 (1986)
Honduras	0.6	14	14 (1987)
Nicaragua	0.4	16	—
Panama	0.3	7	11 (1985)
Suriname	0.1	11	11 (1987)
Guyana	0.04	10	15 (1980)

Column headings:
A: Value added to GDP by manufacturing in 1989 (billions of 1988 dollars)
B: Manufacturing as % of GDP, 1989
C: % of economically active population in manufacturing (year in brackets)

Source: *Economic and Social Progress in Latin America* 1989 and 1990, Inter-American Development Bank

becoming an exporter of manufactured goods. This meant large-scale investments, which had to be funded by foreign capital. Latin America turned to the international loan sharks.

Brazil led the field in both industrialisation and the race for foreign loans. In 1958, it overtook Argentina as the region's leading industrial power. By 1961 it was self-sufficient in electric stoves, refrigerators and television sets. Vehicle production boomed from 31,000 in 1957 to 514,000 in 1971. In 1968 Brazilian industry finally outstripped agriculture as the major wealth producer in the country. By 1988 Brazil's industrial output was twice that of Mexico, and nearly five times greater than Argentina's, and over 300 of Latin America's top 500 companies were Brazilian. The one-time coffee producer had become the region's superpower.

As the factories multiplied, so did the foreign debt. The big borrowers were the state corporations which dominated the politically vital areas of steel, petroleum and electricity production. Over the ensuing years, Mexico's petroleum corporation, Pemex, ran up a debt of $15 billion. State and private banks also borrowed heavily abroad, in order to re-lend to local businesses.

The 'dance of the millions', as the round of frenzied foreign borrowing became known, took off after the oil price rise in 1973-74. OPEC oil producers recycled their new wealth to western banks, who in turn were anxious to find outlets for their 'petrodollars'. Latin America seemed the ideal borrower; it had decades of steady growth and industrialisation already behind it, and countries such as Mexico and Venezuela were sitting on huge oil reserves. Foreign bankers fell over themselves to lend as much as possible, as fast as possible. Since they assumed that governments could not go bankrupt, they paid little attention to where the money was actually going. In the words of one young ex-banker:

> As a loan officer, you are principally in the business of making loans. It is not your job to worry about large and unwieldy abstractions, such as whether what you're doing is threatening the stability of the world economy. In that sense, a young banker is like a soldier on the front lines: he is obedient, aggressive and amoral.

In all, $60 billion in foreign loans entered Latin America between 1975 and 1982. Sixty per cent of the money went to Brazil and Mexico, as they and Argentina became the Third World's top three debtors. In Mexico, the rain of dollars funded exploration and development of the oil industry; in Brazil it fuelled the country's further rise as an industrial power. Brazil was the only country successfully to make the leap to the third stage of industrialisation as an exporter of manufactured goods. From 1970-78 it doubled its proportion of the region's exports, becoming a producer of everything from computers to aircraft.

The results were astonishing. In just 13 years, from 1967 to 1980, Latin America's manufactured exports increased in value forty-fold, from $1 billion to $40 billion. Then the bubble burst.

In August 1982 the Mexican government announced it could no longer pay the interest due on its foreign debt. Many US and other

Capital Flight: as loans poured in, dollars also poured out, as government officials or business leaders siphoned as much as possible into US bank accounts. In many cases this involved corruption, such as taking kickbacks on government contracts, but in Venezuela and Mexico, for example, it was quite legal to export dollars into a US account. Overall figures vary wildly, but according to the Institute of International Economics in Washington, between 1976-82, capital flight from Mexico amounted to $25.7 billion, from Argentina $22.4 billion, and from Venezuela $20.7 billion. Brazil's capital flight was comparatively low at $5.8 billion. According to a banker quoted in Susan George's book, *A Fate Worse then Debt*:

'The most aggressive banks, such as Citibank, have probably accumulated almost as much in assets from poor countries as they have loaned to them. Their real role has been to take funds that Third World elites have stolen from their governments and to loan them back, earning a nice spread each way.'

Megaprojects: banks had to shift large quantities of money as quickly as possible, so they preferred lending to giant projects rather than to smaller ones. Military governments in particular showed a preference for 'pharaonic' enterprises such as vast dams or road-building programmes, which often did great environmental damage as well as costing enormous sums of money. Megaprojects were also accompanied by a high level of waste and corruption.

Arms: the 1970s was a period of military rule in Latin America, and from 1972-82 arms imports grew at an annual rate of 13 per cent. In 1986, the Peruvian Foreign Minister estimated that Latin America's total defence spending over the previous 10 years came to over $114 billion, roughly half of the region's entire foreign debt.

'...SO YOU SEE, THE ENTIRE FUTURE OF THE INTERNATIONAL FINANCIAL SYSTEM HINGES ON YOUR CAPACITY FOR QUICK RECOVERY AND VAST ECONOMIC GROWTH.'

Cartoon: Oliphant

banks suddenly realised that what had seemed a safe and lucrative loans business in Latin America could drive them into bankruptcy, if other countries followed Mexico's lead. The announcement sent a shudder through the international banking community, raising fears of a run on the banks and a possible collapse of the world financial

system. The following weeks established the pattern for years to come. The banks and creditor governments worked together to find a solution — not to the problem of Mexico's excessive debt repayments, but to remove the threat to the banking system. The solution was a band-aid affair whereby the financial system would reschedule debt repayments and lend Mexico new money, purely so that it could give it straight back as interest payments. This would avoid the banks having to write off Mexico's loans as bad debts, which would in turn have damaged their profits and sent their shares plunging on the stock market.

By early 1984, every Latin American nation except Colombia and Paraguay had been forced into similar rescheduling deals. In each case the creditors stuck together, but insisted on negotiating with each debtor nation separately. Rescheduling was good business for the banks, since they could exact particularly high interest rates in exchange for deferring repayments. In return for rescheduling $49.5 billion in loans, the banks earned an extra $1.7 billion. At the same time, they ended virtually all new lending to Latin American nations, other than that needed to pay interest on the original loans.

The immediate cause of the crisis was the sudden rise in US interest rates announced by newly elected President Reagan. Since Latin America's debts had been largely contracted at floating interest rates, this meant a massive increase in its interest payments. Each time the international interest rate rose by one per cent, it added nearly $2 billion a year to the developing countries' bills. At the same time the austerity policies of 'Reaganomics' and the second OPEC price rise of 1979 produced a sharp recession in the industrialised nations which cut demand for Latin America's manufactured exports and sent commodity prices tumbling. Latin America earned less hard currency for its exports, just as it needed to pay more interest on its debt.

The role of the West's debt collector went to the International

Workers scramble to finish a turbine of the giant Itaipú dam and hydro-electric complex, Brazil/Paraguay.

Monetary Fund (IMF), a multilateral funding agency controlled by the wealthy industrialised countries. Its role in the debt crisis earned the IMF another name: the Institute for Misery and Famine. As one Latin American country after another got into difficulties, the IMF bailed them out only after insisting they introduce a package known as 'structural adjustment', a harmless-sounding series of measures designed to open up the economy of the debtor nation to free-market forces. A typical IMF recipe involved:

★ wage controls and interest rate increases to cut domestic consumption

★ devaluation to improve the competitiveness of exports and discourage imports. The resulting trade surplus could then be used to pay debt interest

★ cuts in public spending and an end to subsidies to reduce fiscal deficit and inflationary pressures

★ the end of government controls over prices and imports to encourage a free market to operate

In practice, these apparently anodyne economic measures meant higher food and fuel prices, lower wages, and deteriorating social services. The poor majority were made to bear the brunt of the debt crisis through hunger and increased poverty, while those who had squandered the loans or spirited them abroad remained untouched.

Throughout the region, the debt crisis and IMF structural adjustment packages provoked a terrible recession. In order to earn hard currency for debt repayments, Latin America cut its volume of imports by 60 per cent, while it expanded the volume of exports by 23 per cent.

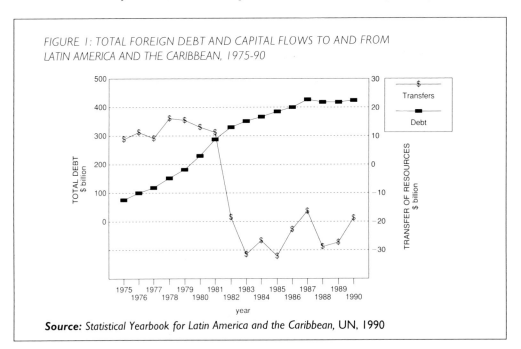

FIGURE 1: TOTAL FOREIGN DEBT AND CAPITAL FLOWS TO AND FROM LATIN AMERICA AND THE CARIBBEAN, 1975-90

Source: *Statistical Yearbook for Latin America and the Caribbean*, UN, 1990

However, this Herculean effort was undermined by the recession in the industrialised world. The collapse in commodity prices meant that despite the increase in the volume of exports, their dollar earnings actually fell by one per cent, while price increases in imports reduced a 60 per cent cut in volume to only a 41 per cent cut in value. Even so, Latin America's trade surplus rose from nothing in 1980 to $38 billion in 1984.

The surplus went towards paying the interest bills. Latin America and the Caribbean sent a total of $198 billion abroad between 1982 and 1990, $70 billion more than all the money that entered the region from 1975-81, and this does not even include capital flight (see figure 1). Despite this haemorrhage of capital, Latin America in 1990 was deeper in debt than ever — the $198 billion had not even met its full interest bill. Since 1982, the poor of Latin America have been subsidising the banking systems of the US, Europe and Japan.

The Lost Decade

'The Third World War has already started — a silent war, not for that reason any the less sinister. This war is tearing down Brazil, Latin America and practically all the Third World. Instead of soldiers dying there are children, instead of millions of wounded there are millions of unemployed; instead of destruction of bridges there is the tearing down of factories, schools, hospitals, and entire economies.'
Luis Inâcio da Silva (Lula), Brazilian labour leader, 1985

For Latin America the 1980s was a lost decade. IMF and western leaders could point to some improvements in the region's economic performance, such as reduced inflation, an end to government over-spending and a large trade surplus, which they claimed paved the way for eventual economic recovery. Nevertheless, in the 1980s countries whose economies had grown steadily since the Second World War went into decline as the IMF's radical economic surgery drove the continent into recession. The rich and powerful elites who had profited from foreign loans proved adept at avoiding the burden of repayment. Businesses laid off workers and cut wages to protect their profits, and many entrepreneurs and financiers could survive hard times by living off the proceeds of their Miami bank accounts. The poor had no such choices.

★ In Mexico real wages halved as unemployment quadrupled between 1982 and 1987. According to Susan George, nearly three-quarters of poor Mexicans were forced to give up eating rice, eggs, fruit, vegetables and milk. These products became luxuries to be eaten only on special feast days about five times a year.

★ Advances in health and nutrition went into reverse; more Latin American children were malnourished or dying in the 1980s than ten years previously. The woman director of a school for disabled children in Argentina reported in 1984:

Of the 115 children in my school, ninety-eight are mentally retarded because of early childhood malnutrition. The children's deficiencies are usually not noticed until they reach the age of primary school — then they're sent to me, and it's too late.

★ The Bolivian government, under IMF pressure in 1986, cut the health budget by two-thirds at a time when over half the population was malnourished.

★ In February 1989 Venezuela's incoming president, Carlos Andrés Pérez, raised food and bus prices in an austerity package agreed with the IMF, in return for an initial $453m credit from the agency. The measures provoked a week of rioting in the normally peaceful country. Tanks took to streets littered with shattered glass, as protesters marched in from the slums to burn shops and vehicles, put up barricades and loot supermarkets. The wave of destruction left an official death toll of 276, but according to Amnesty International, the real figure may have been much higher. In the 1980s 'IMF riots' also occurred in Brazil, Argentina and the Dominican Republic.

★ Throughout the region, millions of sacked or underpaid workers joined the 'informal sector', or left in search of a better life as illegal immigrants to the United States.

Structural adjustment particularly hurt women, either in their role as mothers trying to feed and clothe their families, or as employees of the 'caring professions' of health and education which were hard hit by government cut-backs. In one Buenos Aires shanty town, exhausted young doctors try to run a health centre in the ground floor of a derelict 14-storey former hospital. Paint is peeling off the damp walls. In dank corridors ragged women wait in silence with their babies. On the walls a sign says 'The social workers have stopped working because there are no wages. We won't work until it's been sorted out, March, 1990'.

The recession meant that economies shrank as the population continued to grow. Latin America's per capita GDP fell by 10 per cent in the 1980s. Government deficits rose, fuelling inflation, as administrations printed money to pay their bills and maintain at least some vestiges of social services for the growing numbers of the needy. Governments could no longer afford to invest, while both foreign and domestic private investors took fright. As Latin America in effect mortgaged its economic future to pay its debts, total investment fell by a third between 1980 and 1984, and by 1988 had still only reached 81 per cent of its pre-debt crisis level.

The recession also affected the first world economies. Despite their initial fears, the banks survived the crisis with few casualties, often after being bailed out by western taxpayers. In 1989 government tax relief to British banks on their third world bad debt provisions meant that each British taxpayer subsidised the four main high-street banks to the tune of £62.80. However, the collapse in Latin America's imports meant fewer orders for western industries. Some estimates put the number of manufacturing jobs lost as high as 800,000, especially among companies manufacturing agricultural and other heavy machinery.

From the moment of Mexico's default in 1982, the creditor countries' first priority was to avoid a banking crisis in the US and other major financial centres. Western governments and banks stuck together, insisting on 'case-by-case' negotiations with individual debtor nations. By effectively ganging up on the debtors, the US, Japan and the UK could ensure that negotiations discussed economic policy in the debtor nations, but not their own economic and banking policies, which were at least partly responsible for provoking the crisis in the first place. Above all, the creditor governments worked to prevent the formation of an effective debtors' cartel which could use its power to trigger a worldwide financial crisis in order to negotiate better terms. Apart from occasional ineffectual joint declarations, Latin America's debtor nations were unable to unite, not least because the banks proved adept at using divide-and-rule tactics to buy off countries such as Mexico with slightly better terms than other Latin nations.

Unable to keep up payments, many countries went into 'passive default', while reassuring the banks that they would pay as soon as they were able. Other countries such as Peru and Brazil openly defied the banks, announcing debt moratoria, and in Peru's case refusing to pay more than ten per cent of its export income in interest repayments. But since there was no debtors' cartel they had to act alone, and the creditor countries used financial and political pressure to force them back into line. Moreover, by defying their creditors, countries risked becoming international pariahs, deprived of trade and investment with the outside world. One US Treasury document reportedly asked: 'Have you ever contemplated what would happen to the president of a country if the government couldn't get insulin for its diabetics?' For Latin America's ruling elites, many of whom depended on such links with the industrialised countries for their salaries and status, the price of a debt rebellion was too high.

Once the initial panic was over, and the IMF structural adjustment system was in place, the US and other creditors slowly turned their attention to seeking a long-term solution to the crisis. In late 1985, after three years of case-by-case 'band-aid' reschedulings, the US Treasury Secretary James Baker acknowledged that further action was needed. Rescheduling and structural adjustment were keeping banks afloat at the cost of recession in Latin America, but growth would not resume until capital, in the form of aid and investment, began to flow into, rather than out of, the region. The principal problem was that banks were refusing to lend new funds to what they saw as bad debtors. In response, Baker increased the role of the IMF and World Bank in lending new money to the region, and also attempted to force private banks to resume lending. His efforts were ineffective, and Latin America continued to export capital. Meanwhile, as the banks expanded into other markets and western economies picked up after the recession of the early 1980s, lenders who had been dangerously over-exposed were able to write off bad loans to Latin America and thereby became even less susceptible to pressure to make fresh loans. To the banks, Latin America was becoming a forgotten continent.

In early 1989 another US Treasury Secretary, Nicholas Brady, formulated the 'Brady Plan'. This was an attempt to reduce the overall debt burden through a series of financial mechanisms, many of them extremely baffling to anyone who is not a banker. For example, Latin

Cheap labour. Making shorts for Levi's to reexport to the US, Honduras Free Trade Zone.

American governments were encouraged to use their foreign reserves to clear a portion of their own debt by buying it back at a discount. In late 1990, $100 of Peru's debt could be bought for just $4, since banks considered the value of that country's debt to be so impaired. A host of other measures constituted a 'menu of options' from which banks could choose in trying to convert unpayable debt into some form of asset. Although some countries, notably Mexico, Venezuela and Costa Rica, achieved Brady Plan agreements, the overall success in reducing Latin America's debt burden was negligible. The debt remained at around $420 billion from 1987-90, while the outflow of the region's wealth to the banks continued unabated (see figure 1). Once again, banks largely resisted US pressure for new lending. Over time they have succeeded in transferring an increasing share of the debt burden from themselves to the international financial institutions, funded by governments and taxpayers. As one financier explained with uncharacteristic frankness, 'we foreign bankers are for the free-market system when we are out to make a buck and believe in the state when we're about to lose a buck.'

By the end of the 1980s the debt crisis only made the headlines in the *Financial Times* or *Wall Street Journal*, yet the underlying problems which had provoked Mexico's default in 1982 had changed little. The poorest inhabitants of Latin America had made enormous sacrifices throughout the 1980s in order to safeguard the US and European banking systems, and yet had little to show for it except a bleak panorama of economic stagnation and falling living standards. Now that the western financial system has succeeded in reducing its vulnerability to a debt default, there is less likelihood than ever of Latin America's creditors writing off a debt which has already earned them handsome profits, in order to let the region resume its search for prosperity and development.

Painful Medicine

Together, the exhaustion of the import substitution model of industrialisation and the medicine prescribed by the IMF have reversed Latin America's historic reliance on a state-led model of development. Instead, the 1970s and 1980s saw a rise in the dominance of free-market economic thinking, or neoliberalism, which to some extent foreshadowed the later collapse of the state-run economies of Eastern Europe. Although originating in the US and Western Europe and championed in the 1980s by Margaret Thatcher and Ronald Reagan, neoliberalism was most radically applied in Latin America. Perhaps the most renowned exponent of free market virtues was General Pinochet, the Chilean dictator who seized power in 1973. His example was followed by the Argentine military junta after the coup of 1976. Besides their more infamous activities in the field of human rights, both regimes opened up their markets to foreign competition by removing tax and bureaucratic barriers to imports, while Chile also privatised the vast majority of state companies. The result was to reverse the previous trend towards industrialisation, as cheap foreign imports drove local businesses to the wall. In Chile, this was counterbalanced by diversifying the country's commodity exports, reducing its historic dependence on copper by building up sales of fruit and fish.

In the 1980s, Mexico, one of the continent's great protectionist economies, began to follow suit. After the onset of the debt crisis, the government of the ruling Institutional Revolutionary Party began to privatise hundreds of state-owned companies and entice US and Japanese investors with the promise of low wages (real wages fell by 40 per cent between 1982 and 87) and a quiescent labour force. On a macroeconomic scale, the results were impressive. By the late 1980s, Mexico's border with the US was dotted with 'maquila' industries where US and other companies used cheap Mexican labour to assemble goods for re-export to the US market. In the five years after 1982, manufactured goods rose as a percentage of Mexico's total exports from 16 per cent to 45 per cent. The social cost, however, was a steep rise in unemployment and a drop in the standard of living as the Mexican state cut back on social services and privatised companies which laid off staff.

Other countries adopted the neoliberal orthodoxy, although it was often hard to distinguish real economic changes from free-market rhetoric designed for Washington's consumption. In March 1990 the new Brazilian president, Fernando Collor de Mello, announced that Brazil, which had remained resolutely state-led throughout the military regime from 1964-85, would board the free-market bandwagon. His initial measures caused a massive economic recession. In São Paulo alone, 260,000 people lost their jobs, while Brazil's GDP fell by four per cent in 1990. In August 1990 the *Financial Times* graphically described the lingering barriers to free trade in Brazil, five months after the announcement of the Collor Plan:

> The Argentine nappies on sale in Mappins, one of the country's largest store chains, at half the price of Brazilian ones, required

a long battle. When Mappins began the imports, trucks were held up on the border while Johnson and Johnson, which monopolises the Brazilian nappy market, found a helpful bureaucrat with an ancient regulation classifying nappies as pharmaceutical products which could be imported only if accompanied by a qualified pharmacist, transported and kept in cold storage.

Despite neoliberalism's unpalatable austerity policies, Latin America entered the 1990s with few alternatives on offer. Everywhere governments of all political hues were abandoning state intervention and protectionism in favour of the free market, austerity, and the desperate pursuit of foreign investment.

In June 1991, the Manchester *Guardian* ran a feature saluting Latin America's 'silent revolution'. The article claimed that the regional governments' new-found determination to cut spending and remove barriers to free trade was paving the way to future prosperity. On the same day a single paragraph in the *Independent* noted the arrival in Mexico of a cholera epidemic, the first in the Western Hemisphere since the 1920s. Starting in Peru earlier in the year, the outbreak had killed over 2,000 people by the time it hit Mexico. Cholera is a disease of the poor, spread through polluted wells and ditches, killing when medicines and hospitals are unavailable. Public spending cuts may win international praise, but they inflict a high price on the poor.

The continent's governments have also turned towards the creation of a regional common market as a possible solution to their problems. In March 1991 Argentina, Brazil, Paraguay and Uruguay founded Mercosur, the Southern Cone Common Market, and pledged to end all barriers to internal trade by 1995.

Washington is also keen to build up a hemispheric free trade zone to counter the European and Asian blocs forming around Germany and Japan, and has followed up its free trade agreement with Canada with negotiations to sign a similar pact with Mexico. Despite President Ulysses S. Grant's warnings (see page 17), most Latin American governments remain keen to see a free trade bloc form. As in similar attempts in the 1960s, the likelihood is that such agreements will benefit the stronger economies over the weaker. This is especially true in any agreement which includes the economic might of the US in a free trade zone with countries as small and underdeveloped as Bolivia and Paraguay. Time will tell if the painful medicine of neoliberalism and free trade with its giant northern neighbour cures the Latin American patients or merely accelerates their demise.

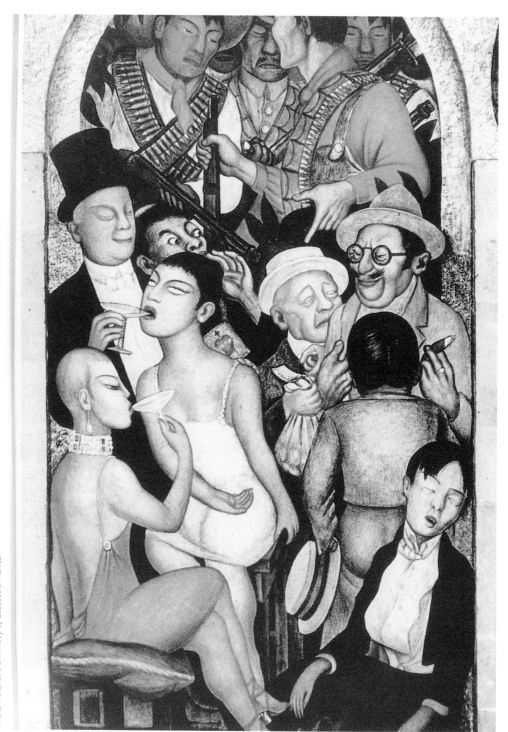

Unacceptable faces. Diego Rivera's portrait of the Mexican elite at the time of the revolution, 1910-17.

Chronology

1896   First moving picture shown in Buenos Aires

1910-17   Mexican revolution begins attempt to construct a new mestizo consciousness, especially through the work of muralists such as Diego Rivera

1923   Brazilian government sets up country's first radio station which soon bows to popular demand for broadcasts of samba music

1959   Cuban revolution promotes attempt to build a radical and distinctive Latin American cultural movement

mid 1960s   First *telenovelas* broadcast in Brazil and Mexico

1967   Miguel Angel Asturias becomes first Latin American novelist to win Nobel prize for literature; Gabriel García Márquez publishes *One Hundred Years of Solitude*

1971   Cuban government arrests the dissident poet, Heberto Padilla

1973   Singer Víctor Jara killed by the army following military coup in Chile

1979   Nicaraguan revolution provides state support for poets and artists

1990   Peruvian novelist Mario Vargas Llosa loses presidential elections to the unknown Alberto Fujimori

Writing on the Wall

6

Culture, Identity and Politics

Every evening the suburbs and shanty towns of Latin America grind to a halt as anyone with a television settles down in front of the latest *telenovela*, or soap opera. TV-less neighbours drop by for the show and an animated discussion about the latest twist in an often bewildering plot. In Mexico in the late 1980s 40 million people — half the country's population, regularly tuned in for 'Cradle of Wolves', a lurid account of a ruthless heroine with an eyepatch who committed a series of gruesome murders. When the last episode was shown, Mexico's underground drivers refused to go to work and the public transport system closed down.

In Europe and North America, Latin America is better known for its literature and music than for its soaps. Salsa and lambada are favourites on European dance floors, like the tango and bossanova before them. Latin American literature has become so popular that, in the words of critic and translator Nick Caistor, it 'has become the equivalent of the Amazon rainforest, providing oxygen for the stale literary lungs of the developed world'. Yet although Latin America's novelists have become international celebrities, at home the audience for one of the top Mexican or Brazilian soaps exceeds the entire continent's readership for writers such as Mexico's Carlos Fuentes, or Peru's Mario Vargas Llosa. In response Gabriel García Márquez, Colombia's Nobel Prize-winning novelist, has announced that his next project will be to write a *telenovela*.

In his work, García Márquez has drawn heavily on the traditional 'popular culture' of his native Colombia, filling his books with the tales of travelling singers and story-tellers, remembered from his childhood. In making the leap to soaps, he challenged those intellectuals and critics who have in the past derided the genre as cheap, tacky melodrama churned out by Latin America's media giants. Such critics frequently hark back to a 'pure' popular culture in the countryside, free of the taint of capitalism and technology, yet such views risk reducing the idea of 'popular culture' to a quaint, but increasingly irrelevant folklore destined for the museum. Popular culture would paradoxically cease to be the culture of the people, with its constantly evolving mix of traditional and modern styles.

Over the 500 years since the Conquest, Latin America's dispossessed peoples: the Indians, descendants of African slaves, and poor mestizos, have developed varied and unique cultural forms by constantly absorbing new influences into a bedrock of tradition. The Indians of the Andes and Central America kept alive pre-conquest textiles and pottery, while adopting Spanish stringed instruments and combining

Rigoberta Rivera/Morococha/TAFOS/Panos

Day of the Dead, Peru. Miners go to the cemetery to be with and remember dead relatives.

them with their own panoply of flutes and drums. Traumatic events such as the Conquest and murder of the Inca emperors are today recalled through the cultural memory of street theatre and dance, yet traditional styles are still evolving. In Guatemala, widows of men killed or 'disappeared' by the military during their counter-insurgency campaigns in the early 1980s now include stylised images of helicopters in their traditional weaving patterns, where they join images of Spaniards on horseback from the time of the Conquest. In Brazil the Kayapo Indians expertly wield imported video cameras to record their traditional dances and rituals for future generations. The Kayapo explain that they find their own ceremonies more interesting than Brazilian national TV. The cameras also come out at meetings with the Brazilian authorities, and past videos are kept to be played back to the bureaucrats should they try to go back on a promise.

The survival of ancient cultural traditions was frequently achieved in defiance of the colonial authorities' attempts to impose European ways. The greatest battleground for the defence of tradition was religion. Traditional Indian religion and culture are inseparable; music, costumes and dance are part of an annual round of rituals and feast-days linked to the seasons and the agricultural cycles of sowing and harvest. To the Catholic Church, charged with a mission to convert the heathen, the pantheon of Indian deities had to be crushed, the temples overthrown and practices such as ancestor worship stamped out. In order to appease the authorities, Indian communities adopted Catholic forms, but subverted their content. The Christian saints took on the characters and powers of the different Indian gods and All Souls Day, known in Spanish as the 'day of the dead', became an opportunity for ancestor worship. Every year on the 2nd of November, Mexican families still go to the cemeteries to picnic with their dead. Throughout the continent the cycle of fiestas, carnivals and saints' days play a central role in community life:

In all of these ceremonies the Mexican opens out. They all give him a chance to reveal himself and to converse with God, country, friends or relations. During these days the silent Mexican whistles, shouts, sings, shoots off fireworks, discharges his pistol into the air. He discharges his soul. This is the night when friends who have not exchanged more than the prescribed courtesies for months get drunk together, trade confidences, weep over the same troubles, discover that they are brothers, and sometimes, to prove it, kill each other.
Octavio Paz, *The Labyrinth of Solitude*, 1950

In Mexico, visions of the Virgin Mary began to occur soon after the Conquest, the most famous being the Virgin of Guadalupe, who appeared to an Indian at Tepeyac, north of Mexico City, the site of a traditional Indian shrine to Tonantzin, the Aztec earth goddess. A flow of miracles forced the disapproving Church authorities to recognise the event and the Virgin of Guadalupe's shrine became the most important holy place in the Americas. She also became a symbol of emergent Mexican identity, representing both earth goddess and dark-skinned Virgin Mary, who had chosen to appear to an Indian rather than to a member of the white elite. In Bolivia, paintings by mestizo artists of the colonial period also transformed the Virgin into Pachamama, the Andean earth goddess. Sometimes the subversion of Catholicism was even more deliberate. The Mexican muralists of the 1920s were particularly influenced by contemporary accounts of a religious dance around the statue of the Virgin in a Puebla village, during which the statue toppled over to reveal a small stone carving depicting the goddess of water, hidden beneath the Virgin's skirts for centuries, and worshipped throughout that time.

In the Bolivian mines, Catholic and pre-Columbian beliefs are fused in the figure of the *tío*. The *tío* (uncle) is the god of the underworld whose domain includes the tin mines where many of Bolivia's Indians toil in unhealthy and dangerous conditions. Since the Christian God resides in heaven, the *tío* has become equated with the Christian devil, but without the qualities of evil normally ascribed to him. In the mines, the *tío* must be placated and asked for help to avert the all-too-frequent rockfalls and explosions. His statue glares out from niches cut into the walls of the mines, but the miners seem on affectionate terms with him, handing him cigarettes or coca to chew. At carnival time they offer him the blood and heart of a llama. As they prepare to cut the llama's throat, the miners, their cheeks bulging with coca, cry out 'for the health and prosperity of our section', 'may there be no more accidents'. Blood collected in a chipped china plate is then smeared on the walls of the mine to bring good luck for another year.

Above ground, the carnival brass bands and 'devil dance' of young men dressed in the elaborate, horned and multicoloured masks of the *tío*, have moved down from the pitheads to the town centre and become a tourist attraction. These days it is the shopkeepers and middle classes who dance in the masks, which have become too elaborate and expensive for a miner to buy. In the dance the Archangel Gabriel, a pink-skinned, blue-eyed European representation of good, fights the devils in ritual combat. The god of the mines, like the miners he protects, comes off worst in this clash of cultures.

In traditional Indian beliefs, sacred properties belonged not just to a God, but filled everyday objects, which could themselves be worshipped or asked to bring good luck. Everything from a hill, to a tree or a carving could be seen as holy. To the Catholic Church, these practices were idolatrous, and public worship of objects (other than saints) was stamped out, but many of the beliefs were passed down through the family, principally from mother to daughter. Along the

---

MAGICAL REALISM

The real as magical — electricity comes to Macondo

'Dazzled by so many and marvellous inventions, the people of Macondo did not know where their amazement began. They stayed up all night looking at the pale electric bulbs fed by the plant that Aureliano Triste had brought back when the train made its second trip, and it took time and effort for them to grow accustomed to its obsessive toom-toom. They became indignant over the living images that the prosperous merchant Bruno Crespi projected in the theatre with the lion-head ticket windows, for a character who had died and was buried in one film and for whose misfortune tears of affliction had been shed would reappear alive and transformed into an Arab in the next one....When someone from the town had the opportunity to test the crude reality of the telephone installed in the railroad station, even the most incredulous were upset. It was as if God had decided to put to the test every capacity for surprise which was keeping the inhabitants of Macondo in a permanent alternation between excitement and disappointment, doubt and revelation, to such an extreme that no one knew for certain where the limits of reality lay.'

The magical as real — Macondo is stricken by a plague of insomnia

'With an inked brush [José Arcadio Buendía] marked everything with its name: *table, chair, clock, door, wall, bed, pan.* He went to the corral and marked the animals and plants: *cow, goat, pig, hen, cassava, caladium, banana.* Little by little, studying the infinite possibilities of a loss of memory, he realized that the day might come when things would be recognized by their inscriptions but that no one would remember their use. Then he was more explicit. The sign that he hung on the neck of the cow was an exemplary proof of the way in which the inhabitants of Macondo were prepared to fight against loss of memory: *This is the cow. She must be milked every morning so that she will produce milk, and the milk must be boiled in order to be mixed with coffee to make coffee and milk.* Thus they went on living in a reality that was slipping away, momentarily captured by words, but which would escape irremediably when they forgot the values of the written letters. At the beginning of the road into the swamp they put up a sign that said MACONDO and another larger one on the main street that said GOD EXISTS.'

Gabriel García Márquez, *One Hundred Years of Solitude*

Susan Cunningham

African-based religions
such as Candomblé have
flourished alongside
Christianity in Brazil.
Candomblé ceremony.

way, they were fragmented and transformed into what became known
as 'folk magic', involving faith healing and other 'magical' practices.
Today, throughout Latin America, such beliefs as *mal de ojo* (evil eye)
and the sale of love potions are commonplace amongst Indians and
mestizos alike. Even such eminently rationalist, western figures as 'The
Liberator', Símon Bolívar, have been turned into quasi-religious icons.
Stores in Venezuela's shanty towns sell 'Liberator' aphrodisiacs and his
name is invoked in faith-healing.

This interweaving of the sacred with everyday life is one reason
why writers such as García Márquez insist that their style, often labelled
'magical realism', is merely an accurate portrayal of the life and stories
of their native world. In Latin America everyday 'magic' and 'reality'
are so interwoven as to be inseparable.

In Brazil, the African slaves on the sugar plantations of the North-East
managed to retain their cultural identity through music and dance.
Plantation owners even encouraged erotic dances to keep up morale
amongst their slaves. Today on Rio's beaches young black men can
still be seen performing *capoeira*, a traditional slave dance combining
both dance and ritualised martial arts. As increasing numbers of blacks
left the sugar plantations and moved to the shanty towns and
tenements of the cities, African religions resurfaced in the shape of
Candomblé. *Candomblé* is based on the personal relationship between
an individual and a pantheon of African deities, each with a different
personality and tastes. As in the Andean religions, music, dance and
worship are inseparable. The gods appear through the possession of
chosen 'sons and daughters' and receive ritual offerings, songs and
dance.

African and Portuguese cultures combined to produce samba and
carnival, a joyous three day euphoria of dance, music, sex and beer
which has become synonymous with Brazil:

In the official parade grounds — the Sambadrome — I thought the silence eerie until I realized it was in fact a solid wall of sound, a percussive din that did not sound like music and advanced gradually towards the spectators on an elaborate loudspeaker system set up on either side of the central 'avenue', or parade space. At the head of the noise was a gigantic waggling lion's head that floated down the avenue and overtook us, giving way to dazzling hordes in red and gold. A marmalade-thick river of people swept past; outlandish dancers in feathers and capes, ball gowns and G-strings, hundreds of drummers, thousands of leaping princes singing at the top of their lungs. Drowning in red and gold, I struggled to focus. In the ocean of feathers and banners faces emerged: brown, white, pink, tan, olive. Young men bopping in sweat-drenched suits; old women in cascades of flounces whirling ecstatically; middle-aged men and women with paunches and eyeglasses bouncing happily in their head-dresses and bikinis.
Guillermoprieto 1990

Carnival's origins lay in festivals brought from Portugal, messy affairs in which the populace pelted each other with flour and water and indulged in gargantuan feats of eating and drinking. Over the years dance and music acquired increasing importance and local carnival associations grew up to organise floats for processions through the streets of Rio. The centre of carnival culture moved from the rich European suburbs to the poor black *favelas*, provoking one well-to-do reader of the *Jornal de noticias* in Bahia to write in 1901:

> The authorities should prohibit those [African drum] sessions and *candomblés* that in such quantity are overflowing on our streets these days, producing such great cacophonous noise, as well as those masquerades dressed in [typical black costumes] singing their traditional samba, because all of that is incompatible with our current civilized state.

The associations metamorphosed into the samba schools, enormous permanent organisations based in Rio's *favelas* which each year take on the task of building the increasingly monumental floats, and organising thousands of drummers and costumed dancers into their various 'wings'. The vast expense of carnival and the elaborate costumes have so far not forced the samba schools out of the *favelas*, but there has been a slow erosion of the *favelas*' involvement in carnival as a whole. Outside designers and artists are now hired to create the floats, costumes are farmed out rather than made by the women of the *favela*, and each school's procession is now fronted by TV stars, usually white.

Two Cultures Clash

In Latin America culture and politics have been inextricably linked since Pizarro's conquistadores ransacked the temples of Cuzco and melted down the Inca empire's finest wrought gold and silver into

Little Tamales from Cambray
To make 4,200,000 small tamales
by Claribel Alegría

Two pounds of mestizo cornmeal
a half-pound loin of Spanish immigrant
all finely chopped and cooked
with a packet of ready-blessed raisins
two tablespoons of Malinche's milk
one cup of troubled water
then fry the conquistador's helmets
with three Jesuit onions
one small sack of multinational gold
two dragon's teeth
add one presidential carrot
two tablespoons of pimps
the fat from Panchimalco Indians
two Ministry tomatoes
half a cup of televised sugar
two drops of volcanic lava
seven pito leaves
(don't get me wrong, it's a soporific)
set it all to boil
over a slow fire
for five hundred years
and you'll discover its unique aroma'

Lovers and Comrades: Women's Resistance Poetry from Central America,
ed Amanda Hopkinson, London, 1989
Note: 4,200,000 is the population of El Salvador, of which *tamales* are
the national dish. Malinche was the name of the Indian mistress of
Cortés, who betrayed the Aztec emperor Cuauhtémoc to the
Spaniards.

ingots to be sent home to Spain. After the Conquest the Spanish
authorities initially banned fiction, fearing it would excite the minds
of the Indians and fan subversion. During the colonial period the social
and economic divide between the white ruling elite and the
dark-skinned masses was mirrored in the gulf between their two
cultures. In their art academies and concert halls Latin America's elites
pursued a purely European aesthetic and made regular visits to its
cultural capitals of Paris or Rome. Werner Herzog's film, *Fitzcarraldo*,
recounts one particularly bizarre example of the forced implantation
of European culture — a rubber baron's folly in the shape of a 2,000
seat opera house in Manaus, in the heart of the Amazon jungle. After
it opened in 1897, companies from Milan, Paris and Madrid sailed up
the Amazon to sing at the theatre, which boasted curtains from Alsace,
stone from Portugal, Venetian crystal and English wrought ironwork.
When the rubber boom came to an end, the theatre closed down, until

its restoration in 1990, when Plácido Domingo came to sing *Carmen* to a full house. Meanwhile, away from the paved streets of the city centres, a rich and separate popular culture was actively combining ingredients of Indian, African and European culture into a uniquely Latin American cocktail.

Many 19th-century writers portrayed popular culture as a form of barbarism which must be fought through the introduction of civilised (ie European) values. However, popular culture also offered middle-class writers and artists an apparent solution to a conundrum that has dogged the continent's intelligentsia since the Conquest, the question of Latin America's identity. After independence, and particularly as modern nation states began to form towards the end of the 19th century, the search for a national and continental identity played an essential role in the formation of a common sense of nationhood. The influence of European romanticism made writers and artists look for such an identity in Latin America's own version of the 'noble savage', a noble and authentic creature untainted by tawdry modernity. In Argentina the romantic figure of the *gaucho*, the self-reliant cowboy of the pampas, spawned a series of novels and poems in the dying years of the century, glorifying rural life at a time of massive migration to the cities. Although a caricature, gauchismo offered a sense of belonging to a distinctive culture, playing much the same role as the glorification of the cowboy and the 'winning of the west' in the US.

The search for a Latin American identity and debate over politics and art took on greater urgency in the political and cultural ferment that followed the Mexican revolution of 1910-17. The revolutionary Mexican government set about forging a new national consciousness. Under the patronage of a dynamic education minister, José Vasconcelos, a group of Mexican artists began to cover the walls and ceilings of public buildings with murals depicting scenes from Mexican history and allegorical portraits of the revolution. By preferring walls to canvas, the muralists sought to make art the property of the people, not a commodity for sale to the highest bidder. The movement came to be dominated by the 'big three', Diego Rivera, José Clemente Orozco and David Alfaro Siqueiros. Between them, they developed what has been called the greatest public revolutionary art of the century, a maelstrom of unforgettable images of Indians, conquistadores, farmers and bloated capitalists. Rivera, in particular, drew heavily on pre-Columbian designs and the popular artists of his time, notably the skull images of José Guadalupe Posada, who had earned fame for his satirical cartoons prior to the revolution.

Although perhaps unintended by the artists, the murals helped the state establish enduring myths of a new Mexico which had thrown out the rich, white capitalists and now belonged to the poor mestizos and Indians. The muralists' combination of revolutionary zeal with an unquestioning faith in technological progress both excited and enraged the US art establishment. In California in 1933, Rivera's patron, John D. Rockefeller, ordered his 'Man at the Crossroads' destroyed because Rivera refused to remove the figure of Lenin from an allegory of progress in the modern age.

The work of the Mexican muralists has inspired political street art

throughout Latin America. In Chile one of General Pinochet's first actions following the 1973 coup was to whitewash the left-wing murals of Santiago, while in Nicaragua following the Sandinista revolution of 1979, the walls of the cities became littered with revolutionary iconography. Figures like Che Guevara, Sandino, Allende and Zapata joined Bolívar and others on the roll call of Latin America's secular saints.

Football crowds celebrate at the Brazilian cup final, Maracaña stadium, Rio, Brazil.

The Mexican experience was the first example of a phenomenon repeated throughout the continent in the coming years. Populist governments took power, combining limited social reform with a drive to turn the major nations such as Mexico, Brazil and Argentina into industrial powers. By promoting a sense of patriotic identity with its own myths and symbols, populist leaders such as Brazil's Getulio Vargas and Argentina's Juan Domingo Perón could build the national unity needed to implement their model of development and ensure the legitimacy of the state. In Brazil, Vargas seized on samba, carnival and football and used state money to turn them into national icons. Vargas built the Maracaña stadium, the biggest football ground in the world, and transformed carnival into a major international event. Both samba and football were ideal for the purpose, being poor people's pastimes which the state could use to weld people together at both local and national level.

Football also acquired an important political role under the military dictatorships in Brazil and Argentina. The 1964 coup came when Brazilian football was at its height, the national team having won two successive world cups and turned their stars into national heroes, many of them black. Unfortunately the generals could not resist the temptation to meddle, appointing a military official as head of the Brazilian Confederation of Sports who sought to impose greater discipline and teamwork on the individualist genius of Brazilian football. The national team promptly went into decline. The 1978 world cup took place in Argentina, two years after a military coup and amidst a wave of army human rights violations and disappearances. The junta used the national team's victory to seek both national and international legitimacy. Two years later, the goals from the cup final were still being shown every lunchtime on the main shopping precincts of Buenos Aires, a source of enduring national pride in a country with a conspicuously fragile sense of identity.

The political importance of literature and art also showed in the great political weight acquired by the intellectual, a figure of far greater status in Latin America than in Britain or the US. Writers and poets such as Chile's Pablo Neruda, Mexico's Carlos Fuentes and Octavio Paz and Guatemala's Miguel Angel Asturias have served their countries as ambassadors, while in 1987 Peru's Mario Vargas Llosa decided to abandon the pen for the campaign trail and run for president. His political career came to an apparent end following his defeat by Alberto Fujimori in the general election of 1990.

Electronic Ambassadors

The rapid pace of urbanisation since the turn of the century has had a massive impact on popular culture. Towns and cities act as the entry point for foreign influences, while the most remote rural areas remain repositories of traditional culture. As the rural poor flocked to the shanty towns around the major cities, they brought with them traditional customs, which blended with the new influences. In Peru this melting pot has produced what is known as *chicha* culture, named after a potent local brew. *Chicha* music has combined the traditional Andean form of the *huaynu* with tropical music and electric guitars to become the sound of Lima's shanty towns, and shows signs of following the lambada and salsa into the international arena.

The introduction of new electronic media has transformed popular culture in the present century. Film, radio and TV have become the main channels of public communication in society, thereby acquiring a central role in creating and passing on cultural values. The mass media has also become a battleground in the struggle to define Latin America's identity. Increased dependence on Western technology has given huge influence to outside film and TV exporters, with the film industry in particular dominated by Hollywood. Other media, such as radio and TV, have shown greater success in becoming largely national in character, playing an important role in forging national identities.

It is difficult to overestimate the importance of the US as a purveyor of mass culture. The record shops of Latin American cities blare out Michael Jackson and Madonna. Middle-class youth covet the latest Levis or US trainers just as much as their North American or European counterparts. Dubbed or subtitled US films of the *Rambo* and *Rocky* school form the staple diet of scruffy cinemas throughout the continent. Especially since the Cuban revolution of 1959, many artists and writers have come to see US influence in the media as another facet of US political and economic domination of the continent. They argue that its domination allows the US to instil its values into Latin Americans,

acting as a subliminal ambassador which can reach into the poorest home with a dazzling image of the giant to the north. Latin America's intellectuals have stressed the political importance of creating and sustaining a separate Latin American culture in the mass media, as a means of building opposition to the US and finding a political alternative to US domination.

Chicha culture achieves a unique and dynamic blend of traditional Indian and modern imported styles and fashions, Peru.

The high cost and advanced technology required in film-making has meant that Latin America's cinema has lived in the shadow of films from the US and other industrialised nations, but at different moments it has managed to produce high quality films which have challenged the Hollywood monopoly. Until the 1960s most Latin American cinema consisted of low budget musicals, comedies and melodramas whose characters and themes were summed up by the critic John King as 'good women who bear the stigma of fate, weak men caught in the trap of a man-eater, rooms and brothels reeking with smoke and moral turpitude, eyes bloodshot with alcohol and grief, innocence, violent death.'

Yet Latin American cinema has also been intimately involved in politics since the days when the Mexican revolutionary, Pancho Villa, signed an exclusive contract with the US Mutual Film Corporation, granting it exclusive rights to film his battles. For $25,000 he agreed to fight in daylight whenever possible, to rerun scenes of battle if the cameras had missed the real thing, and to reschedule firing-squad executions from 4am until after dawn.

The Cuban revolution marked a watershed for the continent's film-makers, as Havana quickly became the centre of a politically committed 'New Cinema', dedicated to portraying Latin America's conflicts, especially with the US, through a brand of social-realist cinema and documentary. The 1960s and early 1970s saw young radical film-makers using a low budget, hand-held camera style to film life, warts and all, in *favelas* and villages across the region, producing classics such as *Blood of the Condor* (Jorge Sanjinés, Bolivia) and *Battle for Chile* (Patricio Guzmán, Chile). Havana became the host of an annual Latin American Film Festival and invited film-makers from every corner of the Third World to come and study at its international film school.

The New Cinema dominated the 1960s, but soon afterwards the optimism began to wear thin as military dictatorships in the Southern Cone drove film directors into exile and the Cuban government started to show growing intolerance towards dissident writers and directors. Cuba illustrates a problem which has beset the Latin American cinema since its inception. In the absence of private capital, it has frequently had to rely on state support, leaving it open to manipulation and censorship, or simply asphyxiation by a state bureaucracy which cares little for artistic innovation. In recent years, many film-makers have got round the shortage of cash by going in for co-productions with European or US companies, using foreign stars, a development which is the antithesis of the New Cinema's hopes for a unique and pure Latin American genre, but has produced some notable films such as *Kiss of the Spider Woman*, made by the Brazilian director Héctor Babenco, starring William Hurt.

Latin America's national TV networks are relatively recent creations — Brazil's system did not become consolidated until the 1960s. Heavily patronised by the state, which recognised its political potential, Latin American TV has grown rapidly with the rise of the *telenovela*. The percentage of foreign programmes shown on Brazilian TV fell from 60 per cent in 1972 to 30 per cent in 1983 in a process analagous to Brazil's drive for import substitution in industry. In a further parallel with their economic development, Brazil and Mexico have even become TV exporters, breaking into the US market to build a large following for their soaps among the growing Hispanic population.

From the mid-1960s, when the first national *telenovela* was filmed, Latin America's soaps have built on the melodramatic tradition in popular theatre and film, developing rapidly into a major cultural commodity dominated by Brazil and Mexico and their giant media conglomerates, TV Globo and Televisa, who now export soaps throughout Latin America. *The Strange Return of Diana Salazar*, shown by Televisa in 1988, described the reincarnation in today's Mexico of a 17th-century aristocratic woman who had been burned as a witch by the Inquisition. The plot illustrated several key themes in the soap genre. It contained a struggle between good and evil, in which one was often mistaken for the other; it included the obligatory love story, complete with a baroque plot which only addicts could disentangle, and it emphasised individual emotion and melodrama, rather than wider social or political themes. In addition, the soap added a new ingredient to the successful recipe — Diana Salazar could exert special powers over computers, another sign of the assimilation of new influences into existing forms.

Such is the influence of television, that it has been credited with creating a new breed of politician, the 'TV populist'. In 1989 Fernando Collor de Mello came from nowhere to be elected as president of

Brazil. His main assets were good looks, a telegenic style, and the backing of Brazil's mighty TV Globo conglomerate.

Sex and violence fail to interest bored film-goers, Mexico.

The Impact of Cuba

The cultural impact of the Cuban revolution spread far beyond the cinema. In a continent preoccupied with its identity, Cuba became a symbol of resistance to US domination and the search for a new Latin America, where culture was at the service of the people. In the early years of the revolution, the Cuban National Ballet performed classical and folk dance in factories during the lunch breaks, mobile cinema vans took film to isolated villages for the first time, and Havana became an international centre for writers, poets, film-makers and musicians. In the 1960s everything was new, 'New Song' in Chile blended traditional Andean music with folk ballads and revolutionary lyrics, 'New Cinema' recorded real life rather than cinematic fantasies, and the 'New Novel' established a worldwide readership for writers like Mexico's Carlos Fuentes, Cuba's Alejo Carpentier, Colombia's Gabriel García Márquez and the Argentine Julio Cortázar.

While the 1960s phenomenon in Europe peaked in 1968, Latin America's cultural boom reached its zenith a year earlier. In 1967 the Guatemalan author Miguel Angel Asturias became the first Latin American novelist to receive the Nobel prize, Gabriel García Márquez published *One Hundred Years of Solitude*, and Che Guevara was killed in Bolivia. With Che died the optimism of a generation who had grown to believe in imminent revolution. In Cuba the beginning of the 1970s saw the government curtailing cultural freedom and arresting the dissident poet Heberto Padilla, leading many leading figures such as Mario Vargas Llosa to part company with the revolution, after fiercely criticising Fidel Castro.

Since the Cuban revolution, students, radicals and social movements throughout Latin America have tried to create more democratic alternatives to the mass media dominated by big business. This conscious attempt to build a counter-culture to national and international TV, film and music involves myriad grass-roots initiatives, using audio cassettes, community radio, theatre, film and video.

In a dusty square in one of Recife's poorer neighbourhoods, 'TV Viva' is showing community videos on a six feet square screen atop a VW van. Their team of radical journalists makes a monthly 50-minute programme which combines cartoons, community news and radical politics, a typical example of the slick, high-tech Brazilian left. Barefoot children run in and out of the crowd as their parents guffaw at street interviews on the theme of 'when did you last have sex'. Another piece shows how property speculators have been moving in on community football pitches — serious politics in Brazil. When a more traditionally 'political' piece on death squad assassinations comes on, two-thirds of the audience drift away — raising awareness is not always easy.

In developing their community video, TV Viva have learned that broadcasting left-wing diatribes is useless; they must adapt their message to the forms of popular culture if they hope to win an audience. In Lima, a community radio broadcast in a market square to a largely female audience only took off when the women were asked to make their own programmes about their home regions' traditions. Out of this experiment grew a radio soap about a woman migrating to the city, full of political content, but based in the lived experience of the audience.

The 1970s saw gloom settle over much of Latin America. Coups in Chile and Uruguay (1973), and Argentina (1976) coupled with the growing intolerance in Havana led to repression and exile for many intellectuals, and a climate of hostility, fear and censorship for those that remained. The clampdown's best-known victim was Víctor Jara, Chile's top exponent of 'New Song'. Jara was murdered, along with thousands of others, in Santiago's infamous football stadium shortly after the coup. In an act of extraordinary malice, the soldiers crushed the guitarist's fingers before killing him. In exile other musicians such as Chile's Inti Illimani toured the world giving concerts for Chile aimed at raising awareness and money for the solidarity movement. Safeguarded by exile and international fame, already established writers responded with novels of dictatorship: Paraguay's Augusto Roa Bastos published *I, The Supreme*, while García Márquez produced *Autumn of the Patriarch*.

The Nicaraguan revolution of 1979 brought a chink of light to an otherwise sombre panorama. Poetry workshops sprang up in such unlikely places as the secret police and army barracks; a national literacy crusade brought the printed word for the first time to hundreds of thousands of peasants; an internationally acclaimed writer, Sergio Ramirez, became vice-president; state-sponsored musicians, dancers and circus performers sought to recover national traditions, and revolutionary murals adorned the walls of even the smallest village. In Ramirez' words: 'Once we lifted the yankee stone which weighed Nicaragua down, everything that was fundamental and authentic had to surface again: dances, songs, popular art and the country's true history.'

In the Southern Cone, the 1980s brought the military's slow retreat from power. In Argentina, war over the Falklands/Malvinas forced the military to treat youth as the saviours of the country, rather than potential delinquents. Radio stations were ordered to stop broadcasting music in English, giving 'national rock' access to the mainstream media for the first time. The military invited rock stars to take part in pro-war concerts, but instead an anti-war movement sprang up, whose anthem became León Gieco's song, 'Sólo le pido a Dios':

I only ask God
not to make me indifferent to war
It is a great monster that tramples on
the poor innocence of the people

Following defeat in the Falklands, the end of the dictatorship led to a new cultural flowering, for example in Argentine cinema, but the debt crisis and economic recession rapidly led to further cuts in state support for the arts, and a climate of disillusionment.

Latin America's literary establishment remains dominated by the grand old men of the 1960s boom, but new novelists and poets have also emerged. One of the most important developments has been the rise of a generation of women writers and poets, after centuries in which recognised writers were almost exclusively male. Authors such as Chile's Isabel Allende, Brazil's Clarice Lispector and Mexico's Elena Poniatowska are gaining growing readerships both within Latin America and abroad. Allende's *House of the Spirits* became the first genuine bestseller by a woman in Latin American history. Poniatowska has developed a style of documentary narrative to provide a 'people's eye view' of key moments in modern Mexican history, such as the social impact of the earthquake of 1985, and the 1968 Tlatelolco massacre of student protesters by the government. She has pioneered a form of writing in which middle-class women journalists and anthropologists work with working-class and peasant women to produce memorable life stories such as *Let Me Speak*, by Domitila Barrios de Chungara and Moema Viezzer, and *I, Rigoberta Menchú*, by Rigoberta Menchú and Elisabeth Burgos-Debray. In recent years Central America has also produced some renowned woman poets, notably Claribel Alegría (El Salvador) and Giaconda Belli (Nicaragua).

Through novels such as *Betrayed by Rita Hayworth*, and *Kiss of the Spider Woman*, Argentina's Manuel Puig has challenged the radical orthodoxy of the 1960s, with its scorn for Hollywood and cheap mass entertainment of the *telenovela* type. Puig argues that writing off the cultural preferences of a large percentage of the population is an elitist mistake by intellectuals from the traditional left. Instead, they should be embracing mass culture. His characters belie the idea that Latin Americans are passive recipients of whatever the media throw at them; they are quite capable of indulging themselves with Hollywood fantasies while keeping a clear sense of their own identities. Puig also deals with issues of gender and sexuality in a way that has moved some women critics to describe him as the best creator of female characters in Latin American fiction.

Although the euphoria of the 1960s has been lost in decades of militarism and economic crisis, its cultural impact lives on in the continued quest for a truly Latin American identity. Through his music, Panama's Rubén Blades has transformed salsa's traditional blend of tropical rhythm and sentimental lyrics into an exploration of contemporary Latin America. In his best-selling album *Buscando America* (Searching for America), Blades, who intends to run for president in Panama, sums up the pressing challenges that lie ahead:

> I'm searching for America and I fear I won't find her
> ...I'm calling America but she doesn't reply
> those who fear truth have hidden her
> ...while there is no justice there can be no peace
> ...if the dream of one is the dream of all let's break the chains
> and begin to walk
> ...I'm calling you, America, our future awaits us
> before we all die, help me to find her.

The quest for identity has been given new urgency by the debate surrounding the Columbus quincentenary in 1992, when Latin Americans must decide whether to identify with the European conquerors or the Indian conquered. Intellectuals and artists throughout the region refuse to allow its traditional cultures, trampled on or ignored for centuries, to be rediscovered only to be consigned to a tourist museum. They hope to prove that the forms of electronic mass culture, the soap operas, comics and photostories, are not merely the modern-day opium of the people, fostering individualism and passivity, but that they too can be combined with popular traditions to be transformed into an authentic culture of the people.

The fat of the land. The Presidential Family, Fernando Botero.

Chronology

1808-26	Latin American independence wars
1928	Caudillo General Plutarco Calles establishes the National Revolutionary Party (later the PRI) in power in Mexico; the PRI goes on to establish an effective one-party state
1930s	Urbanisation and industrialisation produce new political parties, led by populists
1946	Juan Domingo Perón elected president of Argentina
1958	The two main parties in both Venezuela and Colombia agree to share power in order to end decades of instability and military rule.
1964	Military coup in Brazil marks beginning of wave of military takeovers
1973	Salvador Allende, the world's first elected Marxist president, murdered during the military coup which brings General Pinochet to power
1989	Chile's Christian Democrats lead coalition which wins elections to end Pinochet presidency
1989	TV populist Fernando Collor de Mello wins presidential elections in Brazil
Early 1991	Every Latin American country except Cuba ruled by elected leader

Party Pieces   7

Democracy and Politics

By early 1991, every country in Latin America except Cuba was ruled by an elected leader. In every case bar Paraguay, where General Rodríguez won elections after overthrowing his former commander, General Stroessner, that leader was a civilian. Political power was won and lost not in the guerrillas' mountain hideouts nor in the military barracks, but in the more familiar arena of polling booths, national parliaments, presidential palaces, party headquarters, public meetings and the other battlegrounds of constitutional government.

'Democracy' is an elusive and much abused concept in Latin America. Over the last 30 years, it has meant virtually all things to all political actors. In the heady days of the 1960s the region's left-wing guerrilla movements were fond of condemning all elections as mere 'bourgeois democracy', designed to lend a false legitimacy to the state. Armed revolution in the Cuban style, they argued, was the only road to true 'popular' democracy. In the 1970s military juntas repeatedly swore that they were overthrowing elected governments in order to uphold democracy, before launching bloody pogroms against anyone they labelled as subversive. In Central America throughout the 1980s, the US State Department claimed that the periodic holding of elections in El Salvador would bring about democracy, despite the existence of a civil war, an army that constantly violated human rights and a radical opposition which largely refused to participate.

The origin of the word sheds some light on its true meaning. 'Democracy' stems from Greek roots, meaning literally 'people power'. If the empowerment of ordinary people, rather than a periodic trip to the polling booth, becomes the litmus test of democracy, a rather different picture emerges. Few elected governments in Latin America, (or indeed in Europe or North America), would then qualify as truly democratic.

Several factors prevent the formal democratic structures of elections and parliamentary rule from producing real empowerment in Latin America. Firstly, elected governments are not in total control of their own countries — unelected forces such as large foreign investors, the international financial institutions like the IMF, the military or powerful interest groups such as large landowners all exert huge political influence and have the power to frustrate and even overthrow an elected government if it challenges their interests. Although this criticism also applies to democracies in Europe and the US, the limits on governmental action in Latin America are much stricter. In the 1980s, when the debt crisis left Latin American nations crying out for

La Moneda, presidential palace in Santiago, Chile, burns under the air attack which began the military coup of September 1973. President Allende died during the assault.

aid and debt rescheduling, the IMF and major foreign creditors like the US could exert enormous control over a government's economic policy in return for providing temporary financial relief. When Salvador Allende's elected government in Chile nationalised the all-important copper mines and gave out land to the peasants, the result was a military coup backed by Washington and the US copper companies. Allende's overthrow and death in 1973 convinced many on the left of Latin American politics that real democracy could not be achieved through elections alone, since the economic and military elite would always resort to force to prevent radical change.

Secondly, electoral processes themselves are often far from clean. In many Latin American countries polling day frequently involves vote-buying, intimidation and fraud. A memorable film of Chico Mendes, the Brazilian rubber-tappers' leader, showed him running as a Workers' Party candidate for state deputy in the 1986 state elections. As he strolled down the main street in his home town of Xapuri, greeting his many friends and acquaintances, a stream of local people came up to ask how much he was paying for votes. When he explained that he had no money, they wandered off, bemused. He lost the election. As one of his supporters explained: 'We all need to vote for Chico. But he has nothing to give you. He doesn't have any money or shirts to give away.'

Elsewhere, electoral fraud has been even more blatant. Paraguay's General Stroessner, the archetypal dictator from 1954-89, regularly declared himself victor of presidential elections with 90 per cent of the vote.

Further doubt surrounds the democratic potential of elections held in the midst of civil wars. A climate of violence intimidates both candidates and voters. The left is usually the victim. In Colombia between 1985 and 1990, over 1,000 activists and candidates of the

'The problem was how to find something to eat. We were talking this over when Oscar arrived with the news that over at Don Tiberio's they were giving out roast suckling pig because there were elections on Sunday. We rushed over, and it was true. They were handing out meat and beer on a piece of land at the edge of the village decorated with photos of the candidates and Conservative Party flags. Everyone was very friendly. Most of the people there were relatives, plus a few drunks and others filling their bellies as if they'd never eaten before. We tucked in and promised to vote for the Conservatives.

Half drunk, we were wandering off when someone told us that, on the other side of the village, the Liberals were giving out *aguardiente* (cane liquor), so off we went. There was a great party going on, red flags, rockets and booze coming out of our ears! So once again we promised our vote, this time to the great Liberal Party.

The comrades of the Patriotic Union also had their stall to hunt votes, but all they gave people were soft drinks and lots of speeches. We left with our heads full of ideology, ready to vote for the new party.

We ate twice in each political café and in the end we each voted for whoever we liked. Everyone thought we had voted for their party.'

Alfredo Molano, *Aguas Arriba*, Bogotá, 1990, author's translation

left-wing Patriotic Union coalition were killed, including its presidential candidate Bernardo Jaramillo. The killers were right-wing death squads linked to the army and the cocaine cartels. In such circumstances it is almost impossible for a party to find candidates, campaign or build up its membership, and on polling day, many voters are too scared to vote for them. Elsewhere, as in Peru or El Salvador, guerrilla organisations have also tried to intimidate candidates and prevent the local population from voting.

The Salvadorean elections during the 1980s have been criticised as 'demonstration elections', designed by US officials to convince the US Congress that the country had become a democracy and therefore deserved military and economic aid to fight the civil war against the guerrillas of the Farabundo Martí National Liberation Front (FMLN). Here, the elections equals democracy formula has been enormously successful in reducing domestic opposition to US aid to El Salvador, even though elections have failed to reduce the country's economic and social inequalities or to end the army's atrocious human rights abuses.

Given so many limitations on the empowering potential of elections, the most that can be said is that in Latin America, free elections are a necessary but not sufficient condition for achieving true democracy. The other conditions, such as a military that abjures the coup d'etat, freedom from outside interference, and a government's ability to introduce reforms which benefit the poor, even if they harm vested interests, often prove more elusive than the holding of periodic ballots.

In Latin America, political stability has often been achieved at the expense of democracy in the broader sense. The two governments most often held up as shining examples of the merits of stability are those of Mexico and Venezuela, yet in Mexico the ruling Institutional Revolutionary Party (PRI) effectively runs a one-party state. In Venezuela, the two principal parties got together in 1958 to end decades of military rule by dividing power between them. After foreswearing inter-party violence, they agreed to share out cabinet posts and defend the elected government against any attempt at a military coup. Although this has guaranteed a certain level of democracy and economic development, it has prevented any serious alternative emerging to the two-party duopoly on power. In neighbouring Colombia a similar deal the same year between the Liberal and Conservative parties ended the period of anarchy known as *la Violencia*. As in Venezuela, the agreement helped bar the military from government, but the two parties' resulting stranglehold on power meant that those seeking radical change were left little option but to join the country's guerrilla movements.

On the other hand, attempts at empowerment which have gone beyond the formal mechanism of elections, such as those in Chile under the Allende government or in Nicaragua under the Sandinistas, have often led to instability, the eventual downfall of the government and the end of the democratic experiment. Such experiments, and their overthrow at the hands of the military, foreign powers or vested interests, have meant that no Latin American government to date has managed to achieve both empowering democracy and stability.

Mexico's PRI is a unique institution in Latin American politics. Through a combination of popular reforms, appeals to nationalism, coercion, corruption, and electoral fraud, the PRI has ruled Mexico since 1929, changing its name twice along the way. No other political party in Latin America has matched the PRI's staying power.

Although it is one of the most successful electoral fraudsters in the region, the PRI owes its longevity not to elections but to its control of an enormous and complex web of debts and obligations which reaches into every corner of Mexican society. Known as clientilism, this network creates a vast system of personal allegiance, binding ordinary people to the party, and stifling the emergence of any significant opposition. By keeping in with the party, Mexicans can ensure everything from better rubbish collection to a new road for the neighbourhood, or a better job. Clientilism extends beyond the PRI to the whole of Mexican life; one study in the 1970s showed that 38 per cent of factory and office workers admitted obtaining their jobs through personal contacts.

When clientilism is not enough to prevent a threat to its power, the PRI is quite ready to use bribery and repression. But Mexico's relatively clean human rights record, compared to its more savage neighbours in Central America, attests to the PRI's skill in heading off opposition at an earlier stage; protesting student leaders are all too frequently absorbed into the PRI bureaucracy before they can cause any trouble; trade union activists face the sack or exclusion from a PRI-dominated labour movement. Since the rule of law takes second place to personal loyalties, clientilist systems are also fertile breeding grounds for corruption, and in Mexico bribes are routine for everything from

Joe Fish

Many elected governments live under constant threat of military interference. President Cerezo on the Day of the Army, Guatemala, 1987.

finding a parking space to winning a multi-million dollar government contract.

Clientilist networks have provided the power base for Latin America's *caudillos*, establishing them as regional overlords. Regionalism is still a widespread feature of political life, and in countries such as Brazil can undermine both the strength of nationalism and national political parties. In *The Autumn of the Patriarch*, Gabriel García Márquez recalls the heyday of the central *caudillo* figure:

It was hard to admit that the broken-down old man was the same messianic figure who during the beginnings of his regime would appear in towns when least expected with no other escort but a barefooted Guajiro Indian with a cane-cutting machete and a small entourage of congressmen and senators whom he had appointed himself with his finger according to the whims of his digestion, he informed himself about the crop figures and the state of health of the livestock and the behaviour of the people, he would sit in a reed rocking chair in the shadow of the mango trees on the square fanning himself with the foreman's hat he wore in those days, and even though he seemed to be dozing because of the heat he would not let a single detail go by without some explanation in his talks with the men and women he had called together using their names and surnames as if he had a written registry of inhabitants and statistics and problems of the whole nation inside his head, so he called me without opening his eyes, come here Jacinta Morales, he said to me, tell me what happened to the boy he had wrestled with himself and given a fall the year before so he would drink a bottle of castor oil, and you, Juan Prieto, he said to me, how is your breed bull that he had treated himself with prayers against sickness so the worms would drop out of his ears, and you Matilde Peralta, let's see what you're going to give me for bringing back that runaway husband of yours in one piece, there he is, pulled along with a rope around his neck and warned by him in person that he'd rot in the stocks the next time he tried to desert his legitimate spouse, and with the same sense of immediate governance he had ordered a butcher to cut of the hands of a cheating treasurer in a public spectacle and he would pick the tomatoes in a private garden and eat them with the air of a connoisseur in the presence of the agronomists saying that what this soil needs is a good dose of male donkey shit, it should be spread at government expense, he ordered... because in those days there was nothing contrary in everyday life no matter how insignificant which did not have as much importance for him as the gravest matter of state and he believed sincerely that it was possible to distribute happiness and bribe death with the wiles of a soldier.

Joining the Party

During the period after independence, Latin American politics was a game for the rich, except, needless to say, when it spilled over into war. Voting was restricted to literate male landowners, comprising 1-2 per cent of the population. Parties tended to be either Liberals or Conservatives, reflecting the 19th-century power struggles between the Roman Catholic Church and the state, and between the dominant cities and the backward rural areas. Although the ideological distinctions between them were frequently less important than the personal ambitions of their leaders, Conservatives tended to be pro-Church and supported a centralised system of government which favoured the big cities, while Liberals tended to be anti-clerical and federalist. As often as not, they conducted their discussion on the battlefield; 19th-century Colombia witnessed eight national civil wars, 14 regional civil wars and countless local disputes between the two parties.

In Argentina and Chile the growing middle class became frustrated with what was essentially a dispute between different sections of the wealthy elite, and split off from the Liberals to form the Radical parties which advocated extending the franchise and some welfare legislation.

In the late 1980s, Conservatives and Liberals still dominated politics in Colombia and Uruguay, while the Radicals under Raúl Alfonsín held office in Argentina from 1983-9. Yet elsewhere the traditional political parties have been largely superseded by a new generation of organisations which emerged following the Great Depression and the start of industrialisation from the 1930s onwards.

The Great Depression of the 1930s destroyed the world market for Latin America's commodity exports, bringing to an end the era of unquestioned dominance by the agro-exporting elite. The new drive to build up local industries created growing working and middle classes, who gave their support to a new generation of political leaders. This was the era of the populists, a wave of modern *caudillos*, military men like their 19th-century predecessors. They included Getulio Vargas in Brazil and Carlos Ibáñez in Chile, but the greatest of them

all was Juan Domingo Perón, Argentina's populist leader and beloved father-figure. Perón came to power in elections in 1946, and Peronism has dominated Argentine politics ever since, despite Perón's death in 1974. Together with his wife Evita, he became the object of a personality cult, portrayed as the heroic defender of the nation's *descamisados* (the shirtless ones), a man of the people who oversaw the growth of industry, redistribution of income, and the development of a welfare state.

Juan Domingo Perón

Twenty years after his death, saint-like portraits of Juan and Evita adorn walls in the shanty towns of Buenos Aires. In one of them, Ciudad Oculta, where cooking smells mix with the tang of eucalyptus leaves trampled with the rubbish into the muddy street, a mural of blond beautiful Evita looks out at the dark-skinned Paraguayan immigrant families. As one hard-bitten local activist, Juan Cymes, recalls: 'Evita was a goddess for me when I was a kid. I wrote to ask her to help some poor neighbours and she wrote back to me within a week!' Bearing the slogan 'Social Justice will be achieved inexorably, whatever the cost, whoever falls', the freshly painted mural looks like publicity for this year's presidential candidate. Evita died of cancer in 1952.

Perón expounded the doctrine of *justicialismo* (social justice) which he saw as a third way between capitalism and communism in a world gripped by the deepening Cold War. The state replaced the *caudillo* as the all-powerful provider; it mediated in any dispute between different sectors of society, cared for the sick and elderly, as well as taking a commanding role in the economy via a burgeoning network of state-run industries. Perón's support rested on a highly organised and devoutly Peronist trade union movement, which became virtually an arm of government.

In 1955 Perón's conflicts with the military and the Church led to his overthrow and exile in Madrid. He returned only for a brief and chaotic period as president from 1973-74. Nonetheless, despite his exile and death, and years of military prohibition and persecution, Peronism continues to dominate Argentine politics, preventing the emergence of a stable political party structure. When the Justicialista party lost the election in 1983 to Raúl Alfonsín's Radicals, it seemed the Peronists might be a dying force, yet in 1989 they returned in the shape of President Carlos Saúl Menem, a Peronist *caudillo* from the remote rural province of La Rioja.

Perón typifies the damaging impact of populism on Latin America's political party system. Populist leaders like Perón, Panama's Omar Torrijos or Assad Bucaram in Ecuador created political parties as personal vehicles. When the great man died, the party had no clear way of choosing his successor and often disintegrated or lost political direction. As a result, political parties have failed to develop as coherent, long-term institutions. Other factors have added to this instability:

★ The Latin American military's readiness to seize power has meant that civilian politicians often stood a better chance of coming to power on the coat-tails of the generals, than by taking part in elections. In some countries a queue of frustrated politicians begged the armed forces to overthrow their opponents, thereby undermining the legitimacy of party politics and the electoral process.

★ Even more than in the US, Latin American presidents dominate government at the expense of the elected representatives in Congress. They wield vast powers of patronage, and can frequently bypass Congress altogether by issuing presidential decrees or declaring a state of siege. Consequently, political parties often have no serious role between elections.

★ In some countries internal power struggles lead to parties constantly splitting and reforming. In Bolivia, one researcher listed a total of 323 different political parties active in the period 1958-83.

★ In many countries, because of the absence of well-established party machines and party loyalties, the electorate is far more volatile than in the US or the United Kingdom. In Peru, President Belaúnde's party, *Acción Popular*, slipped from a winning 45 per cent of the vote in 1980 to just seven per cent in 1985, while his successor, Alan García, managed a similar feat by reducing his APRA party's support from 53 per cent in 1985 to 19 per cent in 1990.

Despite this chaotic and constantly changing picture, several broad currents exist among the region's political parties.

Traditional parties: in some countries the original Conservative and Liberal parties of the 19th century have survived by adapting and modernising themselves successfully to prevent the emergence of new rivals. In most cases the source of their power remains a clientilist network, fed by patronage. *Examples:* Colombia; Paraguay; Uruguay

Christian democracy: a political movement born in Western Europe in the 1940s and 1950s, rooted largely in the social doctrines of the Roman Catholic Church. Christian democracy is based on the fight for improved social conditions for the poor, 'traditional values' such as

JOSE NAPOLEON DUARTE: A MAN FOR ALL SEASONS

The career of the late President Duarte of El Salvador typifies the twists and U-turns of Latin America's Christian Democrats. Duarte was a man of messianic convictions, given to comparing himself with Moses, leading the Salvadorean people towards a better future. In 1961, Duarte helped found El Salvador's Christian-Democrat party, becoming its first general secretary (1960-64) and a much-loved mayor of the capital, San Salvador (1964-70). In office he was a model local leader, building schools, introducing street lighting and organising rubbish collections. When he tried to go further, however, he came up against the vested interests which have consistently blocked reforms in El Salvador. In 1972 he won a presidential election, but the army used fraud to deny him victory, and then arrested and tortured him, before sending him into a seven-year exile.

Duarte's political ambition blinded him to the impossibility of achieving reforms within the prevailing system. In 1980 he returned to El Salvador to head a military-civilian junta at a time when the army and death squads were murdering a thousand people a month. From being a radical and troublesome mayor, he had become a sad front-man for the army and the coffee barons. After US backing and finance had helped him to win the presidency in 1984, the army allowed the new-look Duarte to take office, whereupon he presided over a disastrous five years of Christian-Democrat mis-government. He saw his ambitious plans for agrarian reform largely shelved after pressure from the big landowners, the army out of control, and a growing civil war and economic crisis. Prevented by law from standing for a second term, he stood down in 1989. The Christian Democrats split over the succession and lost the presidency to the candidate of the right, Alfredo Cristiani. A defeated man, Duarte died of cancer in 1990.

respect for the family and private property and an opposition to materialism of both the Marxist and capitalist varieties.

Christian democracy reached its height in the 1960s when it spread rapidly all over Latin America. In Chile in 1964, Eduardo Frei became the region's first elected Christian-Democrat president. Over time, Christian-Democrat leaderships failed to deliver on promises of reforms (often due to opposition from landowners and big business) and started to drift to the right, alienating their more radical youth wings, who often split off to form the nuclei for the Christian and revolutionary left groups of the 1970s. By 1973 the Chilean Christian-Democrat party had moved so far to the right that it supported the coup which brought General Pinochet to power. However, the savagery and political exclusion of the Pinochet years forced a change of heart, and the Christian Democrats, led by Patricio Aylwin, headed the coalition that won the elections in December 1989. *Examples:* In Central America there have been Christian-Democrat governments in El Salvador (1984-89) and Guatemala (1985-90). The largest and most influential Christian-Democrat parties are in Chile and Venezuela (Organising Committee for Independent Electoral Policy, COPEI)

National revolutionary movements: often created by the populist leaders of the 1940s and 50s, such as Perón in Argentina or Víctor Raúl Haya de la Torre in Peru. The national revolutionary movements stressed the need for national independence, agrarian and other reforms to benefit peasants and the working class, and a central role for the state in developing the nation and redistributing wealth. In countries with large Indian populations, such as Peru and Mexico, the movements stressed the need to recognise the indigenous elements in national culture.

In keeping with their often erratic founders, these movements have wandered widely over the ideological spectrum. In the early 1970s the Peronist party achieved the remarkable feat of containing within its ranks both the left-wing Montonero guerrillas and the right-wing death squads of the Argentine Anticommunist Alliance.

Examples: Peru (American Popular Revolutionary Alliance, APRA); Venezuela (Democratic Action, AD); Mexico (Institutional Revolutionary Party, PRI); Costa Rica (National Liberation Party, PLN); Bolivia (Revolutionary Nationalist Movement, MNR and Movement of the Revolutionary Left, MIR); Argentina (Justicialista Party — Peronists, PJ); Panama (Democratic Revolutionary Party, PRD)

Communist Parties: Latin America's Communist Parties sit uneasily between the parliamentary parties and the extra-parliamentary left described in the next chapter. Their attitude towards parliamentary politics, as with most other issues, has been dominated by the foreign policy considerations of the Soviet Union, and most Latin American CPs followed the same embarrassing U-turns as Moscow repeatedly changed its line. From 1928-35 the Soviet Union preached revolution, and there were CP-led insurrections in Mexico, El Salvador and Brazil. In the early years of the Second World War the Hitler-Stalin pact forced Latin America's CPs to support the Axis powers until Hitler invaded the Soviet Union in 1941, whereupon they promptly changed sides. The Cold War led to prohibition and repression of CPs in countries such as Argentina, Bolivia, Brazil and Venezuela, from which many parties never recovered.

Since the Second World War most CPs have supported 'popular fronts' with other centre and left-wing parties and the 'peaceful road to socialism' espoused by Salvador Allende in Chile. This has led to severe tensions between orthodox CPs and the guerrilla organisations which sprang up in the wake of the Cuban revolution and the Sino-Soviet split of the 1960s, many of them founded by dissident communists. In Colombia the CP adopted armed struggle in 1966, but continued to participate in electoral politics. Local CPs played little part in the Cuban or Nicaraguan revolutions, and in Nicaragua the CP even joined the right-wing coalition which defeated the Sandinistas in the 1990 elections. The row over guerrilla tactics provoked deep disagreements between Moscow and Havana. In recent years the example of the Nicaraguan revolution and obstacles to peaceful change elsewhere have led CPs in Chile, El Salvador and Guatemala to support armed struggle, although the Chilean party has split over the issue.

In Cuba, Soviet aid supported Fidel Castro's regime following the 1959 revolution and the US economic blockade of 1960, and in 1961 Castro pronounced Cuba to be a socialist state. Outside Cuba, the largest CP has been in Chile, where it played a central role in Allende's Popular Unity coalition. Elsewhere, the loss of supporters to the revolutionary left, and continuing repression under military governments kept most CPs from making any electoral impact. Few have ever won more than 10 per cent of the vote in a national election and at the end of the 1980s there were probably fewer than 200,000 CP members in the whole of Latin America, outside Cuba. By the early 1990s, the Soviet Union's internal crisis had thrown even its continued support for Cuba into question, and the future for the region's CPs appeared grim.

Examples: The largest Communist Parties are those of Cuba and Chile, while small CPs exist in most other Latin American countries.

The military parties: in a number of Latin American countries the armed forces set up proxy political parties to do their bidding in civilian politics. Following the 1964 coup in Brazil, the military abolished all existing political parties, before setting up the National Renovating Alliance (ARENA) and the opposition Brazilian Democratic Movement (MDB). It then fixed the electoral rules so that the pro-military ARENA held a majority in Congress until it was wound up in 1979. In Central America, the Salvadorean military set up the National Conciliation Party (PCN) in 1961 and it dominated the National Assembly for the next 18 years. Most such parties have gone into decline over the last decade, following the military's retreat from power.

Examples: ARENA (Brazil), PCN (El Salvador)

Anti-establishment populists: recent years have seen a rise in presidential candidates who present themselves as 'outsiders', willing to take on an unpopular political establishment and promising a radical change from the traditional political parties. In Brazil's 1989 election campaign, Fernando Collor de Mello overcame his lack of party support by cashing in on his charisma and the backing of Brazil's powerful TV Globo media conglomerate. In Peru, Alberto Fujimori's independent 'Change 90' movement came from just 0.5 per cent in the opinion polls to win him the presidency three months later. Once in office, both men found that their lack of a party base forced them to play politics with the traditional parties they had attacked during the campaign. So far, the result has been an erratic form of coalition politics offering few prospects of a better future for the deprived majorities of both countries.

Examples: Alberto Fujimori/Change 90 (Peru), Fernando Collor de Mello/National Reconstruction Party, PRN (Brazil)

The Left

Latin America's left, discussed in detail in the next chapter, has long struggled to achieve forms of democracy which go beyond formal 'bourgeois' democratic structures to achieve real participation and empowerment for the region's poor majority.

The long road to democracy. Voting queue, Managua, Nicaragua, 1984.

Nicaragua under the Sandinista government (1979-90) encapsulates many of the arguments and dilemmas over the left's attitude to formal democracy. The Sandinistas came to power in 1979 as a small guerrilla organisation whose structure and ideas had been forged in the underground war against the Somoza dictatorship. Throughout the period of Sandinista rule, the party itself remained a small, vanguard organisation of hand-picked activists which sought to provide leadership for a wider popular movement.

At first the FSLN appeared to disparage electoral democracy, preferring more direct forms of participation. The party's leaders toured the country conducting face-to-face talks with peasants and workers to hear their complaints, and popular organisations such as trade unions, peasants and women's groups were given seats on a consultative Council of State, established to advise the FSLN in government. The party's cadres were told to act as the eyes and ears of the government, keeping it in touch with ordinary Nicaraguans.

Results were mixed. The emphasis on participation and organisation transformed a large part of Nicaraguan society. Many of the poor gained self-confidence as they learned to read and write and became involved in a myriad of 'mass organisations'. Since these organisations were largely controlled by the party, however, they were often forced to put party or national interests before those of their members. Participation dropped off as people became exhausted by endless meetings, the growing economic crisis and the rigours of the war against the US-trained and financed Contra rebels.

In 1984 the FSLN held presidential elections to try and win international recognition as a legitimate government and thus bring pressure to bear on Washington to stop funding the Contras. Under pressure from the US embassy, some right-wing opposition parties boycotted the ballot, but the FSLN went on to win 67 per cent of a free vote against both right- and left-wing parties, showing that it remained a hugely popular government. Displeased by the result, President Reagan declared the election illegitimate, and the war ground on.

From 1984-90, the FSLN ruled Nicaragua in the dual role of a government that had been freely elected, but which also saw itself as a non-parliamentary vanguard party working directly with the mass organisations. Over time, its views of the role of elections in democracy changed. Instead of a tactical measure designed to forestall US pressure, elections became more central to Sandinista philosophy.

In February 1990 the FSLN was stunned when it lost the election to Violeta Chamorro's UNO coalition. The defeat showed the extent to which the party had lost touch with ordinary Nicaraguans and led to a far-reaching process of self-criticism. The FSLN also surprised its critics by calmly accepting the result and promising to play the role of a loyal opposition. The revolutionary vanguard had assumed the role of opposition in a party political system. In opposition, the FSLN began to discuss its final transformation into a more traditional form of political party.

Elections have come to play a more central role in the left's programme in countries such as Brazil, Colombia and El Salvador. The failure of numerous guerrilla movements and the repression at the hands of military regimes led activists to give greater importance to the legal and constitutional safeguards provided by elected governments. The collapse of one-party states in Eastern Europe also influenced left opinion by showing the dangers that non-elected governments face in becoming isolated from ordinary people.

With the exceptions of Chile (1970) and Nicaragua (1984), the left has won most of its victories at local government level. In Peru the United Left's Alfonso Barrantes became mayor of Lima in 1983, and literally kept the poor alive with a free milk programme during a period of intense economic hardship. In Brazil the Workers' Party (PT) won the giant city of São Paulo and 35 other major towns in November 1988. In late 1989 Uruguay's Broad Front broke the two-party duopoly to take control of the capital city, Montevideo.

At national level, the left revived in the late 1980s and came close to several breakthroughs. In Brazil, the PT leader, Luis Inâcio da Silva (Lula), was narrowly defeated at the hands of Fernando Collor de Mello, while in Mexico's 1988 elections the PRI used fraud to cheat Cuauhtémoc Cárdenas and the Democratic National Front of probable victory. Both Lula and Cárdenas attempted to involve the new social movements in their electoral platforms and campaigns, opening up the exciting prospect of a new form of political organisation which can take power by bridging the gulf between the traditional parties and grassroots movements.

Despite their historic weaknesses, the political parties were the main beneficiaries of the military's retreat from government during the 1980s, described in chapter 12. Their role in driving the generals from power was often secondary to the pressures created by the military's own political and economic failures, but every process of 'democratisation' ended in elections and the chance for a political party to return to power.

The parties suffered under military rule. In Argentina and Chile thousands of activists were tortured or killed and party structures driven underground. Despite this, when the political spaces once again opened up, it was the old parties which reappeared, albeit chastened by their experience and more willing to work together to avoid presenting the military with further reasons to intervene.

The region's democratisation in the 1980s is not its first. There appears to be a regular cycle of dictatorship, followed by a return to elected government. In the 1930s, the Depression destabilised many economies, leading to an upsurge in communist and other protest movements and a wave of military interventions. During the 1950s, democratic governments returned to most of the continent, producing a short-lived optimism that the period of military rule was over. From 1964-76 the generals once again took power, before withdrawing once again during the 1980s.

The process of democratisation in the 1980s coincided with Latin America's deepening economic crisis. Optimism over the return of elected leaders soon faded into despair and disillusionment as poverty and hunger grew. This produced both a growing scepticism towards traditional political parties and an increasing preference for 'anti-politics' candidates, such as Peru's Alberto Fujimori and President Fernando Collor de Mello in Brazil.

Despite the wide ideological range of the political parties in power during the 1980s, the external pressures of the debt crisis, the IMF, and the general acceptance of the failure of the state-led development model of previous decades, has led to an increasing uniformity in their policies, once in office. Free market measures have been introduced by the avowedly statist PRI in Mexico and the Peronists in Argentina, while in Peru in 1990 Alberto Fujimori won the presidency by condemning the free-market ideas of his rival, novelist Mario Vargas Llosa, and then promptly introduced a remarkably similar programme!

One of the tragedies of the debt crisis and the 1980s' 'lost decade of development' has been that it has coincided with the return to civilian rule, which could have been a first step to empowerment for Latin America's poor. Instead, elected governments have been obliged to make the poor pay, through austerity programmes and cutting subsidies, for debts incurred by others. Economic austerity has eroded the hopes that millions had placed in the return to constitutional government. Perhaps their disappointment will make them seek other options for establishing a real empowering democracy in Latin America, for example through the grassroots 'social movements' described in the next chapter. Yet the danger remains that their disillusion will open the doors to a new generation of populists or generals offering crude, brutal and illusory solutions to the continent's problems.

Mike Goldwater/Network

Young radio operators of the FPL guerrillas, El Salvador, 1984. Throughout the 1980s women played an increasingly important role in guerrilla and non-violent movements for change.

Chronology

1910-17	Mexican revolution
1926	Augusto César Sandino returns to Nicaragua to begin a guerrilla war against occupying US forces
1959	Cuban revolution marks first successful guerrilla campaign and leads to wave of *foquista* guerrilla insurgencies throughout Latin America
1967	Death of Che Guevara in Bolivia
1970	Peru's Shining Path movement founded in remote Andean province
1979	Sandinista-led insurrection in Nicaragua becomes second guerrilla victory in the Americas
1979	Founding of Brazilian Workers' Party (PT), based on the support of the new 'social movements'
1980	Founding of Farabundo Martí National Liberation Front (FMLN) in El Salvador
1988	In local elections, Brazil's PT wins São Paulo and 30 other towns and cities
1990	Sandinistas voted from power in presidential elections

The Left

8

Guerrillas and Social Movements

The first sign of the squatters was a huge red flag flapping above a depression in the hills a few hundred yards away. Across two barbed wire fences and an arid, sandy hillside lay the cluster of huts thrown up by 40 landless families weeks before. They had called the encampment Esperança ('Hope'). Already the inhabitants were making the first improvements — tiles were starting to replace plastic sheets on the roofs of the huts, whose walls were made from branches tied together with twine. To provide safety in numbers, 500 people had originally occupied the site. When ten armed policemen promptly arrived to evict them, the children stood in front with stones, then the women and adolescents, followed by the men armed with their primitive farming tools. The policemen backed off without a fight, allowing the squatters to get on with planting their first crops of yams and fennel.

The red flag belongs to Brazil's Movement of Landless Workers, the MST. The MST leads landless peasants and the urban poor in well-organised invasions of waste land in the cities or uncultivated farmland elsewhere. Standing amidst newly ploughed furrows thirsty for rain, one of the squatters explained: 'People came here for land. We weren't interested in riches — land created people and people must live from it. The owner says the land is his, but if he doesn't even farm it, how can that be?' As he talks, the skies open. Rain sheets across the grey fields and through the torn plastic roofs, onto the dripping but delighted farmers.

The MST is one of a number of organisations whose political activity, in this case over the explosive issue of land, takes place outside parliamentary channels. In Latin America's shanty towns, women's organisations pressure local councils for food and milk for their children, and neighbourhood committees demand electricity or paved roads, while in the rural areas peasant organisations lobby for land reform or better credit from the state bank. In Colombia and Central America, human rights organisations demonstrate and protest about the 'disappearance' of their loved ones, and radical priests and nuns set up 'Base Christian Communities' to discuss the Bible and its message for the poor. What such a diverse range of organisations have in common is their use of extra-parliamentary action to gain the attention of the authorities, and a commitment to direct action in order to improve their lives. In 1987 that commitment saw them classified by the annual conference of Latin American and US armies as one of the sinister faces of the 'international communist movement', making them in military eyes a legitimate target for state repression under the

Susan Meiselas/Magnum

The day of triumph. After years fighting in the mountains, Sandinista guerrillas celebrate the overthrow of the Somoza dictatorship, Nicaragua, 1979.

national security doctrine (see chapter 12).

The best known apostles of extra-parliamentary activity are the guerrillas. In the 1970s no western student bedsit seemed complete without its poster of Che Guevara, with beret and beard, gazing mistily off into the middle distance. The real thing can look somewhat different. On a hot afternoon in the hills of a guerrilla-controlled area in El Salvador, the two ragged 'freedom fighters' patrolling the road looked about 11 years old and had great difficulty carrying their M16 rifles. In a nearby town, however, 'Diego', a handsome political officer of the Farabundo Martí National Liberation Front (FMLN) lived up to expectations. In neat fatigues, he personified the myth of the guerrilla fighter, caricatured by Peruvian novelist Mario Vargas Llosa in *The Real Life of Alejandro Mayta*:

> His beard had grown, he was thin, in his eyes there was an unconquerable resolve, and his fingers had grown calloused from squeezing the trigger, lighting fuses and throwing dynamite. Any sign of depression he might feel would disappear as soon as he saw how new militants joined every day, how the front widened, and how there, in the cities, the workers, servants, students and poor employees began understanding that the revolution was for them, belonged to them.

An embarrassed priest served coffee and biscuits as Diego described his political work with the local peasants. Outside, the walls of the village were plastered with FMLN graffiti and posters proclaiming that June was to be a month without alcohol — village meetings convened by the guerrillas had decided that drunkenness was a serious problem. A short drive away lay the last army roadblock — in tiny El Salvador guerrillas and army are rarely more than a few miles apart.

The FMLN, who throughout the 1980s fought a guerrilla war against a US-funded and trained army, are heirs to a long Latin American tradition. In 19th-century Argentina the cowboy Montoneros of the pampas fought an unsuccessful civil war to free the interior from the stranglehold of Buenos Aires. Elsewhere, irregulars helped to win independence from Spain. As the century wore on, such exotic bands passed into folklore as they were replaced by regular standing armies.

The guerrilla tradition was rediscovered in the 1920s by Augusto César Sandino, the Nicaraguan rebel whose distinctive ten-gallon hat became the symbol of revolutionary Nicaragua. In 1912, US marines occupied Sandino's homeland, leaving in 1925 only to return again the following year. As a young man, Sandino had worked in the Mexican oilfields and was influenced by the anti-yankee and socialist ideas of the Mexican revolution. When the marines returned to Nicaragua, Sandino followed. With a band of 29 fighters, he began to harass the US forces. When conventional tactics led to a series of defeats, reducing his company to just six, he developed a new style of fighting which later became the model for guerrilla warfare. According to this model, the successful guerrilla should:

★ avoid set-piece confrontations where the enemy's superior firepower will give it an advantage;

★ use hit-and-run tactics and surprise rather than defend fixed positions. The objective is not to seize and defend territory, but to make the costs of staying unacceptably high to the enemy;

★ stay in small groups to avoid detection and increase mobility;

★ rely on superior knowledge of the terrain and contacts with local people to outwit the enemy.

Sandino's movement gathered force, giving the Nicaraguan brief fame as a romantic hero at the head of 6,000 fighters. When the Kuomintang marched into Peking in 1928, they named a division after Sandino, and a thriving anti-war movement in the US sang his praises. For the first time, the US experienced the frustration of facing an enemy that wouldn't 'fight fair'. In the words of the writer and former Sandinista Vice-President Sergio Ramírez:

> The well-trained and elegantly uniformed yankee soldiers could find only one phrase to describe it: 'damned country'. Rains, mosquitoes, swamps, swollen rivers, wild animals, the horror of suddenly falling into an ambush, fevers, an always invisible enemy.

The words could just as well describe the US nightmare in Vietnam, and the US forces in Sandino's Nicaragua reacted in much the same way, venting their anger on civilians they suspected of supporting the guerrillas and thereby swelling the numbers of Sandino's supporters.

In 1933 the US changed tactics, withdrawing from Nicaragua and setting up a National Guard which soon came under the control of Anastasio Somoza. Sandino's fight had always been primarily a nationalist one, so when the marines left he accepted partial disarmament and peace talks. In 1934 as Sandino and his generals were leaving a dinner in the presidential palace, they were ambushed and shot dead by Somoza's men.

The world forgot about Sandino, and the ensuing Somoza dictatorship did its utmost to wipe out his memory within Nicaragua, but his example inspired a group of radical students in the 1960s, who formed a new guerrilla band, the Sandinista National Liberation Front (FSLN), and took to the hills in Sandino's old strongholds. There they found many ageing Sandinistas willing to help them. One guerrilla leader, Omar Cabezas, recalls the time when a young Sandinista came for the first time to an old farmer's hut. 'See, I knew you'd come back', the *campesino* said with a grin, 'I've got something you left behind last time'. He then dug up an Enfield rifle from the time of the marines, buried for 50 years since the days when Sandino roamed the mountains.

Castro, Cuba and Che

While Sandino's memory smouldered in the Nicaraguan hills, it was the Cuban revolution of 1959 which marked the start of the modern guerrilla era. Cuba under the Batista dictatorship combined misery in the countryside and urban slums with a millionaire's playground of casinos and brothels for US tourists and organised crime. Cuba's guerrilla war began in 1956 when Fidel Castro and 81 men, including the young Argentine Che Guevara, squeezed onto a motor launch called *Granma* and set off from Mexico to invade Cuba. The mission was a disaster; Castro's 26 July Movement had already been infiltrated by Batista's secret service, and the Cuban troops were waiting for them. Fewer than 20 survivors fled to the mountains of the Sierra Maestra to lick their wounds and begin a two-year guerrilla war. Batista's ferocity and intransigence fuelled peasant support for the guerrillas; in 1957 he attempted to forcibly relocate the rural population of the Sierra Maestra. By 1958 opposition political parties, landowners and businesses had joined in, while the guerrilla force had grown into a rebel army which was attacking the government forces on three separate fronts and was able to take and hold fixed positions. Castro mounted a nationwide offensive, during which Che Guevara's soldiers succeeded in splitting the country in two. Batista fled to the Dominican Republic in early 1959 and Fidel Castro swept into Havana.

Cuba had a huge impact on the thinking of the Latin American left. Most of the analysis and theorising occurred after the event, as Guevara and others, such as Parisian intellectual Régis Debray developed the new theory of the guerrilla *foco* (small nucleus of guerrilla fighters). *Foquismo* was based on three conclusions from the Cuba campaign:

★ Irregular forces can defeat a standing army.

★ Revolution can be triggered in underdeveloped countries by *focos* of guerrillas. Previously the Communist Party, which had dominated the debate, had insisted that revolution could only be achieved once the 'objective conditions' for revolution were present. This entailed the creation of a 'bourgeois democracy' and the growth of an industrial proletariat who would then form the vanguard for a predominantly urban revolution.

ERNESTO 'CHE' GUEVARA

The 20th century's most famous guerrilla fighter was born Ernesto Guevara in Argentina in 1928 to middle-class parents, and qualified as a doctor in 1953. Guevara became a committed communist from the time of the 1954 CIA-instigated overthrow of the radical Arbenz government in Guatemala. In that sense, he was much more radical than Fidel Castro, who only embraced communism when US hostility forced revolutionary Cuba into the arms of the Soviet Union.

Guevara, a tall asthmatic man, became a Cuban citizen a month after the revolution. Castro made him President of the National Bank and Minister of Industries. Always a hardliner, he argued that Cuba should seize the Soviet missiles when Kruschev agreed to withdraw them to end the 1962 missile crisis. In 1965 he left Havana on an eight-month tour of revolutionary movements all over the world. Itching for a return to the guerrilla struggle, he embarked in 1966 on the Bolivian episode which led to his death the following year.

Part of Guevara's legacy to Cuba has been insistence on the need for a 'new man', motivated not by profit but by moral commitment to the cause of progress and equality:

'The process is a conscious one. The individual perceives the impact of the new social power and perceives that he is not completely adequate to it. He tries to adjust...He is educating himself. We can see the new man who begins to emerge in this period of the building of socialism.... The [new men] no longer march in complete solitude along lost roads towards far-off longings. They follow their vanguard, composed of the party, of the most advanced workers, of the advanced men who move along bound to the masses and in close communion with them.... The reward is the new society, where human beings will have different characteristics: the society of communist man..... He will thus achieve total awareness of his social being, which is equivalent to his full realization as a human being, having broken the chains of alienation.'

Che Guevara, *Man and Socialism in Cuba*, Havana, 1965

★ In the underdeveloped nations of Latin America the war would be fought in the countryside and depend on the peasantry, again contradicting Communist Party orthodoxy.

Guevara and Debray's ideas triggered a wave of unsuccessful attempts to repeat the Cuban experience in other Latin American countries. Many of the young men and women who took to the guerrilla's harsh life in the mountains did so because they had seen all peaceful means for bringing about change blocked by a combination of electoral fraud and physical repression. In El Salvador the military denied electoral victory to a reforming coalition of political parties in the 1972 and 1977 elections, thereby triggering a spiral of frustration and violence which was to plunge the country into a decade of horror during the 1980s. The young Salvadorean guerrillas were students, peasant organisers or lay preachers of the Catholic Church who had

BECAUSE I WANT PEACE

Because I want peace
and not war
because I don't want to see
hungry children
squalid women
men whose tongues
are silenced
I have to keep on fighting.
Because there are clandestine
cemeteries
and Squadrons of Death
drug-crazed killers
who torture
who maim
who assassinate
I want to keep on fighting.
Because on the peak
of Guazapa
my brothers peer out
from their bunkers
at three battalions
trained in Carolina
and Georgia
I have to keep on fighting.
Because from Huey
helicopters
expert pilots
wipe out villages
with napalm
poison the rivers
and burn the crops
that feed the people
I want to keep on fighting.
Because there are liberated
territories
where people
learn how to read
and the sick are cured
and the fruits of the soil
belong to all
I have to keep on fighting.
Because I want peace
and not war.

Claribel Alegria, *Poesía Viva*, translated by El Salvador Solidarity Campaign

seen their efforts at peaceful protest met with bullets.

To some, the romantic appeal of *foquismo* lay in its offer of a short-cut to power. A few student or intellectual heroes, with sufficient courage and political clarity, could go up into the mountains and lead the people to inevitable victory. For the region's angry and disenchanted middle-class youth, this was a far more exciting prospect than years of toil within the trade union and peasant movement.

Young radicals formed guerrilla groups in Venezuela, Colombia, Peru, Bolivia, Guatemala and Nicaragua, all of which met with failure or were forced radically to rethink their tactics. A generation of young radicals, poets, students and peasant leaders lost their lives.

Guevara's own attempt to bring revolution to Bolivia in 1966 showed many of the fatal errors in the *foquismo* theory. Choosing Bolivia because it was the poorest country in Latin America and 'ripe for revolution', Guevara set off with a team of 16 Cubans and headed for a remote south-eastern province to set up their *foco*. The obstacles proved insuperable; although the guerrillas managed to recruit a few Bolivians, the leadership was entirely Cuban, and none of them could speak Guaraní, the local Indian language, and local people viewed the outsiders with suspicion. Furthermore, the region they chose was more prosperous than surrounding regions, and was so cut off that it had almost no contact with the capital, La Paz, and therefore no-one had suffered directly at the hands of central government.

With intensive counter-insurgency training from the US, the Bolivian army soon tracked down and defeated the isolated 'freedom fighters', and Guevara was shot. Following his death, the *foquismo* theory came in for severe criticism, as new wars in Vietnam and later Nicaragua provided alternative models for guerrilla war.

The late 1960s and early 1970s saw a new phenomenon, the urban guerrilla movements in the more advanced countries to the south. In Argentina, the Montoneros named themselves after the horseback irregulars of the 19th century, while in Uruguay the Tupamaros took their name from Peru's 18th-century Indian rebel leader Túpac Amaru II (see page 165). Similar movements sprang up in Brazil and Colombia. These groups concentrated on spectacular actions, described as 'armed propaganda', intended to win publicity and popular support. Some kidnapped prominent politicians, ambassadors and businessmen, while in Colombia the M-19 guerrilla group announced itself by symbolically stealing the sword of independence hero Simón Bolívar. Such actions, however, won little lasting support and frequently led to severe repression at the hands of the military, who aimed far beyond the guerrillas to attack the whole popular movement. In Argentina, 90 per cent of the 5,000 Montoneros lost their lives. Such groups have been criticised for their lack of political direction and tendency to use methods little different from terrorism.

After the failure of the *foquistas* and the urban guerrilla movements, the armed left continued to seek the right strategy for the seizure of state power. Following the US defeat at the hands of a guerrilla army in Vietnam, guerrilla leaders pored over the writings of strategists such as General Nguyen Giap:

> The political, economic and military aspects are equally important, but most important is the political factor, the 'people' factor. That is why in the last war, with the support of the people, we succeeded in building up relatively safe bases, not only in inaccessible mountainous regions, but also in the midst of the vast, open delta region, criss-crossed with rivers and studded with enemy posts.

Vietnam put the people back at the centre of guerrilla warfare. In what became known as 'prolonged popular war', guerrilla organisations such as the Popular Liberation Forces (FPL) in El Salvador embarked on a patient long-term programme of political work with the peasantry. As a result, guerrilla organisations became less dominated by students, and increasingly came to be genuine peasant armies. The new generation of guerrilla organisations placed greater importance on links with trade union and other popular organisations. These offered the guerrillas support networks, fertile ground for political work and recruitment, and a legal front for organising non-violent protests such as strikes and demonstrations. The thorny question of how far social movements in countries such as El Salvador or Peru are controlled by guerrilla organisations has enabled the military to justify its attacks on social movements as part of its

Andean village wrecked by guerrillas of Sendero Luminoso in Latin America's most brutal civil war, Peru.

counter-insurgency campaign (see chapter 12).

Other experiences enriched guerrilla thinking; the Nicaraguan revolution of 1979 showed the need for unity between different ideological currents on the left and demonstrated how a combination of rural guerrilla warfare and urban insurrection could produce a quick victory. In Peru, the extraordinary advances of Sendero Luminoso (Shining Path) appeared to show that an authoritarian and violent movement built around a god-like leader in Abimael Guzmán ('President Gonzalo') could win over the oppressed Indian communities of the Andes with the promise of unheard-of security. As the years passed, and no magic formula for revolution emerged, guerrilla groups accepted that each struggle had to be rooted in each country's different traditions, populations and terrain.

The debates have led to numerous divisions, sometimes leading to internecine warfare and murder. Although such arguments may seem highly theoretical, they are in fact crucial to the success or failure of guerrilla warfare. Different movements must decide between pursuing painstaking political work in the countryside, thereby risking a rapid counterattack by the local army, or calling for a swift insurrection, whereupon all guerrilla sympathisers have to come into the open, risking death if the insurrection fails. Some organisations propose alliances with middle-class and even military factions as a necessary step, whereas others argue that this opens the way to the revolution being hijacked and eventually betrayed.

Latin America's Main Guerrilla Movements

Colombia: Colombia has the longest guerrilla tradition in Latin America. Many of today's fighters are third-generation guerrillas. There are four principal organisations, all of which have been involved in peace talks with the Colombian government at various points since the early 1980s. Despite sporadic attempts to build a unified umbrella organisation, Colombia's guerrillas have been unable to unite like their counterparts in El Salvador or Guatemala:

ELN (National Liberation Army, *Ejército de Liberación Nacional*). Founded in 1964. A pro-Cuban group of 600-1,000 combatants, which specialises in attacks on oil pipelines belonging to foreign oil companies.

M-19 (19 April Movement, *Movimiento 19 de Abril*). Founded in 1973. Its ideology is an eclectic mixture of radical liberalism, Marxism and social democracy. Specialised in kidnappings, ransoms and sabotage. In 1984 the M-19 became the first guerrilla organisation to sign a ceasefire with the government, allowing it to compete openly in politics. Although the initial agreement broke down, M-19 continued to pursue a return to civilian politics despite the assassination of many of its leaders. In elections, it achieved good results at both local and national level. In December 1990 it became the largest single party in the constituent assembly set up to rewrite Colombia's constitution, leading observers to foresee possible victory in future presidential elections.

EPL (People's Liberation Army, *Ejército Popular de Liberación*). Founded in 1968 by the pro-Chinese Communist Party. Has also been involved in on-off peace talks with the government, leading to ceasefires in 1984 and 1991. Claims 2,000 combatants.

FARC (Revolutionary Armed Forces of Colombia, *Fuerzas Armadas Revolucionarias de Colombia*). Founded in 1964 and adopted two years later by the pro-Moscow Communist Party. Claims 5,000 combatants.

El Salvador: The five guerrilla organisations of El Salvador came together in 1980 to form the Farabundo Martí National Liberation Front (FMLN). During the course of the next decade they proved themselves one of the largest and most durable of Latin America's guerrilla movements, surviving years of bombing, repression and army attack to number some 11,000 fighters in 1984. Three-quarters of the fighters belonged to the FPL and ERP (see below), who along with the Communist Party, exert most influence in the organisation. The different guerrilla organisations forged an increasingly united front, with combined operations in the field, and joint political and diplomatic work elsewhere. As the decade drew to a close, the FMLN made greater efforts to achieve a negotiated peace with the government and army, although it remained acutely aware of the assassinations and destruction experienced by the Colombian guerrillas after they had laid down their arms. The five organisations are:

FPL (Popular Liberation Forces, *Fuerzas Populares de Liberación — Farabundo Martí*). Founded in 1970 by dissidents from the Salvadorean Communist Party, whose ex-General Secretary, Salvador Cayetano Carpio, became its leader, The FPL's stronghold lies in the northern province of Chalatenango. Although initially a strong supporter of prolonged popular war, a violent internal feud in 1983 led it to fall into line with the other organisations' efforts to win a negotiated peace.

ERP (People's Revolutionary Army, *Ejército Revolucionario del Pueblo*). Formed in 1972 by disenchanted Christian Democrats. Its early history was marked by internal division and assassinations, including that of Salvadorean poet Roque Dalton. The ERP has favoured insurrection over the longer-term strategies espoused by the FPL before 1983. The ERP became the strongest military group in the alliance, with its power base in the eastern province of Morazán.

PCS (Salvadorean Communist Party, *Partido Comunista Salvadoreño*). Set up in 1930 and based on urban trade unions. In 1972 it stood as a partner of the Christian Democrats and others in an electoral alliance, but was deprived of victory through fraud. After a similar experience in 1977, the PCS eventually accepted the need for armed struggle. Within the FMLN it has few fighters, but great political influence.

The other, less influential, FMLN guerrilla organisations are the RN (National Resistance) and the PRTC (Revolutionary Party of Central American Workers).

Guatemala: A little known guerrilla war has been going on in Guatemala since 1962, when the FAR (see below) commenced operations. The guerrillas reached their high point in the early 1980s, when Guatemala appeared poised to follow Nicaragua into revolution. Instead, the government and army unleashed a merciless counter-insurgency campaign which killed tens of thousands of guerrilla sympathisers in the Indian highlands. Nevertheless, the guerrillas survived, grouped together in the URNG (Guatemalan National Revolutionary Unity, *Unidad Revolucionaria Nacional Guatemalteca*) from 1982. By the late 1980s they were claiming 3,000 combatants, though others put their numbers as low as 1,500. The three main guerrilla organisations are:

FAR (Rebel Armed Forces, *Fuerzas Armadas Rebeldes*). Founded in 1962 by dissident young army officers after a failed military revolt. The FAR broke free from Communist Party control in 1968 and by the end of the decade were effectively defeated by a US-assisted counter-insurgency campaign. The survivors regrouped in the remote northern department of Petén which became their stronghold, and resumed working with the Communist Party.

EGP (Guerrilla Army of the Poor, *Ejército Guerrillero de los Pobres*). Set up in 1972, espousing a prolonged popular war strategy. The EGP was the first group to involve large numbers of Guatemala's impoverished Indians, based in the Indian highlands of Quiché and Huehuetenango. The EGP was particularly hard hit by the army's massacres of its Indian supporters.

ORPA (Organisation of the People in Arms, *Organización del Pueblo en Armas*). Publicly launched in 1979, both it and the EGP were set up by dissidents from the FAR. The ORPA, like the EGP, incorporated large numbers of Indians in its ranks, but emphasised military action, rather than long-term political work. Strongholds in San Marcos and around Lake Atitlán.

The URNG also includes factions of the small and divided Guatemalan Communist Party (PGT)

Peru: *Sendero Luminoso* (Shining Path). Full name: the Communist Party of Peru — for the Shining Path of José Carlos Mariátegui. Mariátegui (1895-1930) was the founder of Peruvian communism. A maoist organisation set up in 1970 under the leadership of Abimael Guzmán, Shining Path believes in a prolonged popular war of up to 50 years, surrounding the cities from the countryside and simultaneously leading urban armed struggle. From its original base in Ayacucho, Shining Path has spread out until it now operates in 21 of Peru's 24 departments. By the mid-1980s it was believed to have 2-3,000 regular fighters with many more in part-time militia and urban cells. Shining Path is unique among Latin American guerrilla organisations in its rejection of all alliances — many of its attacks have been on other guerrilla organisations or social movements not controlled by itself. Among Indian communities it exercises a form of violent retributive justice using corporal punishment and execution against petty criminals, government officials, thieves, drunks and adulterers. Despite its brutality, it has won peasant support, especially from women, by imposing order on a disintegrating Andean society. Although Shining Path has committed well documented atrocities, most of the 15,000 deaths in the civil war up to mid-1988 were undoubtedly the work of the armed forces in a bloody and often indiscriminate counter-insurgency campaign.

In the early 1980s Shining Path also established a presence in the upper Huallaga valley, Peru's main coca growing region. After a series of pitched battles, it succeeded in driving out the police, army, other guerrilla organisations and even the drug traffickers' gunmen. Shining Path was then able to collect an estimated $40m a year in taxes on the cocaine trade. Unlike guerrilla organisations in Colombia, El Salvador and Guatemala, Shining Path shows no interest in a negotiated peace, preferring to fight for an eventual total victory, however high the cost.

MRTA (Túpac Amaru Revolutionary Movement, *Movimiento Revolucionario Túpac Amaru*). Shining Path's chief rival, set up in 1983 and named after the 18th-century Indian rebel leader. Smaller and weaker than Shining Path, it numbers only a few hundred militants and has suffered both at their hands and those of the army.

Victorious Revolutions

Despite the idealism and courage of generations of guerrillas, the only two successes they have to show for 30 years of fighting and bloodshed are Cuba and Nicaragua. In both instances, the crudeness and intransigence of the previous regime had at least as much to do with eventual victory as the guerrillas themselves. In Nicaragua, the Sandinistas were toppled in 1990 with the aid of the Contras, themselves midway between a genuine guerrilla group, and a band of hired thugs. By the end of 1990 Fidel Castro's regime also appeared in difficulties.

A number of factors account for this dismal record of guerrilla achievement:

★ The state and army invariably possess an overwhelming advantage

Margarita Montealegre

in firepower, troops and logistical support.

★ The difficulty of reconciling military and political work, both of which are needed for eventual victory. Military success requires a small tightly disciplined group, able to keep mobile, preferably in secret, not defending fixed positions. Political support requires steady contact with the 'masses', staying put to build up a relationship, and the ability to defend them against any ensuing attack by the army.

★ The US has placed enormous importance on preventing first 'another Cuba' then 'another Nicaragua' in its hemisphere. Since Vietnam, the Pentagon has tried to develop effective counter-guerrilla strategies, which have come to be known as 'low intensity conflict'. These have combined elements of reform ('winning hearts and minds') with anti-guerrilla military tactics. Often counter-insurgency has involved severe repression of civilians judged sympathetic to the guerrillas, and Washington's readiness to support human rights abusers in El Salvador and Nicaragua has lost it many friends in the region.

Nicaragua and Cuba show that military victory only heralds the start of a revolution's problems. Both governments only managed to survive a US economic and political siege by turning to the Soviet Union for oil and other supplies. Radical governments in Bolivia (1952-6) and Chile (1970-73) which did not have eastern bloc support soon fell or caved in to a combination of pressure from the US and local economic and military elites. Since the USSR's economic collapse means that Soviet aid is no longer available, any future revolutionary government in Latin America will either have to assuage historic US hostility to radical regimes or find another sponsor in Europe or Japan. Neither option looks likely as long as Latin America remains firmly in the US sphere of influence.

'We are not birds to live from the air, nor fish that live from the sea — we are men who live on the land'. Peasants on their way to take over unused land soon after the revolution which brought the Sandinistas to power, Nicaragua, 1980.

'By day, San Miguel is a world of women and children. Men leave by the busload at dawn in search of a day's wage, and women are left to produce the miracle of survival, a task which has required collective action. For example, it was women, exasperated from washing babies, dishes and laundry on a barrel of water a week, who stood for hours outside city hall demanding access to city water.

Women's involvement in the [residents'] association set off hundreds of household 'revolutions' some negotiated, some violent, as women began to challenge their husbands' and in-laws' dictates and stepped into new roles. Although most of the work of the association was being carried out by women during the day, decisions were made during late-night assemblies. The few women who could be present at such hours rarely spoke.

In 1982 half a dozen activists came together to form the *Grupo de Mujeres en Lucha* (Group of Women in Struggle) as a committee of the association, to promote women's participation in leadership. The new group focused on the issues of rape and battering. Arguing that domestic violence is not a private matter, but rather a crime against the community, the women's group intervened directly, removing the batterer and locking him in the meeting hall all night, and then verbally confronting him in the morning before releasing him. In others, they worked with local Alcoholics Anonymous members to have alcoholic batterers committed to AA programmes, and then raised funds to support the battered women and their children. Such actions had a tremendous impact on the community. Yet it was only after the economic crash of 1982, when *Mujeres en Lucha* began to focus on economic survival issues — children's breakfasts, milk, coupons for subsidised tortilas, that it began to grow beyond a handful of activists. For the first time, women not only filled the ranks of marches and sit-ins, but also negotiated demands with authorities and developed distribution systems for the resources they won (children's breakfast rations, milk cards, tortilla coupons, toys). By integrating consciousness-raising workshops into their organising process, they worked to ensure that women who first dared step out of the house in search of cheaper tortillas stayed on to become an active part of the movement.'

Elaine Burns, 'Squatters' Power in San Miguel Toronto', *Report on the Americas*, New York, November/December 1989

Trade Unions and Social Movements

Trade unions in Latin America occupy a very different place in society than in Europe or the US, since they represent that minority of workers who have stable jobs in the formal sector of the economy and are therefore relatively privileged compared to the mass of peasant farmers and the urban poor. In relative terms, their members have benefited from the status quo, and trade unions have often been unwilling to rock the political boat in case their members end up worse off. Nevertheless, some trade unions have been at the forefront of the

radical left. In Chile they were the first to take to the streets to begin the long campaign to topple General Pinochet, while in Brazil from 1978 the unions led an anti-military fightback similar to that waged by the Solidarity movement in Poland.

In countries such as Venezuela or Mexico, however, unions have acted as the defenders of a 'labour aristocracy', and have often been coopted by the state. The crisis of the 1980s has renewed efforts in these countries to establish a new unionism independent of the state.

The last 30 years have seen a spectacular growth in so-called new social movements. Shanty-town dwellers, women's groups and human rights organisations have joined radicalised trade unions and peasant associations to create a new form of grass-roots democracy which involves large numbers of people who previously had little role in the party political process. Although the social movements form a broad category, they have certain points in common:

★ They are often based on a locality rather than a workplace, unlike traditional trade unions;

★ They organise around specific and immediate demands, rather than wider appeals for structural change;

★ They practise a much higher degree of internal democracy and show a far greater level of women's participation than either left-wing political parties or guerrilla groups;

★ They generally demand improvements from the state rather than confront vested interest groups such as landowners, the military and big business.

So called 'catalyst' groups such as radical priests, social workers, feminist groups and political party activists often play an important role in helping to establish groups by encouraging organisation and

Land occupation, Peru. All over Latin America landless peasants are forced to seize land in order to grow food crops.

discussion. The more traditional catalysts often found it hard to let the new groups take control:

> I still thank the church for having opened my eyes. Working with the mothers' clubs, I learned how important we women are and how important it was for us to get organised. We managed to set up dozens of mothers' clubs. The women were well organised, and were taking on all sorts of activities.
>
> Then all of a sudden the church pulled the rug out from under us. It stopped the programme and took away all our funds. Why? They said there was no more money, but we don't think that's what happened. We think they were afraid of how far we'd gone. It was the church that first started organising us women. I'd never done anything before getting involved in the mothers' clubs. The church forged the path for us, but they wanted us to follow behind. And when we started to walk ahead of them, they decided that maybe organising the women wasn't such a good idea after all.
>
> Elvia Alvarado, *Don't Be Afraid Gringo*, San Francisco, 1987

Social movements have frequently been unsung political actors, outstripping the politicians in ideas and energy. In Chile under the radical government of Salvador Allende, militant peasant organisations continually occupied land, while trade unions seized factories and shanty town dwellers invaded waste ground. In each case the government followed behind, legalising some of the actions and trying to prevent or reverse others. When the military seized power in 1973, it directed its venom against the social movements more than any other target. Since there were no obvious leaders to kill or buy off, mass repression was the only way to quell the movement.

In Nicaragua the insurrection which overthrew Somoza in 1979 was largely out of Sandinista control. Once again peasants and the urban poor took matters into their own hands and the political parties followed. Although at times the FSLN attempted to dominate the social movements and prevent them from making too many demands, the Sandinista government proved more responsive to their needs than any other Latin American government, relying on the social movements for much of its support.

The upsurge of social movements in the 1980s was both a reaction to the continent's worsening economic crisis and a consequence of the traditional political parties' failures to deliver improvements for the poor. In Argentina the human rights organisations forced the Alfonsín government to jail the former military dictators for the first time in Latin American history. In El Salvador the military and death squads had laid waste to the popular movement in 1980-82, and yet by 1985 the trade unions were back on the streets again, demanding peace and economic development from a government incapable of providing either. In Brazil, after 20 years of military rule, land invasions, factory

Hands that rock the cradle. Women form the core of the new social movements which have sprung up all over Latin America. Demonstration in Mexico.

occupations and mass protests became almost routine.

Despite this extraordinary level of political effervescence, social movements have run up against serious obstacles. Local problems and their solutions, such as land distribution or greater spending on social services, often require action by the national government. Recognising this, many social movements have attempted to link up their vast array of groups into broader regional and even national networks in order to lobby the government. In growing to such a size, however, they risk losing the internal democracy which distinguishes them from orthodox political parties. After decades of co-option and betrayal, social movements are understandably wary of giving power away even to elected leaders, and attempts at wider coalition building have often broken down or have been hijacked by populists who promise the earth without ever being able to deliver.

The process of building a national organisation for the social movements most advanced in Brazil, where the Workers' Party (PT) has transformed the political landscape. The PT was set up in 1979 under the military government by the social movements themselves, led by a new generation of radical trade unionists such as 1989's PT presidential candidate, Luis Inâcio da Silva (Lula). The trade unionists came together with rural unions, radical Catholics, left-wing intellectuals, shanty town movements and a number of other currents to try and set up a party controlled by the membership which would avoid being absorbed into the Brazilian political establishment. In an astonishingly short time the PT became a major national force. In 1988 it won São Paulo and over 30 other towns, while the following year it narrowly lost the election for president to Fernando Collor de Mello. Although the PT has suffered debilitating splits and arguments through its attempt to reconcile its diverse membership with internal openness and democracy, its successes and rapid rise to political maturity have given many social movements hope that they can build a national party which will remain true to its origins.

Woman hoeing on squatted land, Honduras. Twenty women occupied the land and began to grow melons and corn.

Chronology

1930s on	Mechanisation of agriculture and growth of cities encourages young women to migrate from the countryside to the towns
1961	Paraguay becomes last Latin American country to give women the vote
1971	US Peace Corps expelled from Bolivia, accused of sterilising Indian women without their knowledge
1975-85	UN Decade for Women encourages some improved legislation on gender issues
1975	Cuban government passes law making childcare and housework equal responsibility of men and women
Late 1970s	Women in Brazil's Cost of Living Movement lead opposition to military rule
1976-83	Argentina's Mothers of the Disappeared lead opposition to military rule; inspiring similar movements in Central America and the Andes
1979	Nicaraguan revolution: women head health ministry and police and government bans use of women's bodies in advertising
1985	Women in São Paulo earn 53% of men's average income
1990	Violeta Chamorro wins Nicaraguan presidential elections

Women's Work

Gender and Politics

9

Penha is an imposing figure, a big confident woman who has risen to become president of the Alagoa Grande Rural Workers' Union in Brazil's drought-prone and poverty-ridden North-East. She recounts her life story, the words half lost in the drumming of a sudden downpour which turns the street into a river of rubbish from the nearby market. A broken home, starting work aged seven, a mother who died from TB when Penha was 12, early marriage and struggling to feed her six children — the story of countless poor Latin American women. Then came transformation as she became involved in the union, inspired by a charismatic woman leader named Margarida Maria Alves. When Margarida was assassinated, probably by local landowners, Penha took over.

Earlier, out on her rounds, Pehna had been trying to persuade an impoverished farming community to join the union. Pot-bellied children with skinny arms played at the feet of men and women as the banter and serious talk rolled easily along. Penha guided the conversation with a blend of authority, humour and kindness, letting others speak and enjoying the jokes, as the impromptu discussion developed into a full-blown community meeting about the causes of poverty in Brazil. As dusk fell, the meeting turned into music and dance, in honour of the visitors.

Although generalisations are always dangerous in a continent with such a variety of cultures and lifestyles, there has been an undeniable transformation in women's lives over the last 20 years. In the past, descriptions of Latin American society have either ignored its women altogether or portrayed them as the submissive victims of a male-dominated order perpetuated by the Catholic Church. Women were shown as helpless figures, condemned to endless pregnancies which destroy their health and confine them to the house, subject to the burden of childcare and dependent on often unreliable and violent men. In the title of one book, they were 'the slaves of slaves'. But in recent years, as more women have gone out to do paid work, some, like Penha, have fought for recognition in male-dominated trades unions. Others, described in chapter 8, have built a new form of politics through the social movements, bypassing traditional political parties.

Women's lives and expectations may have changed, but so far there is little evidence of parallel developments among Latin American men. A dictionary translation of the Spanish word *macho* captures the essence of Latin American masculinity. Besides male and masculine, the word means tough, strong, stupid, big, huge, splendid, terrific and doubles as a slang term for a sledgehammer. Machismo is an extreme form of patriarchy, the social system of male dominance which exists through much of the world. The Latin American variety has its roots in Mediterranean culture and the Catholic Church's contorted attitude towards women. As Virgin and Mother, Mary combines its impossible and contradictory ideals of Latin American womanhood. Machismo stresses the opposition between male and female; men are fearless, authoritarian, aggressive and promiscuous, while women are naturally submissive, dependent, quiet and devoted to the family and home. Machismo is often greater among the mestizo population. In Indian societies men and women commonly have sharply divided tasks, both at work and in the home, yet anthropologists describe their roles as complementary, rather than the subordination of women by men.

Nowhere is the nature of machismo more graphically outlined than in Latin America's rich vocabulary of curses, with their ornate combinations of the central concepts of mother, whore and virgin. Threats to this world view, such as the feminist movement or homosexuality in men or women, excite fear and hatred. Women have their inferiority drummed into them from birth; in Peru the midwife receives a sheep for delivering a baby boy, while a girl merits only two chickens. Under the ideological barrage, women often internalise these ideas of femininity and submissiveness, giving rise to a female counterpart to machismo, known as *marianismo*, after the Virgin Mary.

Latin America's most famous women have often filled these submissive and maternal roles. Evita Perón, a gifted politician and the darling of the Argentine masses, described her relationship with her husband as 'He the figure, I the shadow', while Violeta Chamorro became president of Nicaragua in 1990 by playing on her position as the widow of a national hero and presenting herself as the healing mother of the nation who could reconcile her divided children. Following an injury early on in the electoral campaign, she had to be carried through the crowds, coming to resemble one of the saints held aloft in Latin America's innumerable religious processions.

Family Ties

'...girls get married so young — at 14 years old — and then they have a baby immediately. From then on, you have one load strapped to your back, one on your head, your baby inside and children around your feet.'
Bolivian woman in Bronstein 1982

Traditionally, girls are groomed from the cradle for their future role as wife and mother. Bolivian parents call their baby daughters *mamita* (little mother), and within a few years they can be seen hauling their baby brothers and sisters on their backs around the villages of the Andes. In rural Latin America, families usually have numerous children so that enough will survive high child death rates to work the family farm and to look after their parents in old age. For women this has led to the health problems associated with frequent pregnancies, compounded by malnourishment and poor or non-existent medical care. Large families lack even the most basic services such as running

Lou Dematteis

water, and need constantly to make do and mend. Together, these pressures create the archetypal Latin American mother who never rests: cooking, cleaning, changing nappies, looking after children with frequent illnesses, queuing for scarce food, mending clothes or making food to sell outside the home consume every waking hour. In rural areas fetching water or firewood and the long haul to sell left-over produce in the local market impose further strains on women's workload.

Violeta Chamorro carried aloft on the campaign trail to victory over the Sandinistas in the 1990 presidential elections.

My day begins at four in the morning, especially when my *compañero* is on the first shift. I prepare his breakfast. Then I have to prepare the *salteñas* [small meat pies], because I make about one hundred *salteñas* every day and I sell them in the street. I do this in order to make up for what my husband's wage doesn't cover in terms of necessities. The night before, we prepare the dough and at four in the morning I make the *salteñas* while I feed the kids. The kids help me: they peel potatoes and carrots and make the dough.

Then the ones that go to school in the morning have to get ready, while I wash the clothes I left soaking overnight. At eight I go out to sell. The kids that go to school in the afternoon help me. We have to go to the company store and bring home the basics. And in the store there are immensely long queues and you have to wait there until eleven in order to stock up. You have to queue up for meat, for vegetables, for oil. So it's just one line after another. Since everything's in a different place, that's how it has to be. So all the time I'm selling *salteñas*, I line up to buy my supplies at the store. I run up to the counter to get the things and the kids sell. Then the kids line up and I sell. That's how we do it.

Domitila Barrios de Chungara, *Let Me Speak*, New York, 1978

TABLE 7: CONTRACEPTIVE METHODS USED IN LATIN AMERICA, circa
1983

Female Sterilisation	36%
Pill	29%
IUD (coil)	9%
Rhythm	9%
Withdrawal	6%
Other	4%
Condom	3%
Injectable	2%
Vaginal Barrier (diaphragm)	1%
Male Sterilisation	1%
Total	100%

Source: 'Levels and Trends of Contraceptive Use — As Assessed in 1988',
United Nations, New York, 1989

The size of the average family has dropped during the last 50 years.
The fall in infant mortality figures has enabled parents to have fewer
children, safe in the knowledge that enough will survive to care for
them. Access to education and the wider availability of contraceptives
have also helped women to take control of their fertility. Urbanisation
and the growing number of women who go out to work have further
reduced the number of women having large families.

In recent years there has been an explosion in the rate of breakdown
of couples, and the number of female-headed households now stands
at an average of 20 per cent across the continent. These are often
among the poorest families, with women forced to perform a gruelling
combination of housework and wage-earning, often in the informal
sector, to keep their children from starvation.

In the last 20 years, contraception has become more widely
available. In the 1980s the number of couples using contraception
varied widely from 23 per cent in Guatemala to 70 per cent in Costa
Rica. Nevertheless, the issue remains far more controversial than in the
US or Western Europe. Not only is the Catholic Church fiercely hostile
to all forms of contraception, but the health problems provoked by the
often unsupervised use of the Pill, IUDs and injectables such as Depo
Provera have created widespread suspicion. Contraception is
anathema to many Latin American men, who see their wives' regular
pregnancies as proof of their virility. In only 4 per cent of couples do
men take responsibility for contraception via condoms or sterilisation.

In some cases, foreign agencies have been implicated in sterilising
women without fully informing them of the consequences. Such
incidents led to the expulsion of the US Peace Corps from Peru and
Bolivia in the 1970s. As a result, some Latin Americans see the West's
emphasis on birth control as a plot to maintain its dominance. In the
words of one Guatemalan Indian man:

They say it is better to have only two or three children because

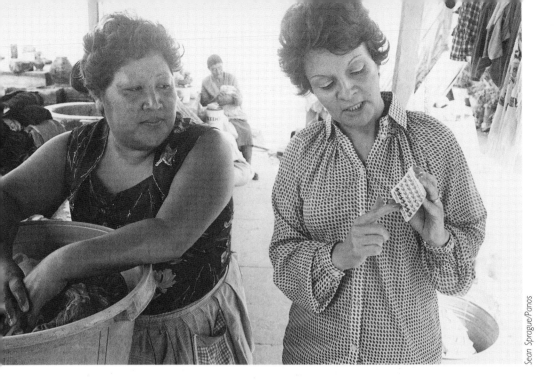

Sean Sprague/Panos

there isn't enough land. But who is saying that there isn't enough land? There is plenty of land, but only a few people own it all. And they want all the Indians to disappear, so they can keep all the land, and we won't be a threat to them. That's why they keep sending so many people to Guatemala to talk about birth control, and teach it. We know that these things are not good for women's bodies. To me it is a form of violence.
Bronstein 1982

Family planning adviser explains the use of the pill at a public washhouse, Guatemala.

One consequence of suspicion, ignorance and the shortage of contraceptives is a high abortion rate. Except for Cuba, abortion on request is illegal in all Latin American countries, forcing women unable to afford a medically safe abortion to resort to back-street practitioners or their own efforts. Botched abortion is the greatest killer of women of child-bearing age. By one estimate in 1974, there were five million abortions a year in the region, or 400 abortions for every 1,000 live births. Not surprisingly, in view of its more liberal legislation, Cuba has the lowest incidence of maternal death from abortion in the region.

Literacy plays a vital role in empowering women, making it easier for them to find better-paid work, and to wade through the avalanche of printed information resulting from almost any contact with the state. In Nicaragua, the Sandinista literacy crusade of 1980-81 sent 80,000 secondary school students out into the most remote corners of the country to teach *campesinos* to read. The crusade cut illiteracy from 50 per cent to 12 per cent and marked the first step in the Sandinistas' efforts to increase women's active participation in changing society.

Illiteracy is higher among women than men in every Latin American country, in some cases reaching 90 per cent among elderly women. The figure for both sexes is higher in rural than in urban areas, since schools are often scarce, and parents may need the children to work on the farm. Many families prefer to keep girls at home to help with the household tasks and learn how to keep house, while believing that boys must study to prepare themselves for the outside world. Illiteracy rates for rural women range from 15 per cent in Argentina to 68 per cent in Bolivia, compared to urban figures for the same countries of 4.5 per cent and 23.2 per cent. However, the situation is improving rapidly as the expansion in primary and secondary education from 1950 onwards starts to feed into the statistics.

Among the middle classes, the situation is already very different. By 1985 almost half of students in higher education were women, although a large number of them were concentrated in the traditional female spheres of teaching and health care.

The ideology of machismo has influenced legislation affecting women. In most countries adultery is only sufficient grounds for divorce if committed by the wife, while divorce is only available in exceptional cases in countries such as Argentina, Brazil and Colombia. Under El Salvador's Penal Code, a married woman is liable to a jail sentence of six months to two years if she is found guilty of 'carnal access to any man other than her husband', yet the husband is only breaking the law if he *keeps* his mistress, and thereby fails to meet his family obligations. In Brazil until recently, one law required a woman to have explicit permission from her husband before going out to work.

Thanks to the work of women's lobby groups and the UN Decade for Women (1975-85) many governments have improved their legislation and established agencies to promote the status of women and ensure equal rights. Yet despite such paper safeguards, social attitudes and the implementation of equal rights laws lag far behind. Statutory rights on maternity benefits or equal pay are frequently ignored by both employers and male-oriented Ministries of Labour, and legislation often appears irrelevant to the poor. Most women work in the unregulated informal sector and so do not even have a theoretical right to maternity benefits. Since formal marriage is the exception among poor families, the niceties of divorce law hold little meaning.

Attitudes and legislation over homosexuality vary enormously across the continent. In general, Latin American machismo finds homosexuality in men deeply threatening and lesbianism incomprehensible, although more liberal climates exist in Brazil and Costa Rica. In many countries homosexuality is not specifically outlawed, but more general laws such as 'offences against morality' are used to harass gays and lesbians. In stark contrast to its progressive legislation and education work on women's rights, Cuba is particularly repressive towards gay men. Cuban law imposes a maximum 20 year sentence for public expression of homosexuality, and obliges parents to report homosexual children to the authorities. Homosexuals are also stigmatised by Cuban government AIDS policy. Cuba is the only country known to use more or less forcible means to isolate AIDS sufferers from the rest of society in sanatoria cut off by barbed wire fences.

Working for Wages

The number of women in the economically active population, a definition that excludes those involved in unwaged work in the home or on the farm, more than tripled between 1950 and 1980, rising to 26 per cent. Despite this rise in numbers, the kinds of jobs have changed little, with a strong emphasis on 'women's work' which merely extends their caring role in the home.

Fewer women work in rural areas than in towns and cities, where as many as half the women employed are domestic servants, most of them young unskilled migrants from the countryside who average only three years of school education. The other main categories of paid women's work are the informal sector (market women, street sellers), caring professions, such as teaching and nursing, and office work. Women's participation in agriculture and manufacturing actually fell between 1960-80, as mechanisation reduced the proportion of unskilled jobs traditionally performed by women. In agriculture women largely do seasonal work, especially at harvest time, while in manufacturing they are concentrated in industries such as textiles, clothing and the booming *maquila* (assembly plants) in northern Mexico and the Caribbean basin.

Besides being segregated by the jobs they do, women also earn far less than men, even though their educational qualifications for comparable jobs are generally higher. In São Paulo in 1985 women received just 53 per cent of average male income.

The Domestic Worker

Usually young unskilled migrants from the countryside, servants are among the most exploited and invisible of the region's women. Ignorant of their rights or life in the city, and isolated in their employer's house, they are on virtual 24-hour standby, and vulnerable to verbal, sexual and physical abuse by their employers. Young girls emotionally dependent on their employers often absorb their values, feeling self-loathing and contempt for their own families and backgrounds, especially in countries where the employers are white, and the servants Indian:

> The old lady explained everything to me, and little by little she made me aware of my class, using words like 'Indians' and 'Yokels' and saying 'You shouldn't be like that, you're going to get civilised here.'
>
> When you hear it that often you end up being ashamed and uncomfortable about your own class and finally you find yourself supporting the class of your boss. I thought she loved me because she told me: 'I love you like a daughter; here you have everything.' And I accepted it all.
>
> The truth is that the bosses use us even through love. Without realising, we end up loving them and so we say, 'Ay, my señora is good, she loves me a lot.' We look after her things as though they were our own, and after a while you start identifying totally with her mentality.

Ana María Condori, *Mi Despertar*, La Paz, 1988, author's translation

The Street Seller

Market women and street sellers are perhaps the most conspicuous of Latin American women workers, lining the streets of major cities with stalls offering home-made cakes, imported toiletries, vegetables or soft drinks. Their daily contact with the public and unscrupulous wholesalers has made market women a self-confident and fiercely individualistic group. As Anita, a 28-year old Nicaraguan market woman, explains:

> I'm better off working in the market. If I don't want to sell, I don't have to. I can go home whenever I want to, we can bring our children to work and no-one bosses you about and tells you when to come and when to leave. I don't want to work for a boss again.

Duncan Green, *Nicaraguans Talking*, London, 1989

Maquiladoras

Since the mid-1960s, Mexican industry has been transformed by the growth of *maquila* plants along its northern border with the US. Others have sprouted elsewhere in Central America and the Caribbean. These factories, largely owned by US, Japanese and other foreign electronics or textile companies, use cheap local labour to assemble products for export to the US. In the Caribbean, women are also used to perform cut-price data processing for US companies. Over three quarters of *maquiladora* employees are women, usually single and in their late teens or early twenties. Young women are ideal because, in the words of one plant manager, 'they are willing to accept lower wages', and 'girls are educated to obey at home. It is easier to get their confidence... they are loyal to the company.'

> Then I joined the 'Maidenform' bra factory. There were about 30 sewing machines..and four work-benches. I earned a dollar a day, and worked for eight hours. As the factory was only getting under way and I wanted to earn more, in practice I worked nearer nine or ten hours... They brought the fabric and everything in from the United States. They re-exported the finished products, had them packaged, then they came back to El Salvador to be sold.

Marina, Salvadorean *maquiladora* worker

> A US employee would have earned at least $35 a day for the work this woman was paid one dollar to do. Maidenform saved $320,000 a year just by exploiting Marina and her 29 workmates as a source of cheap labour.

CAHRC, *Women in Central America*, London, 1988

Women's growing role in the workforce has brought them mixed blessings. Although paid jobs have often increased women's economic independence and self-confidence, there has been no compensating reduction in housework, with the result that working women are expected to perform what is known as a 'double shift'. A study of women in Chile during the early 1980s showed that working women did an average 12-hour day, seven days a week, between workplace and home. When women did manage to reduce their housework, it was by employing poor women as domestic servants — men did no more housework than before, despite the decline in their role as breadwinner. For any macho man, scrubbing floors or cooking is the ultimate shame. In Cuba, where women's participation in the paid workforce has grown rapidly over the last 20 years, one writer noted that although male Communist Party militants may offer to do the washing, they insist their wives hang it out to dry so that the neighbours won't find out!

In the past, most women in rural areas were members of extended peasant farming families. Their duties included childcare, maintaining the home, and a number of specialised jobs on the farm. Often women tended the animals and a small vegetable plot, while the men looked after the main food crops. Housework in peasant farms can be far more time-consuming than in the cities, since women may have to carry water over long distances, collect firewood, and make long trips to markets in nearby villages.

As commercial agriculture has encroached on the traditional peasant farms, this pattern has been disrupted. Peasant farms have been squeezed by large landowners and by subdivision between members of each new generation, so that they are rarely productive enough to maintain a family. This forces their owners to find work on the big commercial farms. Men's greater access to education and training has meant that they take the permanent jobs on new mechanised farms, and women have been relegated to temporary work at harvest time.

With food in short supply, parents favour boys to stay and eventually inherit the farm, and many young girls are packed off to the city as domestic servants. As a result, young women have outnumbered men in the exodus to the cities which has marked the last 50 years of Latin American history.

Women still supply most of the workers in a number of labour-intensive export industries. They pick coffee, tobacco or cotton, and produce new export crops such as strawberries in Mexico or peanuts in Brazil. In Colombia the women weed, fumigate, pick and package carnations for Europe's florists, suffering frequent respiratory problems and miscarriages from the pesticides to which they are constantly exposed.

Latin America's agrarian reform processes (see chapter 2), have largely failed to benefit women, their apparent 'gender blindness' masking discrimination in favour of men. Most reforms hand out land to individuals identified as 'heads of household', by custom a man, except for widows and single mothers. Instead of being treated as producers in their own right, peasant women are seen as the equivalent of urban housewives and hence as dependents. In traditional Andean culture, farms are owned equally by husband and wife, so the new reforms marked a step backwards for women. In most cases the reforms helped permanent workers, rather than seasonal workers. When General Velasco expropriated Peru's cotton plantations in the late 1960s, women represented 40 per cent of their seasonal workforce,

TABLE 8: DATE OF WOMEN'S SUFFRAGE IN LATIN AMERICA

Country	Date
Ecuador	1929
Brazil	1932
Uruguay	1932
El Salvador	1939
Guatemala	1945
Panama	1945
Argentina	1947
Venezuela	1947
Chile	1949
Costa Rica	1949
Bolivia	1952
Mexico	1953
Honduras	1955
Nicaragua	1955
Peru	1955
Colombia	1957
Paraguay	1961

Source: J Nash and H Safa, *Sex and Class in Latin America*, New York, 1980

but held few permanent jobs. The reform gave the plantations to their permanent workers organised into co-operatives, and as a result women made up only two per cent of members on the new cotton co-operatives. In Chile and Venezuela, agrarian reform law specifically decreed that land given out under the reform should be passed to the beneficiary's sons when he died.

The economic recession unleashed by the debt crisis in 1982, and continuing into the 1990s, has hit women hardest. As employers shed jobs, they have preferred to sack women, since they are not seen as breadwinners and are generally under-represented in trade unions. Public spending cuts have targeted 'female' professions in health and education, and the limited choice of jobs open to women has made it hard for them to find other employment. Between 1982-85 unemployment among women quintupled in Bogotá and doubled in Caracas. Poor women have increasingly turned to the informal sector and part-time work to make ends meet.

In their role as mothers, women have been hit by the structural adjustment programmes adopted by most governments in the region under IMF pressure. Price rises in basic foods as subsidies are cut have made it increasingly difficult to feed a family. When services are cut off through unpaid bills, women must replace electricity by searching for fuelwood. Clothes must be endlessly patched when there is no money to buy replacements. All these tasks add to the growing burden of keeping the family afloat. The growing stress of family life has also led to increased cases of alcohol abuse among men, leaving women to face the frequent domestic violence and family breakdown which follow. As one Bolivian miner says: 'In my work I am happy. I joke with my *compañeros*, I work in peace. And then I come home and I see my wife and children undernourished, poorly clothed. It is then that I have a sense of the problems in my life and I get filled with rage.'

Women in Politics

Driven in part by a need to unite to confront the economic crisis of recent years, growing numbers of women have begun to participate directly in political life. In the new social movements such as Mothers' Clubs, Base Christian Communities and neighbourhood associations, women have built a bridge between the traditionally female world of home and family, and the predominantly male sphere of political activism.

Before the social movements appeared, women were largely excluded from political life. Although a small suffrage movement of largely middle-class women had won the vote in the whole of Latin America by 1961, this did not lead to the expected upsurge in political participation.

In Argentina, Juan and Evita Perón mobilised women as their footsoldiers in the Peronist Women's Party, led by Evita. Yet despite some progressive legislation, the 'father and mother of the nation' never challenged the ideal of wifely submission displayed by Evita herself. The Peronists introduced women's suffrage in 1947 and gave children born out of marriage equal rights before the law. In 1955 Perón's decision to legalise divorce alienated the Catholic Church and helped bring brought about his downfall at the hands of the military.

Elsewhere, political parties and trade unions remained exclusively male preserves. In cases where women were politically active at the grass-roots level, for example in textile workers' unions, they thinned out rapidly further up the union hierarchy. During the left-wing Popular Unity government of Salvador Allende in Chile, women divided along class lines; middle-class women organised 'marches of the empty pots' to protest at food shortages and economic chaos, while women in the shanty towns worked in support of the Allende government. In Chile and elsewhere, many left-wing men were suspicious of an independent women's movement, arguing that it would prove to be a right-wing defender of the status quo, but also unwilling to give up their own privileged status in the home. As Yanci, an activist in El Salvador's women's movement comments: 'In all the key moments of our history, women have always participated, but we have been anonymous. Women have made the coffee so the *compañeros* could think better. Women cook while the men take the important decisions!'

Unlike the left, which often ignored women in their political programmes, the right and the military regimes of the 1970s and 1980s stressed the importance of the family, paying homage to the traditional Latin American icon of the long-suffering mother. The names of right-wing pro-military organisations such as Argentina's 'Tradition, Family and Property' encapsulated the conservative Catholic message. Such an ideology recognised and applauded women only as long as they remained safely in the 'female sphere'. When women dared to trespass into public politics, the military's chivalry proved short-lived.

In Argentina, 30 per cent of those 'disappeared' by the military were women. The traumatised mothers of disappeared children, meeting on their fruitless round of the different military barracks in search of news, came together to form the Mothers and Grandmothers of the Plaza de Mayo. Every Thursday under the military government, a small but indomitable band of women wearing white headscarves walked silently around the Plaza de Mayo in front of the Presidential Palace in Buenos Aires, their placards carrying old, fading photographs of their children. As one mother described it, 'from washing, ironing and cooking we went out on to the streets to fight for the lives of our children'. The human rights movement they created grew to play a crucial role first in forcing the generals to hand power over to an elected government, and then in putting the military's leaders in jail for killing their children.

The Mothers of the Disappeared were able to protest because they did so *as mothers*, effectively preventing the military from using outright repression as they did against virtually all other protest movements. By using the generals' own ideology against them, the women of the Plaza de Mayo opened up the first possibilities of public resistance, which grew into the mass protest movement which helped remove the military from power.

Military rule forced women to take to the public arena to defend their families in many other countries. In Brazil, opposition to the military took off in the late 1970s with the Cost of Living Movement, made up of women protesting at the suffering being inflicted on poor families by the military's economic policies. In El Salvador and Guatemala, organisations of mothers and relatives of the disappeared have yet to obtain answers from a military that kills their sons and daughters with virtual impunity. In each case the crushing of traditional political parties has enabled women's organisations to expand into the political vacuum, sowing the seeds of the region's new social movements.

The nature and tactics of the new social movements reflect their predominantly female origin. Stressing the need for internal democracy, social movements aim to improve local communities, usually by putting pressure on local or national governments. They fiercely defend their independence from political parties or the state, both male-dominated. Many of their demands reflect women's immediate needs: campaigns for day nurseries for working women, for better health care or street lighting, running water or electricity are often seen by the women involved as extensions of the struggles they face as wives and mothers. On occasion, the movements' strengths have also proved to be their weaknesses. Once immediate demands have been achieved, for example, the local authority has agreed to put in street lighting, the movement often disintegrates. After the return to civilian government in Argentina, the Mothers of the Disappeared found it hard to maintain the unity and determination they showed under military rule. Nevertheless, the experience of meeting other women and organising successful campaigns has transformed many women's lives and could lay the foundations of a new and democratic politics for the future.

Eduardo Longoni

Lone voices. Mothers of the Plaza de Mayo confront police, Buenos Aires, Argentina.

The experience of women in Cuba after the 1959 revolution showed that passing legislation is simple compared to the monumental task of changing social structures and attitudes. From the outset, the revolution preached the emancipation of women, yet by the late 1960s little had changed; women only made up a quarter of the work force, and were almost invisible in the higher reaches of the Communist Party. In response, the government acknowledged the need to change men and women's attitudes to issues like housework and childcare which were preventing women from participating as workers or political activists. In 1975 it committed the ultimate crime against machismo by passing legislation making childcare and housework the equal duty of men and women! Slowly, women's participation started to rise.

The Nicaraguan revolution, arriving in 1979 when feminism had come of age as an influential political movement in the West, put greater emphasis on gender issues than the Cubans had in 1959. Thirty per cent of the Sandinista guerrillas were women, many of them in leadership positions. In Nicaraguan society, nearly half the households were headed by women, who were therefore more used to fighting for survival in the public as well as private spheres. In revolutionary Nicaragua women quickly emerged in the second tier of leadership, although all nine members of the Sandinista party's National Directorate were men. Women headed the health ministry and the police force and occupied a number of senior party positions. On the ground, however, women continued to be under-represented in trade unions and peasant organisations, and soon dropped out of the army. One controversial subject in both Nicaragua and Cuba has been whether women should put their gender or class interests first. Many feminists from Europe and the US have argued that if there is a choice to be made, gender should come first, whereas women's organisations in both Cuba and Nicaragua have repeatedly argued that the defence of the revolution is an essential prerequisite for any expansion in women's emancipation. These differences emerged in the debate over abortion law. Although many women activists felt the Sandinistas should legalise abortion, the party leadership insisted that to do so would destroy its attempts to make peace with the Catholic Church and alienate both men and women in Nicaragua's more conservative regions. The women's movement eventually agreed that the gender demand of a legal right to abortion should take second place to the overall aim of national unity at a time of undeclared war with the US.

During 11 years of Sandinista rule, Nicaraguan women achieved some notable successes. The government banned the use of women's bodies in advertising; the literacy crusade empowered innumerable peasant women, and a women's section in the main agricultural workers' union vastly increased the level of women's organisation in the countryside. Discussions of issues like abortion and contraception brought them into the public arena for the first time, ridding these subjects of some of their shame and fear. In a paradox that will be familiar to British readers, the election in 1990 of Nicaragua's first woman president, Violeta Chamorro, marked the start of an attempt to roll back the achievements of the Nicaraguan revolution, including those in the field of women's emancipation. The Education Ministry has closed down women's centres working on sex education, there is no longer the political will to enforce legislation on domestic violence, and a conservative Catholic morality once more pervades the Nicaraguan media.

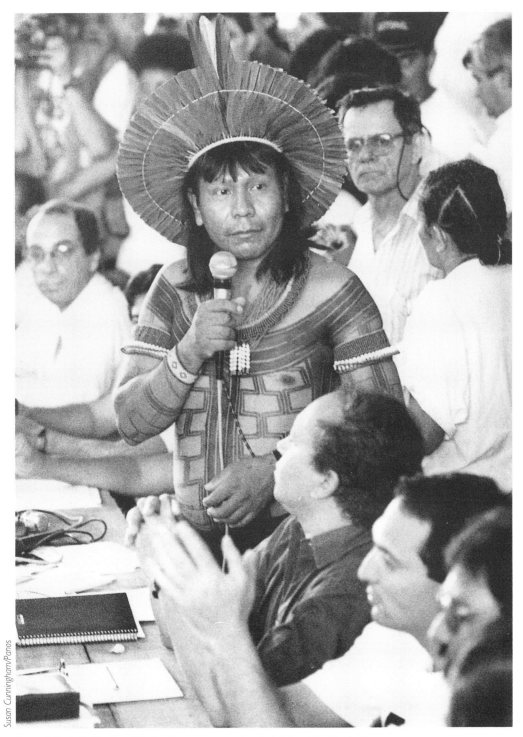

Kayapo Indian leader Bep Koroti Payakan Kayapo protests against the building of the Altamira dam on Kayapo territory in Amazonia, Brazil.

Chronology

30,000BC	First people reach the Americas across the Bering Straits from Asia
1492	Columbus arrives in the Americas, to be met by friendly Arawak Indians
1519	Cortés invades Mexico with 600 men
1535	Pizarro completes conquest of Inca empire
mid 16th century	Arawak population of the Caribbean extinct within 50 years of Columbus' arrival
1781	Túpac Amaru lays seige to Cuzco, the former Inca capital, in Indian rebellion. Amaru captured and executed
1960s	Officials of Brazil's government agency for Indians use poison, machine guns and disease to 'clear' land for large landowners
early 1980s	400 Indian villages destroyed, 40,000 killed in counter-insurgency operations in Guatemala
1989	Brazil's Kayapo Indians hold meeting at Altamira to protest dam-building on tribal lands.
1992	Indigenous groups throughout the Americas condemn the official celebrations of the quincentenary of Columbus' arrival in the Americas

Race Against Time

Indigenous Peoples

10

Cabo Domingo (Cape Sunday) is a lonely place. Low, dark hills under an enormous sky sink towards the ocean at the southern tip of the Americas. At this spot one Sunday in the 1920s a German landowner held a banquet for the local Yaganes Indians. When they were drunk, his hidden henchmen opened fire with a machine gun. The Yaganes died because, unaccustomed to the concept of private property, they had killed and eaten the landowner's sheep. The Indians of Tierra del Fuego were an almost stone-age people dressed in skins and using flint hand-tools. When the whites started to colonise the region in the 1880s, the various tribes soon succumbed to disease and slaughter. Today only a few impoverished old folk remain of the people whose permanent camp fires gave Tierra del Fuego (Land of Fire) its name.

Several thousand miles north, at the Altamira gathering in February 1989, the Kayapo Indians of Brazil were fighting to avoid the same fate as the Yaganes. In organising a campaign to prevent a massive hydroelectric dam flooding their lands, they made full use of modern technology and their own appeal to foreign liberals. Dressed in little more than exotic feather headdresses, warlike Kayapo men danced, debated and expertly wielded video cameras to record the proceedings for the people back home. The dramatic highlight came during a pompous speech by an uncomfortable-looking engineer from Electronorte, the Brazilian electricity company. As he tried to impress a hall full of angry Kayapo warriors with technical jargon, an old Indian woman jumped up and ceremonially slapped him about the face with the flat blade of her machete. Cameras flashed as the engineer sat stoically through it all. The Indians had turned the tables. Now they were treating *him* like a child. Five hundred assorted ecologists, journalists and aid agency representatives jostled for a view of the event, which galvanised international opposition to the dam scheme.

The Kayapo's dynamism belies the conventional western image of fatalistic Indians calmly awaiting extinction. Latin America's history is full of the uprisings and resistance of peoples whose civilisations were in many ways far in advance of Europe's at the time of the Conquest.

The Americas' original inhabitants came from Asia, crossing the Bering Straits about 30,000 years ago and migrating slowly south until every part of the continent was populated, albeit thinly, with Indian groups. The original migrants were hunter-gatherers, and groups like the Yaganes and Kayapo changed little over the millenia. Elsewhere, however, Indian groups developed agriculture about 5,000 years ago. Once settled on the land, they swiftly built the highly complex and cultured civilisations which dazzled the first European visitors.

The Mayas were a nation of astronomers and architects, already in decline before the Spaniards came. They were brilliant mathematicians, developing the concept of zero long before any other civilisation, and making astronomical calculations of astonishing accuracy. Their ornate temples are still being rescued from the jungles of Central America, and it is not yet clear what caused the Mayan empire to go into a sudden decline around 1000 AD.

The Incas covered the largest area of any of the pre-Columbian empires, spanning present-day Peru, Ecuador, Bolivia and parts of Colombia, Chile, Argentina and Brazil. Their extraordinary level of social organisation can still be seen in the mammoth stone buildings of Cuzco and Machu Picchu and the remains of agricultural terracing that line many Andean valleys, often still being farmed by the Incas' descendants.

The Aztecs, at their height when Cortés and his band of conquistadores arrived in Mexico, lived on a permanent war footing. In their capital city of Tenochtitlan, site of today's Mexico City, they sacrificed up to 20,000 prisoners of war in a single day to the gods of war, rain and harvest. Their empire was built on a constant thirst for booty and fresh sacrifices, and the Spanish proved skillful in using the subject tribes' hatred of the Aztecs in their overthrow.

Despite their vast numerical superiority (Cortés invaded Mexico with just 600 men), the mighty Indian empires crumbled before the Spanish. In part, the conquistadores' success came from their superior technology of warfare: they used armour, horses, cannon and muskets against Indian soldiers armed with spears and arrows. The Spanish also proved adept at playing off rival Indian peoples against each other and at capitalising on the Inca and Aztec empires' extreme dependence on a single emperor. Both Cortés in Mexico and Pizarro in Peru first took the emperor prisoner then murdered them, leaving the empires leaderless before the Spanish onslaught.

Once the centre had been removed, the Spanish viceroy replaced the emperor as the supreme authority and the former empires fell into

TABLE 9: ESTIMATED INDIGENOUS POPULATION OF AMERICA AT THE TIME OF EUROPEAN CONTACT

	Estimated population (million)	% of total
North America	4.4	7.7
Mexico	21.4	37.3
Central America	5.65	9.9
Caribbean	5.85	10.2
Andes	11.5	20.1
Lowland South America	8.5	14.8
Total	57.3	100.0

Source: William M Denevan (ed), The Native Population of the Americas in 1492, University of Wisconsin Press, 1976.

their hands. Where Indian groups were less advanced and centralised, the Spanish encountered much greater difficulties. In southern Chile and Argentina the native Mapuche peoples successfully resisted the colonial forces, finally losing their fight to the new Chilean and Argentine armies following Latin America's independence from Spain. As always, the victors write the history, and Argentine schoolchildren now learn the names of the heroes of the 'War of the South', a 19th-century campaign to exterminate the Indians, during which soldiers were paid a reward for each pair of Indian testicles they brought in to their commanders. The extermination of the Indians opened up the south of Argentina for sheep and cattle ranching.

A further legacy of the Conquest was the misnomer, 'Indian', dating from Columbus' first landfall in the Americas, when thanks to a miscalculation of the circumference of the globe, he was convinced he had reached Asia. In the furore surrounding the Columbus quincentenary in 1992, many indigenous Latin Americans not only reject the term 'Indian', which in Spanish carries distinctly derogatory overtones, but even object to the words 'Latin American'. The region's native peoples point out that they are not in any sense Latin, and object to being called American, since the term stems from the name of another European explorer, Amerigo Vespucci.

Military victory marked the beginning of a process of extermination. Within a century of the Conquest, Latin America's Indian population fell from 100 million to ten million, by one estimate. In the Caribbean, the Arawak peoples who first greeted Columbus with delight soon rued the day they had paddled their canoes out to his ships, bearing gifts for the exhausted sailors. Enslaved to the Spanish lust for gold, those Indians who survived smallpox, influenza, measles and the other new diseases committed mass suicide by poisoning and hanging.

Women at Sololá market, Guatemala. Guatemala and Bolivia are the only countries in Latin America with majority Indian populations.

Mothers even slaughtered their newborn babies to prevent them being enslaved by the Spanish. Within 25 years of Columbus' arrival, only 3,000 Arawaks remained of an original population of 600,000, and by the mid-16th century they were extinct. Five centuries later, the youth of Brazil's Kaiowa Indians met the same threat in the same way. In 1990 alone, 20 boys and girls from the threatened tribe, all aged between 13 and 18, killed themselves by hanging or poisoning. Thirty others tried but were saved. On February 3, 1991, 15-year old Maura Ramírez hung herself from a tree. Her mother said, 'she was sad. She dreamt Helena was calling her.' Helena, Maura's elder sister, had committed suicide three months earlier. Psychologists blamed the deaths on the dislocation caused by going away to work on the sugar plantations.

Although more Indians fell victim to the diseases introduced by the Spanish and Portuguese than died in the mines, plantations or battlefields, the level of economic exploitation and misery inflicted by the Europeans was at least partially responsible for making the Indians so vulnerable to illness. Millions were literally worked to death.

The colonial authorities adopted various systems for exacting tribute and labour from their Indian 'vassals'. During the initial period the *encomienda* system rewarded Spanish officers and favourites with whole Indian communities. In return for supposedly bringing their allocated Indians to Christianity, the *encomenderos* were authorised to demand tribute and unpaid labour. In the densely populated regions of Mexico and the Andes, this left Indian villages more or less intact. In more sparsely peopled regions, the *encomienda* system degenerated into raiding parties to abduct slaves.

In the Andes an adapted version of this scheme, known as the *mita*, persisted through to independence, while in Mexico and Central America, the authorities preferred a 'free' labour force. European writers and theologians put forward a variety of ideological justifications to show that the natural inferiority of the Indians made their enslavement both necessary and an act of mercy.

As the centuries passed, racial boundaries became blurred. Since men far outnumbered women in the European colonial communities, Indian women were frequently obliged to have sex by their owners and the subsequent intermingling of blood created a growing mixed-race population, known as mestizos. Other Indians abandoned their traditional dress and learned Spanish, often moving to the cities. Over time, cultural criteria, rather than physical characteristics, became the means of identifying ethnic background. An 'Indian' wore non-European dress and spoke little or no Spanish, whereas a 'mestizo' adopted both the white language and western dress. In the coastal regions of Latin America, Indians were swiftly wiped out on the plantations and were replaced with African slaves who added a further ingredient to the continent's racial mix.

The independence wars of the early 19th century were largely a dispute between the local *criollo* ruling class and the Spanish, and little changed for the continent's indigenous peoples. The 19th century brought further encroachments on the Indians' traditional communal lands as liberal administrations in many countries made it illegal to hold land in common and insisted on private ownership. The Indians' traditional collectivism was anathema to governments trying to introduce notions of private property and individual enterprise, although their cohesion as communities made them better able to resist. The new legislation paved the way for large landowners to move in and buy or seize Indian lands for new crops such as coffee.

Modern Indians

The continent's Indian survivors now make up five per cent of its total population and fall into two distinct groups. The first, and by far the largest, is that of the highland Indians, descendants of the Inca, Aztec and Mayan empires. The second are the lowland Indians, like the Kayapo, largely confined to the Amazon basin and Central America. In both Guatemala and Bolivia, over half the population is Indian, while the largest numbers live in Peru and Mexico. Although highland Indians number some 22 million, lowland Indians do not exceed one million, of whom about a quarter live in Brazil, with smaller numbers in the other countries of the Amazon basin: Venezuela, Colombia, Ecuador, Peru and Bolivia. Isolated groups of lowland Indians also survive in the Central American countries of Panama, Nicaragua and Honduras.

When not tied to the *haciendas* of the big landowners, highland Indian communities farm the land in much the same way as they did five centuries ago. They grow the traditional crops — maize, beans and squash in Mexico, potatoes and maize in the Andes, using mainly the simple technology of the digging stick and hoe. Communities stick together, and members are encouraged not to sell land to outsiders and to marry within the village. Although their lifestyles are often romanticised by outsiders, Indian farming communities suffer the high

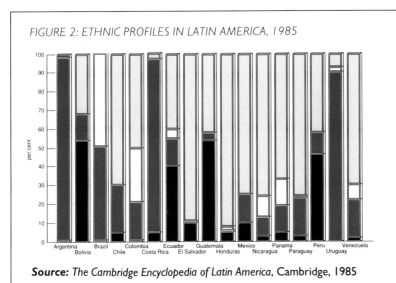

FIGURE 2: ETHNIC PROFILES IN LATIN AMERICA, 1985

Amerindian

European

Afro-American

Mestizo

Source: *The Cambridge Encyclopedia of Latin America*, Cambridge, 1985

levels of infant mortality and insecurity common to all peasant farmers.

Where they have managed to retain a level of independence, such communities frequently enjoy a rich cultural life. In Guatemala, each highland village has its own distinctive costume, with unique designs passed on from mother to daughter for generations. Many traditional practices have survived the efforts of the colonial authorities. Faith healers combine herbal medicine and magic, and the religion of the European invaders has been fused with its predecessors into an original form of folk Catholicism. Communities attach great importance to ritual cycles involving saints' days, feast days and ceremonies such as baptism, marriage and funerals.

In the course of this century modern influences have gradually eroded this traditional pattern. Improved roads have increased trading and involvement in the money economy; improved education and contact with the outside world have enabled most Indians to speak Spanish; and growing numbers of protestant missionaries have both converted Indian groups and persuaded them to abandon their

Willy Cárdenas/Cusco/TAFOS/Panos

traditional customs. The old ways persist most stubbornly in Guatemala, where many speakers of the country's 21 Indian languages still know no more than a few words of Spanish. In most areas men are assimilated into non-Indian ways faster than women, since men have more contact with the money economy through wage labour, and women less frequently go to school, where Spanish is often the only permitted language.

A healer practising a ritual, Peru.

Another major cause of what is known as 'acculturation', the Indians' loss of their traditional culture, is urbanisation. The exodus to the cities brings contact with poor mestizos and Indians from other communities, and Spanish frequently becomes the common language. The disruption of the move often leaves few vestiges of traditional culture intact.

War and repression also accelerate the process. In Guatemala, a ferocious army counter-insurgency campaign in the Indian highlands since the early 1980s left 40,000 dead and over 400 Indian villages destroyed. Many more Indians fled their villages to seek refuge in the cities, where they sought anonymity by abandoning their traditional dress and customs. Over a million people have been displaced from their homes in what borders on a race war against the Indians. In the mid-1980s one Guatemalan President warned 'we must get rid of the words "indigenous" and "Indian"'. Peru's civil war between the Shining Path guerrillas and the army has also driven many Indian families into the swelling shanty towns around Lima.

Violent racism persists in most countries with a significant Indian population. In Guatemala the enormous divide between poor, non-Spanish speaking Indians and wealthy white landowners and entrepreneurs closely resembles apartheid.

'We called all the Indians together, along with their families, in a ravine or at the mouth of a river and there, in the presence of the Indian authorities, we advanced them: one shirt, one machete, some knives to make the cuts [in the rubber trees], a belt so that they didn't fall out of the trees, and of course, any goods they wanted. Throughout the year, we advanced them anything they, or their women, asked for. The women were their ruin and our business, because they fancied everything. Vanity does not respect colour, nor age, nor sex. They wanted combs, perfumes, mirrors and coloured beads, cloth and more cloth, high-heeled shoes and ribbons for their hair. The men asked for drink, Italian sweets and German radios. They liked music and partying.

Every day around 4pm the line of Indians would arrive with the latex, which was weighed on scales and then each Indian's amount was entered in a book. The scales didn't measure the true weight, and the amount we wrote in the book wasn't the amount on the scales. The [German missionary] did a lot of damage because she taught the 'cousins' figures and they began to cause trouble the whole time. When they got unhappy, they'd run away. So we had to invent the pass — no boss would give them an advance if the Indians couldn't show a pass signed by their previous boss to prove that they had paid off their debts. Some Indians managed to pay off their debts, and even earned some money on top, but others didn't. Everything depended on their boss. Some bosses fiddled the books so they never managed to pay it off. But others were very humane and only wrote down what the Indian asked for.'

Alfredo Molano, *Aguas Arriba*, Bogotá, 1990, author's translation

Lowland Indians

'No one sells his own son or his mother, because he loves them. In the same way, it is an absurd idea for an Indian to sell his land. We can't change our feelings for our land, which is where our ancestors are buried.'
Taxáua Indian, Brazil

In contrast to the highland Indians' stable agriculture based on herding and crop rotation, lowland Indians usually practise mobile slash-and-burn forms of farming, combined with fishing and hunting. Both groups, however, share an overwhelming and mystical bond with the land. Lowland Indians, like those of the highlands, have strong religious traditions in which worship of aspects of the natural world is mediated through shamans who speak to the deities in a trance.

Lowland Indians typically live more communally than highlanders, often in communal houses, known as *malocas*, which can hold several hundred people. *Malocas* have been criticised by protestant missionaries for encouraging promiscuity and in many cases have been abandoned in favour of family houses. Many hundreds of different language groups exist, some comprising only a few hundred speakers.

Victor Englebert/Survival

Whereas highland Indians have been in contact with whites virtually since the first days of the Conquest, lowland Indians have frequently lived in inaccessible areas, especially those in the Amazon basin, which outsiders have only recently penetrated. There are still believed to be a few groups, numbering perhaps a few thousand, of 'uncontacted' Indians in the area. When contact does occur, it is frequently as disastrous for the Indians as it was in the 16th century, leading to epidemics of disease and violent confrontations with settlers, such as those that have recently befallen the Yanomami Indians (see chapter 3).

Lowland Indians have suffered the same 'curse of wealth' as their highland relatives. In the rubber boom at the end of the 19th century, unscrupulous rubber companies trapped and enslaved large numbers of Indian tribes as latex collectors. In the Putumayo region of Colombia, 40,000 Indians were killed by these rubber barons between 1886 and 1919. After rubber came oil, African palm, cattle and oil, each new commodity penetrating new areas of the forest and absorbing or driving out the local Indian groups.

The other main source of encroachment on Indian lands has been the colonisation programmes, either spontaneous or government-run, through which landless mestizo peasants have moved into the forest, cutting down the trees to make way for food crops. This has provoked frequent armed conflict between peasants and Indians.

Government attitudes to the lowland Indians have generally alternated between cynical disregard and a desire to 'integrate' the Indians into national life, a process anthropologists condemn as 'ethnocide'. One Brazilian government official proudly described his policy to a visiting journalist:

Yanomami Indians, Amazonia, on the border between Brazil and Venezuela. The Yanomami are Amazonia's largest tribal group, but are declining rapidly as gold prospectors and roads invade their territory, spreading diseases and disrupting communities.

'The civilised people invade, kill our children. We have no support. People let cattle loose all over the land of the Indians. The oldest shamans are dying off. The young ones don't have the knowledge that the old ones had. ...The Xerentes have feasts and dances — the feasts of yam, of honey, of the cutting of hair. They have their own language. When they return from hunting, they don't rest immediately, but wait for the old shaman. Then they relax slowly, while the shaman sings and prays to God.

When a son is born, they go on a diet. The father doesn't eat manioc flour. He doesn't kill snakes. He doesn't collect feathers. Only after spreading honey on his face does he eat honey. When someone dies, he weeps.

When the Indian is about to travel, people join with him and sing and cry with him. When he returns, there is another feast of joy — because he went and he returned. When the moon is beautiful everyone sings. They sing with bowed heads. Only the chief looks at the moon.

Every full moon they sing and celebrate. But ever since civilisation came, they have suffered tremendously. Flu, which they never had in the past, has appeared. The shamans are no longer able to carry out cures. Tuberculosis is what most effects the Xerente today....They used to take medicines from the forest, but there is nothing to deal with the sicknesses of the civilised people. They tried medicines from the forest, but they don't help. They asked the priest to get them some medicine for the sicknesses of the civilised people, and now they are a bit better. This year there was no big sickness.'

Indian spokesman, in Branford and Glock 1985

We resettle them as quickly as possible in new villages and then remove the children and begin to educate them. We give them the benefit of our medicine and our education, and, once they are completely integrated citizens like you and me and the Minister here, we let them go out into the world.

Once out in the world, 'integrated' Indians often end up on the social scrapheap, surviving as beggars or prostitutes on the fringes of the frontier boom-towns of the Amazon. Sometimes the ethnocide was more deliberate. In Brazil in the early 1960s, a subsequent government enquiry found that corrupt officials of its own Indian agency had connived with local landowners to massacre entire tribes using dynamite, machine guns and poisoned sugar. Other investigations showed that tribes in the Mato Grosso had been deliberately infected with smallpox, influenza, tuberculosis and measles.

Rebellion and Resistance

The slow genocide of the Indian nations provoked fierce resistance. In some cases, as in the Caribbean or Brazil, Indian groups opted for mass suicide rather than bow to the dictates of the whites. Many others

'In 1781 Túpac Amaru laid siege to Cuzco. This mestizo chief, a direct descendant of the Inca emperors, headed the broadest of messianic revolutionary movements. The rebellion broke out in Tinta province, which had been almost depopulated by enforced service in the Cerro Rico mines. Mounted on his white horse, Túpac Amaru entered the plaza of Tungasuca and announced to the sound of drums and *pututus* [conch-shell trumpets] that he had condemned the royal Corregidor Antonio Juan de Arriaga to the gallows and put an end to the Potosí *mita*. A few days later Túpac issued a decree liberating the slaves. He abolished all taxes and forced labour in all forms. The Indians rallied by the thousands to the forces of the 'father of all the poor and all the wretched and helpless'. He moved against Cuzco at the head of his guerrilleros, promising that all who died while under his orders in this war would return to life to enjoy the happiness and wealth the invaders had wrested from them. Victories and defeat followed; in the end, betrayed and captured by one of his own chiefs, Túpac was handed over in chains to the royalists. The Examiner Areche entered his cell to demand, in exchange for promises, the names of his rebel accomplices. Túpac Amaru replied scornfully, "There are no accomplices here except you and I. You as oppressor, I as liberator, deserve to die."

Túpac was tortured, along with his wife, his children and his chief aides, in Cuzco's Plaza del Wacaypata. His tongue was cut out; his arms and legs were tied to four horses with the intention of quartering him, but his body would not break; he was finally beheaded at the foot of the gallows. His head was sent to Tinta, one arm to Tungasuca and the other to Carabaya, one leg to Santa Rosa and the other to Livitaca.'

Galeano 1973

retreated into the most inaccessible areas of the continent to escape the burden of constant tributes and forced labour. Some took up arms against the Spanish authorities, the most famous being Peru's Túpac Amaru. Yet neither Indian revolts nor independence succeeded in re-establishing Indian self-rule. In the endless cycle of revolt and defeat, the Indians learned the wisdom of the advice given by Quintín Lame, a Colombian Indian revolutionary leader: 'Do not believe in the friendship of the white man or the mestizo; distrust gifts and flattery; never consult a white lawyer; do not allow yourself to be hoodwinked by the chattering politicians of any party.'

Elsewhere, Indian resistance to oppression was more subtle, but no less stubborn.

In those days we dressed in dark colours decorated with flowers, black *awayos*. We always wore dark blue. But we had to put on coloured clothes because the landowner scolded us: 'How long are you going to continue going around in black, when will you change?' The foremen would go from house to house and whip those wearing dark blue skirts and destroy the tubs used for dying. But we carried on wearing our clothes. That landowner is dead now. The foremen would beat us up and say furiously:

Sebastián Turpo/Ayaviri/TAFOS/Panos

Wedding arch and
procession, Peru.
Ceremonies and rituals
form a central part of the
Indian calendar.

'Damn you, don't you have ears?' We would escape to some
corners of the river and change our clothes: the dark skirt that
we had on underneath we put on top and the other underneath
it.

Andean Oral History Workshop, 'Indigenous Women and
Community Resistance: History and Memory', Jelin (ed) 1990

According to Guatemalan Indian leader Rigoberta Menchú, this passive
refusal to follow orders explains the reputation for passivity which the
Indians acquired in the eyes of outsiders:

This is why Indians are thought to be stupid. They can't think,
they don't know anything, they say. But we have hidden our
identity because we needed to resist, we wanted to protect what
governments have wanted to take away from us. They have tried
to take our things away and impose others on us, be it through
religion, through dividing up the land, through schools, through
books, through radio, through all things modern.

Through this combination of both passive and violent resistance, Latin
America's Indian peoples have achieved their most remarkable victory
— survival. In the face of five centuries of a military, epidemic, cultural
and economic onslaught, the Indians have survived, and are now
increasing in numbers. However, most remain outsiders in their own
lands, condemned to poverty, racism and persecution. The last 25
years have seen attempts to build a politics based on the indigenous
peoples' growing sense of identity and self-confidence, producing an
upsurge in Indian resistance. Among highland groups, Indians have
organised peasant associations and taken up arms to become involved
in civil wars in Guatemala and Peru, while in the lowland areas a
plethora of Indian organisations has sprung up, demanding land and

help from the government, and defending themselves against the invasions of agribusiness, mining companies and poor peasant colonisers. Mario Juruna, the first Indian to become a deputy in Brazil's parliament, made his people's demands quite clear:

> Indian wealth lies in customs and communal traditions and land which is sacred. Indians can and want to choose their own road, and this road is not civilisation made by whites ... Indian civilisation is more human. We do not want paternalistic protection from whites. Indians today ... want political power.

Indian organisations typically rely on individual communities as their basic building blocks. Federations of communities then grow to cover an area, in some cases combining to form regional and even national confederations. Some cross border cooperation has also begun, for example in producing a joint response to the 500th anniversary of Columbus' first voyage to the Americas. In the words of Indian groups from the seven countries of Central America: 'The value of our people has been hidden and ignored by the West ... they call our medicine witchcraft; our religion, superstition; our history, myths; our art, folklore and our languages, dialect.'

Several problems have dogged these attempts at organisation. The first has been the difficulty of building alliances between different indigenous groups and between highland and lowland Indians. But even more thorny has been the problem of the relationship between Indian and non-Indian organisations. Indian organisations are often understandably suspicious of non-Indian political parties and peasant organisations, fearing that they see the world purely in terms of class divisions, and fail to recognise and respect the Indians' right to be culturally distinct. Conflicts between Indians and poor colonists can further sour the relationship between Indians and peasants. In Bolivia, one Indian woman gave voice to the extreme 'indigenist' position: 'To the Indian, the Spaniard is only a tenant. And we have to hit him, complain about him and tell him to leave, because we are the owners and we are going to return.'

Despite these obstacles, the political strength of Indian organisation has grown steadily in recent years, forcing parties, social movements and governments alike to take their demands seriously. Some of the greatest recent advances have been in Bolivia, where the Katarista movement has given a strong voice and political presence to the highland Indians, and in the Brazilian Amazon, where in the wake of Chico Mendes' murder, Indians, rubber-tappers and peasant groups overcame their traditional antipathies and formed the Forest Peoples' Alliance to press for the establishment of sustainable 'extractive reserves' (see chapter 3) and other demands. Indian groups have also had much of their programme adopted by the Brazilian Workers' Party (PT).

Such initiatives have helped boost the low morale of many lowland Indian groups, and Indian populations in some areas have once again started to rise. Yet, although Indian groups have successfully won worldwide recognition and support from pressure groups such as Survival International, they frequently face extreme forms of discrimination and contempt at home. When two Kayapo leaders returned to Brazil in 1988, following a trip to the World Bank to lobby against a dam project which would have flooded their lands, they were arrested and tried under a law forbidding foreigners to intervene in Brazil's internal affairs. Similar anti-Indian sentiments would sit equally well with the ruling white and mestizo elites of Guatemala, Bolivia or Peru.

In the long term, Indians and non-Indians are likely to continue to merge in a process of social and economic 'integration' which in reality means the destruction of the Indians' cultures in return for a place at the bottom of mestizo society. However the recent resurgence of Indian organisation offers the possibility — albeit remote — of a future where Indians and non-Indians live in mutual respect and different cultures can flourish side by side.

Joe Fish

Indian preacher, Guatemala.

Chronology

1494   In the Treaty of Tordesillas the Vatican divides up the New World between Spain and Portugal

1826 on   Independence leaders sign concordats with the Vatican, maintaining Catholicism as the state religion

1926-29   Mexican Church suspends public worship to protest at state harassment. Ninety priests executed during the 'Cristero rebellion'.

1962-65   Second Vatican Council commits the Catholic Church to work for human rights, justice and freedom.

1960s on   Born-again protestant churches begin to expand rapidly throughout Latin America

1968   Meeting of the Latin American bishops in Medellín, Colombia adopts a 'preferential option for the poor'.

1978   Pope John Paul II becomes Pope and leads conservative offensive within Church against 'liberation theology'

1980   Assassination of radical Archbishop Oscar Romero of San Salvador

1990   Estimated number of protestants rises to 40 million from five million in 1970

1991   Guatemala's Jorge Serrano becomes the region's first elected evangelical president

Thy Kingdom Come   11

The Church

The priest, a tall, bearded Scotsman named Michael, was saying mass for the refugees. Salvadoreans of all ages clustered round him, their faces lit by a single naked lightbulb. Everyone was standing, since there were no chairs. With the aid of a microphone and an out-of-tune guitar, the hymns started as the latest refugees arrived, fleeing a new army operation in the guerrilla strongholds to the north.

The Latin American Church has many faces. A few hundred miles south, in Nicaragua, Cardinal Obando y Bravo, fiercely anti-Sandinista, was preaching to a different kind of audience in the little white church of Las Sierritas on the outskirts of Managua. Outside, the cars of the middle-class congregation blocked the street. In the church the air was thick with perfume. As the audience sang 'Glory to my Lord' they clasped hands and raised them above their heads to form a forest of chubby flesh, heavy gold rings and expensive watches.

Beyond the different faces of the Roman Catholic Church, a new force is rising. While beautiful but empty colonial churches crumble in the city centres, ugly evangelical 'temples' are springing up in the shanty towns and villages, crammed with euphoric, chanting, swaying congregations. The crusading zeal of the evangelical protestants is winning millions of new converts every year, threatening a new Reformation in Latin America.

Christopher Columbus had a triple purpose when he set sail for what he imagined to be Asia in 1492. In the words of Bernal Díaz del Castillo, a comrade of Hernan Cortés in the conquest of Mexico, Columbus and the conquistadores who followed went 'to serve God and His Majesty and also to get riches'. In the year that Columbus 'discovered' America, the Spanish led by Ferdinand and Isabella finally drove the last Muslim king out of Granada, bringing to an end the 500-year war to expel the Moors from Spanish soil. That same year, a royal decree expelled all Jews from Spain. With Spain united, the Vatican, at that time under Spanish control, looked to the Americas as the next great crusade. Two years after Columbus landed, in the Treaty of Tordesillas, the Pope decreed that Spain and Portugal could divide up the New World, with a mission to evangelise the heathen.

Since saving souls took precedence over physical well-being, the Crown saw no contradiction between evangelisation and mass-extermination of the Indians through disease and slavery. When Columbus despatched the first 500 Indian slaves back to Spain, he commented in his diary, 'Let us in the name of the Holy Trinity go on sending all the slaves that can be sold'. Under the *encomienda* system, Spanish officers were granted large numbers of Indian slaves, in return for bringing them to Christ. It is not clear how many were successfully converted before dying in the mines or on the haciendas.

From the start, there were dissident friars who expressed their revulsion at the treatment of the Indians. Just 19 years after Columbus first landed, a Dominican named Antonio de Montesinos on the island of Hispaniola (today the Dominican Republic), outraged his Christmas congregation with his questions: 'by what right do you keep these Indians in such a cruel and horrible servitude? ... you kill them with your desire to extract and acquire gold every day.. Are these not men? Have they not rational souls? Are you not bound to love them as you love yourselves?' Five centuries on, many church workers are still asking the same questions of Latin America's rulers.

The sermon changed the life of one young landowner in Montesinos' congregation, a man by the name of Bartolomé de las Casas. Shortly afterwards, de las Casas gave up 'his' Indians and travelled to Spain to begin a lifetime's crusade to persuade the Spanish Crown to end the extermination of the continent's native peoples. First as a Dominican friar, then as a bishop, de las Casas became the Indians' foremost defender, and his book *History of the Indies* a graphic portrayal of their suffering under the conquistadores. In one famous debate in 1550, the 76-year old bishop took on the leading Spanish scholar of his day, Juan Ginés de Sepúlveda, to argue that the enslavement of the Indians was theologically unacceptable, and that Indian civilisation was in many ways superior to that of the Europeans.

Not only the Dominicans, but also the Franciscans and the Jesuits brought a more enlightened version of Christianity. In the early 17th century the Jesuits set up vast 'reductions' covering much of Paraguay, where Guaraní Indians could live and work safe from the depredations of Portuguese slavers. In these sanctuaries, the Indians devoted their great skills to working metal, stone and wood to levels of artistry matching anything in Europe. In the end, however, the Jesuits were driven out and the Indians captured.

From its earliest days in Latin America, the Roman Catholic Church supported the colonial authorities, in return for being made the official religion. In consequence, an increasingly complacent and materialist priesthood lost touch with the poor. In 1748, one report to the Spanish king by naval officers commented:

> it seems relevant to mention here what a priest from the province of Quito told us, during his visitation of this parish, in which — between feasts and memorial services for the dead — he received each year over 200 sheep, 6000 poultry, 4000 Indian pigs and 50,000 eggs. Nor is his parish one of the more lucrative ones.

The independence wars of the early 19th century threatened this cosy relationship and split the Church between pro- and anti-Spanish factions. Usually the upper echelons of the Church supported the old ways, while local priests like Miguel Hidalgo and José María Morelos in Mexico went as far as taking up arms in the independence cause. Both were captured and executed. Despite these schisms, independence leaders subsequently swore allegiance to Rome, and soon came to a series of agreements with the Vatican which maintained

Walter Silvera/San Marcos/TAFOS/Panos

Catholicism as the state religion.

Religious procession, Peru.

Later in the century, the Church paid the price for backing the most backward sections of the elite, usually via the Conservative parties, when Liberal reformers severed the Church-state relationship in Ecuador, Brazil, Cuba, Honduras, Nicaragua, Panama, Chile and Mexico. Liberal governments limited Church control over education and confiscated its property. The countries where the Church was disestablished later became the most fertile ground for the growth of the radical Catholic Church and the evangelical protestants. Anti-clericalism reached its height in post-revolutionary Mexico, where the tensions between Church and state following the Mexican revolution of 1910-17 led the Church to suspend public worship for three years from 1926-29. Ninety priests were executed during the ensuing Cristero rebellion of Church militants, whose name came from their battle cry '*Viva Cristo Rey*' ('Long live Christ the King'). A wartime speech by one Mexican general, J.B.Vargas, encapsulated the virulence of anti-clerical feeling:

> It is enough to have some idea of the terrible history of the Inquisition for one to realise that priests and cassocks reek of prostitution and crime. Confession is an industry invented to seduce maidens, to win over Catholic ladies and transform fathers and husbands into chaste replicas of Saint Joseph ... The Pope is a crafty foreigner who accumulates wealth in collaboration with the exploiting Friars who swindle the foolish people for the benefit of a country quite other than their own ... Nowadays, if Jesus Christ were to come down, the first thing he would do would be to hang them like rabid dogs.'

The rebellion ended when the government backed down and allowed limited autonomy for the Church, though with greatly reduced

THY KINGDOM COME **173**

influence.

While Roman Catholicism remained essentially European at the top, cultural cross-fertilisation was occurring at a local level. From the earliest days of the Conquest, many traditional Indian beliefs and practices were incorporated into a 'folk catholicism', where Catholic saints rubbed shoulders with Andean gods on the niches and altars. In Bolivia's historic mining town of Potosí, the wild baroque carvings of the San Francisco Church look distinctly pagan. Bare-breasted goddesses are interwoven with the ubiquitous symbols of sun and moon, while at the very top of the building, an Inca warrior looks out sternly over the city. A minute, red-cheeked Indian boy explains, 'we built this for ourselves when we Indians weren't allowed in the Cathedral'. African slaves also introduced their spirit religions, which became voodoo in Haiti, Santería in Cuba or the Macumba, Candomblé and Umbanda cults in Brazil.

The Modern Church

The social turmoil of the 1930s, with broader suffrage, the beginnings of urbanisation and the rise of mass politics in the cities, brought home the growing irrelevance of the Church's traditional allies, the Conservative parties and land-owning elites. The Vatican began to wake up to the disastrous condition of its Latin American operation. Grown fat and lazy through its links to the rich, the Church had only the shallowest roots among the poor majority with which to confront a new era of change and mass involvement in politics. Paradoxically, in a continent where the overwhelming majority declared themselves Catholic, few went to church and the ratio of priests to parishioners was far lower than elsewhere in the Vatican's empire.

The Church embarked on a crusade, loosely termed Catholic Action, to organise its lay members and extend its influence within groups such as students, peasants, women, workers and the middle classes. The new emphasis was on social issues, and the movement grew with the emergence of Christian-Democrat parties after the Second World War. Church leaders also saw such organisations as a bulwark against the expansion of communism, and religious organisations in the US contributed funds and personnel as the Cold War gathered momentum in the 1950s. Yet, although the Church acquired renewed political influence, it failed to increase significantly the numbers of active worshippers and reduce its social isolation. In the 1960s only 20 per cent of baptised Catholics regularly attended mass, compared with 80 per cent in Poland or Ireland; there was only one priest for every 5,700 believers compared to a ratio of 1:830 in the US. In addition, the first signs of the imminent explosion of protestant evangelism were beginning to alarm the bishops.

As the 1960s wore on, events threatened to overtake the Vatican. The Cuban revolution in 1959 and the failure of Christian-Democrat governments to deliver reforms led to the radicalisation of many grass-roots Church workers and activists. Many student sections split off from the Christian-Democrat parties to become the nuclei for guerrilla organisations. In Colombia, a radical young priest, Camilo

Torres, took up arms to fight with the National Liberation Army (ELN), declaring, 'the Catholic who is not a revolutionary is living in mortal sin'. Torres died in a shoot-out with the army in 1966.

The speed of events gave an added urgency to the Second Vatican Council, a massive shake-up ordered by Pope John XXIII to drag Roman Catholicism into the modern era. In four years of meetings with 2,500 bishops from around the world, the Vatican charted a new direction. It changed its vertical chain of command for a looser structure based on consultation with local churches, and redirected its attention to the material world, emphasising issues like human rights, justice and freedom. The Church had a duty to pass moral judgements on the state when it contravened basic human rights.

Vatican II, as it became known, had a seismic effect on the Latin American Church, leading in 1968 to the meeting of Latin American bishops in Medellín, Colombia. Medellín took the Latin American Church far beyond Vatican II. In a new doctrine which became known as Liberation Theology, it identified unjust social structures with sin, and came close to justifying guerrilla warfare as a response to 'institutionalised violence':

> One cannot help seeing that in many parts of Latin America there is a situation of institutionalised violence, because the actual structures violate fundamental rights and this situation demands global changes of a bold, urgent and deeply new kind. We should not be surprised that 'the temptation for violence' arises in Latin America.

The bishops then went on to establish a new organisational model to implement these revolutionary new ideas. They suggested the setting up of Base Christian Communities (CEBs), grass-roots groups of working-class or peasant Catholics who would study and reflect on the Bible and use it as a basis for action. This pastoral expression of Liberation Theology was called the 'preferential option for the poor'.

Medellín was a political and theological explosion. The Church abandoned nearly five centuries of largely cosy cohabitation with Latin America's elites in favour of an active commitment to the poor and oppressed. The picture varied enormously between countries; in Chile the Catholic Church was a centre of opposition to the Pinochet dictatorship, and through its *Vicaría de la Solidaridad* played a vital role in documenting and publicising the army's violation of human rights. Radicals also gained substantial influence in Brazil and Central America, whereas the Colombian and Argentine Churches remained true to their conservative past.

The CEBs became a crucible for a process known as *conscientización*, whereby the poor became conscious of injustice and organised to change their lives. As one Salvadorean peasant leader recalls, many went on to lead social movements or even guerrilla organisations:

> What made me first join the farmworkers' union was when I compared the conditions we were living in with those that I saw in the Scriptures; the situation of the Israelites for example ...

Severo Salazar/Ayavini/TAFOS/Panos

Option for the poor.
Open air mass in the
Peruvian Andes.

where Moses had to struggle to take them out of Egypt to the Promised Land ... then I compared it with the situation of slavery in which we were living. Our struggle is the same: Moses and his people had to cross the desert, as we are crossing one right now, and for me, I find that we are crossing a desert full of a thousand hardships, of hunger, misery and exploitation.
Pearce 1986

CEBs treated the Bible as a manual for action. The story of Jesus throwing out the money-lenders acquired enormous political impact when brought up to date through a CEB Bible study group. The groups also had a democratising effect, since the shortage of priests meant that many groups were led by local lay catechists, both men and women, many of whom went on to become popular leaders in their own right. One of them was Rigoberta Menchú, a Guatemalan Indian woman who became a peasant leader. In her autobiography, *I, Rigoberta Menchú*, she describes the impact of becoming a catechist:

> When I first became a catechist, I thought that there was a God and that we had to serve him. I thought that God was up there and that he had a kingdom for the poor. But we realised that it is not God's will that we should live in suffering, that God did not give us that destiny, but that men on earth have imposed this suffering, poverty, misery and discrimination on us.

CEBs took firmest roots in Brazil, where they were instrumental in starting the protest movement which helped drive the military government from power in 1985. They also formed an essential part of the social movements which went on to challenge for power through the Workers Party (PT). Estimates put their numbers at 100,000, comprising some two to three million people. They also

You are the God of the poor,
a human and a simple God.
The God who sweats in the street,
the God of the withered face.
That's why I speak to you,
just like my people speak,
because you are the worker God,
the labouring Christ.'

From the *Misa Campesina* (Peasant Mass) by Nicaraguan singer Carlos
Mejía Godoy

A Base Christian Community in Brazil

'I went to a first communion class on the periphery of São Paulo where
I experienced a practical lesson in theology. The theme that fortnight
was that Jesus was born poor and humble and shares our life, and the
question was 'Why?'. The women present were all poor. None had had
much formal education. Most were migrants from rural areas. All knew
real hardship. They could easily identify with a poor family on the move
whose baby had been born in a stable. Indeed a one-minute reading of
St Luke's account of the nativity provoked a one-hour discussion of the
injustices, humiliations and hardships that the mothers themselves
experienced.

They discussed the terrible health services available in the area and
how a local woman's baby had been born while she was waiting in the
queue to see the doctor (the baby died). They swapped accounts of
having to wait in shops while better dressed people were served first and
how as domestic servants they were treated without respect by their
mistresses. They talked of the high price of food in the local shops ...

After an hour the catechist put the question "Why did Jesus *choose*
to be born poor and humble?"

"Maybe," said one woman, a mother of ten of whom three had died
and only two were working, "maybe it was to show these rich people
that we are important too."

A ripple of excitement went through the room. Was God really such
a clear statement about *their* humanity? About *their* rights as people? The
discussion progressed, but with an electric charge in the air. Half an hour
later, a young woman said "I think we still haven't got the right answer
to the first question!" A complete hush. "I think", she went on, "that
God chose his son to be born like us so that we can realise that we are
important. It is not just to show the bosses. It's to show us too!"'

James Pitt, 'Good News to All', Report for Bishop Victor Guazelli,
CAFOD, London, 1990

The progressive Church's most famous martyr, Oscar Arnulfo Romero was an essentially conservative man, radicalised by his contact with El Salvador's poor and the worsening violence of the army and its associated death squads. As Archbishop of San Salvador, Romero publicly attacked both the economic system and human rights abuses in weekly sermons which were picked up on dilapidated radios in peasant huts and shanty towns throughout the country.

On the economy:

'The cause of all our ills is the oligarchy — that handful of families who care nothing for the hunger of the people but need that hunger in order to have cheap, abundant labour to raise and export their crops.'

On violence:

'Profound religion leads to political commitment, and in a country such as ours where injustice reigns, conflict is inevitable.... Christians have no fear of combat; they know how to fight but they prefer to speak the language of peace. Nevertheless, when a dictatorship violates human rights and attacks the common good of the nation, when it becomes unbearable and closes all channels of dialogue, of understanding, of rationality, when this happens, the Church speaks of the legitimate right of insurrectional violence.'

On 23 March 1980 he signed his death warrant by appealing directly to the soldiers carrying out attacks:

'In the name of God, and in the name of this suffering people whose laments rise to heaven every day more tumultuous, I beg you, I ask you, I order you in the name of God: Stop the repression.'

The next day he was killed with a single shot while saying mass at a local hospital chapel. Ten years on, no one has yet been charged for his assassination, although a variety of sources have laid responsibility at the door of Major Roberto d'Aubuisson, death-squad leader and Honorary Life President of the ruling ARENA party.

played a vital role in Central America, where the radical Church supported the insurrection which overthrew the Somoza dictatorship and then supplied three priest-ministers to the Sandinista government. In El Salvador, the CEBs were at the forefront of the upsurge in the protest movement which ended in a bloodbath in the early 1980s and a prolonged civil war.

Yet the Church paid a high price for its 'option for the poor'. Within the church hierarchy, conservative bishops began to backtrack on the Medellín commitments almost as soon as the conference was over. Their efforts were greatly helped by the appointment of a fiercely anti-communist Polish Pope, John Paul II, in 1978. An increasingly acrimonious dispute between radicals and conservatives threatened to divide the Church from top to bottom.

The new radical Church also became a target for repression. 'Be a patriot, kill a priest', ran one death-squad slogan in El Salvador in the

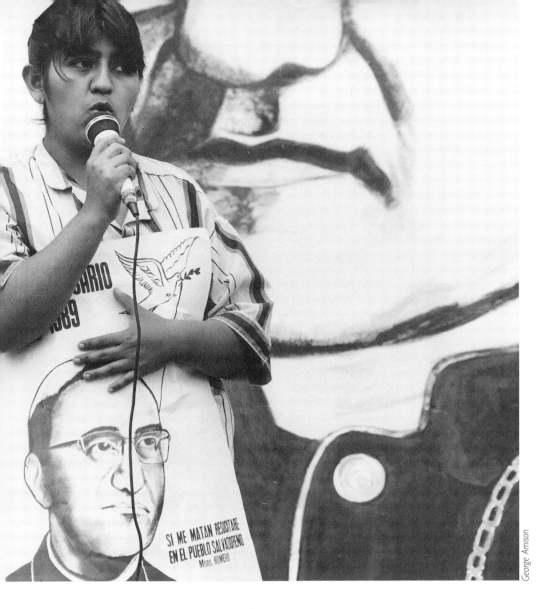

late 1970s. Although dozens of clerics were killed, the most celebrated being Archbishop Romero and four North American nuns killed in El Salvador in 1980, an even greater slaughter awaited the lay preachers, who died in their hundreds. As a result, the Salvadorean CEB movement was devastated, although it stubbornly refused to die and began slowly to rebuild when the repression eased off in the late 1980s.

A New Reformation

The remoteness of both traditional Catholic and protestant churches created a spiritual vacuum into which a new kind of US-based born-again protestantism began to expand. From the 1960s onwards, groups like the Assemblies of God began to attract millions of converts. In subsequent years the divisions within the Roman Catholic Church

A modern martyr. Ninth anniversary of the murder of Archbishop Oscar Arnulfo Romero. Romero was assassinated for calling on the Salvadorean army to disobey orders and end the repression of their own people.

and the growing repression against the CEBs allowed the new churches to grow even faster.

'Evangelicals', as they are commonly called in Latin America, are born-again Christians committed to converting others to their own brand of Christianity. Evangelical services typically involve rhythmic clapping, chanting and swaying, leading to a cathartic mass euphoria. The most dynamic strain of evangelism in Latin America is the Pentecostal movement, which believes that true Christians are taken over by the Holy Spirit during religious gatherings, culminating in speaking in tongues and faith healing. The name comes from a biblical reference to the 'Day of the Pentecost' (a Jewish holiday), when Jesus' disciples were visited by the Holy Spirit and received the 'gift of tongues' to enable them to preach and evangelise in other languages.

The tide of Pentecostalism has rapidly swamped the traditional protestant churches of Latin America, such as the Lutherans and Presbyterians. These are small groups generally set up by immigrants from northern Europe, and have largely middle-class congregations. Many of them have only recently begun to hold their services in Spanish and appoint Latin American-born bishops. In 1936, Pentecostals represented just two per cent of Central American protestants; by 1990 the figure was closer to 90 per cent.

With the exception of the Assemblies of God, the evangelical movement in Latin America is divided up into innumerable separate 'sects', often the personal vehicle of a single pastor. When a congregation grows, it will often subdivide into new sects. Although this reduces the coherence and influence of the movement as a whole, it means that evangelical churches remain rooted in their communities. Pastors display a zeal rarely encountered in their Catholic counterparts. In the middle of a war zone in Nicaragua in the 1980s, evangelical pastors could be found three days from the nearest road, walking between peasant huts in search of converts. The Catholic Church was nowhere to be seen.

The social message of the evangelicals is usually one of individualism, hard work and sobriety. Evangelical pastors are fiercely hostile to collective organisations such as trade unions. Critics, especially radical Catholics, have accused them of encouraging political passivity which only benefits the powerful and denies the poor the ability to organise to improve their lot. Evangelicals respond that true salvation lies in an individual's relationship to God, and, as one Costa Rican group sings, 'I've got nothing in this world, but a mansion in the next'. Carlos Chávez, a 46-year old evangelical of the Elim Church in San Salvador, explains: 'The Lord changes the evangelical's life. He makes him more patient, more passive, more humble, more loving, more centred in what he does.' Carlos shows a typically evangelical view of El Salvador's bloody civil war:

> The war is the fulfilment of the prophesies — the Lord told his disciples there would be wars, plagues, famines and earthquakes, and these would be signs of his coming. As evangelicals, the war doesn't torment us, it brings us joy, because it's a sign that Jesus is coming soon. We don't intervene in the conflict. What we do

'The film *Jesus* has been showing for free for several nights each week. The California-based Campus Crusade for Christ has brought the *Gospel of Luke* here on the silver screen as part of its Central America-wide evangelisation campaign. The film's Jesus is a gentle, white miracle worker, who speaks serpentine parables in an authoritative tone, with a deep Spanish voice-over on the soundtrack.

As a twinkling cross fades from the screen at the film's end, a local evangelist leaps on to the makeshift stage: "Step forward those of you who want eternal life! Who among you here wants to spend the rest of your days with JESUS? Who is ready to take the first step forward with Jesus, just come up to the altar, take that step!" On the face of it, it seems implausible that this American-made product should sell well in revolutionary Ocotal. But singly, or in twos and threes, they come forward slowly.

They are stepping up for a package of beliefs which, as put forward by Campus Crusade, leaves no room in their earthly lives to work for social gains. Caesar must not compete with the Heavenly Father; preoccupation with this world would mean serving two masters. The task of the evangelical is to bring about the glorious return and Kingdom of Jesus. That is 'the only real revolution' writes Campus Crusade's founder and director Bill Bright.'

Deborah Huntington, 'The Prophet Motive', *Report on the Americas*, New York, January 1984

is pray to God that things should change. Today God's people don't struggle with arms, but with prayer.

With very few exceptions, evangelical pastors preach a political philosophy somewhere between neutral indifference and rabid anti-communism. Evangelicals are frequently taught to detest Catholics almost as much as communists, and the rivalry has split many communities.

This essentially conservative message contrasts with the more progressive doctrines gradually being adopted by many of the traditional protestant churches. Grouped together in the Latin American Council of Churches (CLAI), these groups have built ecumenical links with the more radical Catholic Church, although not endorsing the full content of Liberation Theology. CLAI has attempted to turn protestant attention to issues such as the drug war and the debt crisis, but remains a small voice with very limited influence within the Pentecostal movement.

Evangelical churches flourish during periods of social disruption and suffering. Peasant migration to the cities severs an individual's links to the community, resulting in isolation and confusion. In such circumstances, evangelism can offer both a supportive community and a strong sense of purpose and identity. The emphasis on sobriety is particularly attractive to many women whose partners have alcohol problems. The Pentecostals have also picked up men and women who have found the CEBs too secular in their stance and seek a more spiritual message. Others found the traditional Catholic Church too oppressive:

> My grandmother did the circuit of each saint, repeating 'forgive my sins'. I imitated everything she did, I knelt, I repeated 'forgive me, forgive me'. I had no idea what it was all about. You had to keep quiet, look at the saints without saying anything to them, pray, light candles and you can't even cough. When you left, you felt like you were emerging from a cellar, because the churches are huge, dark and full of relics and echoes. The Catholic Church made me very upset. In the Baptists we can talk normally, it is more communicative. If you want you can express all your feelings. All that stuff about imitating the prayers of the priest just seemed stupid to me.
>
> Ana María Condori, *Mi Despertar*, La Paz, 1988, author's translation

In the last two decades the number of protestants in Latin America has risen eight-fold to 40 million. The highest numbers are in Guatemala, where over a third are protestant, Brazil, Chile and Nicaragua (20 per cent), and Costa Rica (16 per cent). Although 40 million people only represents about 10 per cent of the total population, and most of the rest describe themselves as Roman Catholics, virtually all protestants are active churchgoers, whereas the rate among Catholics may be as low as 15 per cent. In terms of active participation, protestants may already outnumber Catholics in several countries, leading to predictions that Latin America is ripe for Reformation.

Although the growth of the evangelical churches has fed on social chaos, suffering and the divisions within the Catholic Church, other influences have attracted severe criticism from progressives of both catholic and protestant backgrounds. The Latin American evangelical movement is financed and heavily influenced by evangelical groups in the US, who in the 1980s constituted the backbone of Ronald Reagan's 'New Right'. US groups have sent thousands of missionaries, run aid projects which also serve as recruitment drives, and trained new generations of local pastors to spread the word. 'Televangelical' preachers like Jimmy Swaggart and Pat Robertson are household names in many Latin American nations, where the resources of the multi-million dollar Bible Belt TV and radio chains buy hours of airtime. A new breed of US-based Spanish-speaking 'super preachers' like Luis Palau and Alberto Mottesi have now joined their ranks.

One key organisation in the evangelical crusade is the Wycliffe Bible Translators (WBT), also known as the Summer Institute of Linguistics. WBT has translated the Bible into dozens of Indian languages and trained local pastors to preach from it. An analysis by anthropologists of one of their dictionaries for the Tzotzil people of Mayan descent showed that the WBT had failed to translate political words such as 'class', 'community' or 'exploitation' despite their existence in both languages, while their examples of contexts for other words were politically loaded. They included:

Protestant evangelical preacher, Guatemala. The rise of pentecostal protestant groups is on the verge of creating a Latin American reformation.

Right: Man has a right to punish his children when they behave poorly.
Boss: The boss is good. He treats us well and pays us a good wage.

The link between the US fundamentalist New Right and Latin America's evangelicals has been strongest in Central America. Believers from the southern states of the US raised millions of dollars for Guatemala when General Ríos Montt seized power in 1982 to become Latin America's first evangelical dictator. The New Right became an apologist for the Guatemalan regime as Ríos Montt launched a counter-insurgency campaign which killed thousands of civilians and wiped out whole Indian communities. Ríos Montt was a member of the El Verbo (The Word) church, a mission of the California-based Gospel Outreach. In a video distributed by the California Verbo community, US missionary Ronny Gilmore revealed a chilling side to his work with the Guatemalan army:

> One soldier in particular was an evangelical and he said that he didn't know if God could forgive him because he had taken children and their mothers and put them into a house and then set then on fire, under orders from the captain. I shared with him God's love for him and told him that he could be forgiven.

The US evangelical networks also played an important role in fund-raising for the Contra rebels in Nicaragua, as part of Oliver North's shadowy Irangate network. One organisation, International Love Lift Mission, runs campaigns in Nicaragua, Brazil and Guatemala, calling itself 'America's most effective contribution to the cause of Freedom in the Latin World'.

Although some radical Catholics claim the evangelical movement is entirely funded and controlled by Washington, the reality is less clear. As a movement hostile to the growth of radical catholicism and opposed to political activism, it undoubtedly serves the interests of the US and local elites by creating a passive, unorganised, diligent workforce. However, many local sects have few ties to the US and the astonishing speed of their expansion shows that they meet a real spiritual and social need in the region. Evangelicals seem to alternate between periods of political indifference and right-wing activity, such as surrounded Ríos Montt's dictatorship. So far, their political influence has failed to match their extraordinary growth rate, although in the first days of 1991, Guatemala achieved another first by providing the continent's first elected evangelical president in Jorge Serrano.

If the Pentecostal church does embark on a period of sustained political involvement with the poor, it could undergo the same kind of radical political conversion as occurred within the Roman Catholic Church in the 1960s. However, there is so far little evidence for such a change, and its links to right-wing US sects would act as a brake on any such development. As a result, people in poor communities throughout Latin America are facing an increasingly polarised choice between the distant and formal tone of the traditional Catholic Church, the progressive, but harshly realistic voice of the CEBs, and the conservative, but spiritually comforting message of the Pentecostals.

Mike Goldwater/Network

Atlacatl brigade on anti-guerrilla sweep, El Salvador, 1982. The Atlacatl have been involved in some of the worst human rights abuses in the country's 12 year-old civil war.

Chronology

1808-26	Wars of independence free Spanish America from colonial rule
1939-45	Second World War establishes US as dominant military power in Latin America
1949	Brazilian Higher War School founded, becoming central to spread of cold-war national security doctrine
1959	Cuban revolution and ensuing support for other guerrilla movements seen by military as proof of international communist conspiracy
1964	Military seize power in Brazil and rule for 25 years
end 1976	At least two-thirds of people on mainland Latin America live under dictatorial rule
1982	Argentina loses South Atlantic war, and military government falls; senior officers subsequently imprisoned on human rights charges
1981-90	US arms and trains Contras to fight proxy war against Nicaragua
1989	US invasion of Panama
1990	Chile's General Pinochet becomes the last of the great dictators to leave office

Men at Arms   12

The Military

G eneral Albano Harguindeguy sat on the sofa in his Buenos Aires
flat. Now a retired Latin American patriarch, his genial back-
slapping style must once have made him popular with his men. Over
a Scotch he reflected on his period in office as Argentina's Minister of
the Interior, priding himself on his grasp of world events. While his
wife served pizza, he mused over what he would have done differently
if he had the chance to be in government all over again. 'Not so many
disappeared people — we should have used the law instead', he
concluded.

The bluff general in his cardigan and slippers was in charge of
internal security during the worst years of the military junta which
seized power in 1976. During the period of the 'dirty war',
Harguindeguy's men took thousands of young men and women from
their homes, often at night, and drove them away in the sinister
unmarked Ford Falcons favoured by the security forces. Their relatives
and friends never heard from them again, amid rumours of torture
cells, concentration camps and mass graves. After the military regime
fell, the rumours proved to be true. The number of documented
'disappearances' exceeds 9,000, and the real number could be two or
three times that amount.

Argentina's dark hours of fear and doubt have been repeated up and
down Latin America. In *Mothers of the Disappeared*, by Jo Fisher, Aída
de Suárez remembers how her son disappeared:

> On 2 December 1977 at four o'clock in the morning, twenty
> armed men broke into our house with rifles and pistols pointed
> at us. They were nervous. They opened and closed the
> cupboards, the fridge. They were looking for things, guns
> apparently. They took everything of any value they could carry,
> the few things of value that a working-class family has in their
> home, sentimental things. But that wasn't important to me. They
> could have taken everything, but my son, no. He was sitting on
> the bed, trying to get dressed. One man shouted, 'There's one
> in here!' and then two huge men with guns in their hands told
> me not to move. They asked only if he was Hugo Héctor Suárez
> and that he had to go with them.
>
> 'Who are you?', I screamed. 'We are the security forces.' They
> were in civilian suits but underneath they were wearing army
> fatigues and boots, and green bullet-proof vests, the colour of
> the army. So it was the army. I said, 'Why? My son has done
> nothing, he's not a criminal. Why have you come in like this,

frightening the children with guns pointed at everyone?' — twenty armed men for a child of 21, an old woman like me, and two young children. 'We've come to take him away for questioning.' 'Why?' I asked and they pushed me and threw me against the wall. They took my son. That was the last time I saw him.

By the end of 1976 two-thirds of people on the Latin American mainland lived under dictatorial rule. Among the major countries, only Mexico, Venezuela, Colombia and Costa Rica had no general in the presidential palace. Pinochet, Stroessner, Videla; the continent became synonymous with vicious military dictators in sunglasses and the midnight knock on the door. As the 1980s passed, the generals began to return to the barracks, some in defeat and humiliation, others managing to retain a significant voice in politics. In March 1990, Chile's General Augusto Pinochet became the last of the great Latin American dictators to leave power when he reluctantly handed over the presidency to the elected Christian-Democrat leader Patricio Aylwin. By early 1991, Fidel Castro's Cuban regime remained the last unelected government in the western hemisphere, yet in many Latin American countries the military retained considerable power, and there was no guarantee they would not once again leave their barracks to seize the presidential palace.

Unlike the UK or US, where civilian political control over the armed forces has long been taken for granted, the military in Latin America have always been an independent political force. The nature of the Spanish Conquest, led by soldiers who defeated the Aztec and Inca empires and were rewarded with land, slaves and booty, was in marked contrast to the methods and lifestyle of the civilian settlers who emigrated to start a new life in the US and Canada. When Spanish power collapsed, Latin America won its independence through the exploits of military heroes like Simón Bolívar and José de San Martín. Today, the streets of every Latin American capital are littered with statues of heroic military figures on horseback, swords raised, and schoolchildren diligently learn the names of the military fathers of the nation.

In the absence of strong political institutions, the independence leaders rapidly became charismatic paternalist figures, known as *caudillos*. As one Venezuelan *caudillo* wrote to Bolívar, 'the people bring me all their problems — how to build a house, whom to marry, how to settle a family dispute, and what seeds to plant'. In Latin America's rigidly stratified society, the military offered one of the few vehicles for ambition and social mobility, and *caudillos* and their personal retinues fought endless wars. In *One Hundred Years of Solitude*, Gabriel García Márquez describes a classic *caudillo*, Colonel Aureliano Buendía:

> Colonel Aureliano Buendía organised 32 armed uprisings and he lost them all. He had 17 male children by 17 different women and they were exterminated one after the other on a single night before the oldest one had reached the age of 35. He survived 14 attempts on his life, 73 ambushes, and a firing squad. He lived

through a dose of strychnine in his coffee that was enough to kill a horse. He refused the Order of Merit which the President of the Republic awarded him. He rose to be Commander in Chief of the Revolutionary Forces.

Caudillos' local armies often far outnumbered the national standing army — in Venezuela's Federal War of 1859-64, 40,000 men died although the regular army numbered only 3,500. The private armies became a massive and unproductive burden on society, holding back economic progress and creating constant political instability as 'revolving door generals' successively seized power. Even today, the *caudillo* tradition remains a strong political influence in many rural areas.

Heroes of Independence

Between 1808 and 1826, wars of liberation raged through the whole of Spanish America. The growing anti-Spanish feeling among the locally-born elite of white *criollos* was finally turned into rebellion by Napoleon's invasion of Spain in 1808. With the colonial power weakened, armed uprisings turned into liberation armies which marched across the continent in two great arcs: in the south, General José de San Martín's (1778-1852) Army of the Andes crossed the pampas from Buenos Aires, marched over the Andes into Chile and then moved up towards Peru. In the north, Simón Bolívar's (1783-1830) followers marched from Venezuela into Colombia and down to liberate Ecuador. The two armies converged on Peru, where they decisively defeated the remaining Spanish forces at the Battle of Ayacucho in 1824. In Mexico, violent social rebellion followed a course of its own. By 1826 Spain had lost everything except Cuba and Puerto Rico. Brazil declared its independence from Portugal in 1822, but in contrast to the republics of Spanish America, the new nation emerged as a monarchy ruled by the emperor Pedro II, a member of the Portuguese royal family. Brazil did not become a republic until 1889.

The independence armies were led by the small *criollo* class fighting to seize power from Spain, but otherwise intent on maintaining Latin America's social structures largely unchanged. 'Liberation' brought few benefits for the Indian population. Black slaves were, however, promised their freedom in exchange for fighting, and formed much of San Martín's Army of the Andes. Indians were press-ganged to fight by both sides. The white leaders of both sides feared revolt by the blacks and Indians more than they feared each other — when the Spanish viceroy decided to abandon Lima in 1821, the terrified and hitherto royalist citizens asked San Martín for protection against a feared black uprising.

Bolívar was the outstanding independence leader, and remains a venerated figure throughout the region. His beliefs were a complex and often contradictory mixture of enlightenment-inspired republicanism and the authoritarianism of the *caudillo*. Shortly before his death, disillusioned by his compatriots' lack of experience in government and the chaos unleashed by the independence wars, he

Eduardo Longoni

Military ceremony, Buenos Aires, Argentina. The military form a separate caste in Argentine society, and have regularly seized power from civilian politicians.

wrote the Bolivian constitution. In it, Bolívar created a president-for-life, able to choose his own successor, thereby avoiding 'the changing administration caused by party government and the excitement which too frequent elections produce.'

Bolívar's dream of a United States of Latin America soon foundered on the rivalries and geographical and cultural differences which helped to divide up the region into today's republics. In the year of Bolívar's death, 'Great Colombia' disintegrated into Venezuela, Colombia and Ecuador; the former 'kingdom of Guatemala' splintered into the numerous feuding Central American republics. Each division took Latin America further from the path to prosperity and power followed by the US to the north.

During the 19th-century *caudillo* period, the military were often no more than armed members of the peasantry. Since then, a process of professionalisation has taken place, transforming the military from an irregular army in the hands of local chieftains into a sophisticated institution, while never removing their taste for occupying the presidential palace.

Professionalisation has involved building a national army with a proper career structure and a separate value system, encouraging its self-image as a caste apart from, and often superior to, the rest of society. Military schools and staff colleges were set up to forge young boys into tomorrow's generals. The schools take boys in their early teens and impose military discipline and values. A high percentage of the intake are sons of officers, which only increases the sense of separation from society. Once the boy has entered the military structure, he will often stay isolated from civilian society until he is a high-ranking officer — his life will revolve around the school and the barracks:

The isolation of the [Argentine] armed forces intensified over the course of the 20th century. Beginning in the 1920s, special neighbourhoods and clubs were constructed for officers and their families. These new institutions included free country clubs or *circulos* used for recreation, business functions and weddings of officers and their children. Paid for out of the military budget, these clubs — like the special apartment complexes erected near major military installations — accentuated the officers' ignorance of civilian values and aspirations. Usually only those with the rank of colonel or above could acquire their own apartments in civilian neighbourhoods. The virtual apartheid separating officers from both enlisted soldiers and civilians was epitomized in the rules governing elevators in military buildings: one set of lifts used by officers and another for civilians and lower-ranking soldiers.
Emilio Mignone, 'The Military: What is to be Done?', *Report on the Americas*, New York, July 1987

In the absence of combat experience, most Latin American armies place enormous importance on educational qualifications as the path to promotion. The standard of education in military schools is often higher than in civilian life, reinforcing the officers' sense of innate superiority.

Once the officers reach the rank of colonel, a new panorama opens. At this point they start to acquire significant political power, a coterie of civilian advisers, and contact with the civilian economic elites and overseas diplomats. In large economies like Brazil and Argentina, military officers are highly sought after to sit on the boards of both state and private businesses, and opportunities for self enrichment begin to appear. In less sophisticated economies, officers must settle for more straightforward methods; in Paraguay General Stroessner kept his officers happy by cutting them in on the smuggling trade with Brazil; in Panama General Noriega bought his men's loyalty and silence by involving them in everything from protection rackets to prostitution; in El Salvador local commanders leave soldiers killed in action on the battalion's books and pocket their wages. As one army leader in the Mexican revolution of 1910 commented, 'there is no general who can withstand a bombardment of 50,000 pesos.'

From the early days of import substitution, some of the region's most developed armies began to assemble a military-industrial complex which gave them enormous economic muscle. In Brazil and Argentina, military conglomerates came to control everything from arms manufacture to petrochemicals. Brazil has even come to rival Israel as the Third World's foremost arms exporter. One side effect of Central America's increasing militarisation has been the growing economic strength of the newly expanded armies. In El Salvador the army has its own banks, pension funds and (appropriately) funeral parlours, while in Guatemala the army has long been a major player in the economy. In many countries, the military's growing economic strength has enabled it to pursue an increasingly independent political line.

The social gulf between officers and men in Latin America's armies is exacerbated by the widespread use of conscription. Many of the young men who shivered in the Argentine trenches during the Falklands/Malvinas war of 1982 were conscripts with little interest in fighting. In countries such as El Salvador, the army raids cinemas or stops buses and press-gangs young men into the ranks, where they face a highly motivated volunteer guerrilla army.

Joe Fish

The Spectre of Communism

Members of Guatemala's elite gather for cocktails on the Day of the Army, Guatemala.

Following the Second World War, Latin America's militaries increasingly adopted a Cold War ideology. This world view was refined at the military's staff colleges, where high-flying young officers were prepared for the High Command. In Brazil, the military set up the Higher War School (*Escola Superior de Guerra*, ESG) in 1949, where young officers studied not only military tactics, but also politics, economics and sociology. From the outset, the ESG also recruited among the civilian elite — business leaders, top civil servants, politicians and judges who by 1966 comprised half the graduates. The ESG thus served both to train the future military top brass and establish firm links between them and Brazil's civilian rulers.

The ESG was instrumental in developing what became known as national security doctrine, an all-embracing viewpoint which saw the military as the guardians of order in the broadest sense, including economic development and the prevention of internal political or social divisions. The enemy of the continent's social order was the spectre of international communism, which was conducting a stealthy war of internal subversion against pro-western governments throughout Latin America.

National security doctrine became established as the linchpin of military thinking following the Cuban revolution of 1959, which the generals saw as proof of the international communist conspiracy. The doctrine provided the intellectual justification for the military to make the defeat of 'internal subversion' its top priority. Subversion was defined as anything which threatened the status quo — trade unionism, peasant movements, socialist politics, or student protest. Since this was a 'Third World War' against the communist menace, human rights

In late 1987 the armies of the Americas held their seventeenth conference in Mar Del Plata, Argentina. The meeting was secret, but the minutes were subsequently leaked, giving a unique portrait of the military's view of the world, and in particular of what it calls the 'International Communist Movement' (ICM). The generals believed that, having largely won the military war against the guerrillas, they now faced the ICM in a new guise, the so-called 'Solidarity Organisations' — social movements devoted to human rights, religious work amongst the poor, trade unions and peasants' organisations. To the military men, all such individuals and organisations were either dupes or willing accomplices of a Moscow-run international conspiracy to overthrow the West.

On the Communist Threat
'The international Soviet communist strategy tries to consolidate its actions in El Salvador, Cuba and Nicaragua in order to extend its geo-political dominance towards Guatemala, Honduras, and Costa Rica, then to take control of the Panama Canal.'

'The ICM objective of Marxist-Leninist infiltration in South America is a fact in the Armed Forces, in the Church, in workers' and students organisations. All the social manifestations are part of the plans of subversion.'

On the Radical Church
'... Liberation Theology transformed the "preferential option for the poor" into a concept far from the meaning of the faith, in agreement with the Marxist idea of "class struggle as the path toward a society without classes", emptying it of its fundamental Christian, ecclesiastical, and pastoral content. In this way, the modality of theological reflection reduces the figure of Jesus to that of a political and social leader.'

'... These positions [of Liberation Theology] ... are a conscious assumption and manipulation of the truly liberating Christian message of salvation to further the objectives of the Communist revolution.'

On 'Solidarity Organisations'
'The organisations [of the ICM] infiltrated organisations, pacifist movements, among others, many of which hold "consultative status" at the UN, working together ... to complete a pincer manoeuvre from the outside, condemning the target country in international forums.'

'The Solidarity Organisations constitute a significant part of the ICM's strategic mechanism ... They serve the revolutionary struggle as instruments to preserve or protect imprisoned cadres; they allow for the execution of "surface politics" that are prohibited to leftist political-military organs ... In essence, we find the importance of the Solidarity Organisations in their capacity to neutralise much of the support of the popular organisations and of certain juridical-institutional resources of countries in their STRUGGLE AGAINST TERRORISM [caps in original], and to change military victories of the Liberal Forces into political defeats.'

> By portraying all opposition as part of the ICM, the military denies the social movements their true roots in Latin America's chronic inequality, human rights abuses or a progressive reading of the bible. Such a view also legitimises repression of social movements as part of the struggle against international communism. The document identified Father Ignacio Ellacuría, rector of the Catholic University in El Salvador, as a Marxist liberation theologian. Two years later Salvadorean soldiers dragged Father Ellacuría from his bed and shot him, along with five other Jesuit priests, in the name of the 'war on communism'.
>
> *Total War Against the Poor* 1990

considerations and the rule of law became redundant, opening the way for the atrocities, disappearances and bloodshed which followed.

Some of the wilder excesses of national security doctrine had a tragicomic air — in the late 1970s the Argentine junta reportedly burnt books on Cubism under the mistaken belief that they expounded the philosophy of Fidel Castro. Junta members were much given to describing themselves as the defenders of western Christian democracy despite their aversion to elections. The Argentine military's perception of what constituted a threat to western Christendom has always been broad; in the 1960s General Ongania defended the sanctity of the family by outlawing miniskirts.

Up until the Second World War US influence was greatest in its traditional backyard of Central America and the Caribbean. In the early years of the century, Washington regularly sent in the marines to overthrow governments, before setting up client armies like General Somoza's National Guard in Nicaragua which enabled it to retreat to its bases in the Panama Canal Zone. Further south, in Brazil, Chile and Argentina, the German army had considerable influence in the early professionalisation of regular armies.

However, the Second World War destroyed Germany as a regional influence and established the US as the supreme foreign power throughout Latin America. US military missions spread across Latin America to supply and train the region's armies, in the process ensuring that future military leaderships would be firmly pro-US. As the Cold War gathered pace, US influence was crucial in forging national security doctrine. In Brazil, US advisers helped set up the ESG and taught there until 1960. Writing in *Military Review* in 1958, one US colonel showed the warped reasoning which saw Latin American independence struggles as tools of Soviet expansionism, and therefore as a legitimate target for repression:

> One of the most successful Soviet weapons during the Cold War has been to agitate among so-called colonial populations so that they fight for their independence and reject what has become termed 'foreign economic exploitation'.

In addition to sending military missions to the various countries, the US trained thousands of Latin American officers and future military leaders in the US or at the School of the Americas in the Panama Canal Zone, earning it the name 'School of the Dictators'.

As a result of President Carter's short-lived human rights policy in the 1970s, brutal military regimes in Latin America found their arms supplies from Washington reduced or cut off. Their response was to look elsewhere for suppliers and develop their own armaments industries. This has undermined US supremacy in the region as arms suppliers from the UK, France, Italy, Germany, the Soviet Union and Israel have broken into the market.

In 1981 President Reagan took office, determined to end Carter's human rights policy, which he blamed for the US 'losing' Nicaragua as a client state through the 1979 revolution. One of the key right-wing thinktanks behind Reagan's new policy, the Council for Inter-American Security, painted a lurid picture of US strategy in Latin America:

> World War III is almost over. The Soviet Union, operating under the cover of increasing nuclear superiority, is strangling the Western industrialized nations ... America is everywhere in retreat. The Caribbean, America's maritime crossroad and petroleum refining centre, is becoming a Marxist-Leninist lake.

President Reagan chose to 'draw the line against communism' in Central America and the Caribbean. US marines invaded Grenada in 1983 and overthrew its left-wing government, while in Nicaragua and El Salvador US strategists refined Vietnam style counter-guerrilla tactics into a more general technique known as 'low intensity conflict'. This attempted to defeat the guerrilla movement in El Salvador and the Sandinista government in Nicaragua through the use of proxy armies in order to avoid the use of US troops which might lead to an anti-war backlash at home. In El Salvador the army was encouraged to 'win hearts and minds' among the peasantry, but at the same time had the conflicting objective of striking at anyone considered sympathetic to the guerrillas. In the end repression took precedence over reform. In Nicaragua the Contras played a significant part in the downfall of the left-wing Sandinista government by sabotaging the economy and forcing the government to divert scarce resources into defence.

General Unrest

The quintessentially Latin American phenomenon of the military coup and military government long preceded the invention of national security doctrine. Prior to the Second World War, military interventions usually aimed to return power to the military's civilian allies, or took place in response to threats against the military as an institution, such as government attempts to interfere in the promotion system or cut the military budget. However, with national security doctrine came not only the notion that government was a legitimate role for the military, but that squabbling civilian politicians were often less fit to govern than well-educated military men with only their country's interests at heart. When the Brazilian military took power in 1964, even the US ambassador expected them to hand over power to a suitable civilian government within the year. Instead they ruled for two decades. Only

> 'The evening of that mild spring day, Tuesday 11 September, General Augusto Pinochet had been in power for a few hours. The guests were assembled in the main hall of the Hotel Carrera, a sumptuous room three storeys high ... The new regime had decreed a curfew. The doors were barred.
>
> People sat around on the sofas or at the little copper-topped tables. They talked animatedly, the suave men and the elegant ladies. They laughed and joked and drank noisily, the sound of their celebration bouncing and echoing off the shiny walls. Every so often there was an expectant hush when the television came up with a *bando*, some new message from the new masters of Chile. When it was ended there were cheers, more champagne corks popped and from ladies' slippers toasts were drunk to Pinochet and his brave companions.
>
> In the corner the service door opened from time to time and groups of waiters peered timidly out. The juxtaposition of the stylish carousers and the apprehensive serving staff was dramatic and served like nothing else to bring home the social impact of the putsch above and beyond the patriotic and martial music that the radio and the television were broadcasting. The waiters and the rest of those below stairs knew what military rule was going to bring and they were afraid.'

O'Shaughnessy 1988

bitter experience and the wreck of several economies disposed of the myth of the military as competent economic managers.

In most cases, military coups take place with the support of at least a section of the civilian political leadership. In Chile Christian Democrat leader Patricio Aylwin openly supported the coup which brought General Pinochet to power in 1973, presumably hoping that once his socialist rival, President Salvador Allende, was removed, the army would then hand power to Aylwin's party before retiring to their barracks. Instead Pinochet kept power for himself and remained in the presidential palace for the next 17 years, until a chastened Aylwin led the campaign which secured his departure.

The military's willingness to interfere, and civilian leaders' readiness to encourage them, destabilised democratic civilian politics by offering politicians a short-cut to power which seemed more seductive than the prospect of long years in opposition. Parties no longer needed to succeed by developing sound policies to win more support than their rivals, but could gain power by currying favour with the high command. The art of conspiracy became the successful politician's chief weapon.

In many third world countries the military have suffered severe damage from meddling in politics. Power politicises the military as an institution, opening the way to factional rivalries and threatening the vertical discipline on which armies depend. Yet Latin American armies have resisted the corrosive impact of military rule better than most. In Argentina the army has had to alternate periods of rule with periods back in the barracks, when it has licked its wounds and restored its

INTERVIEW WITH GENERAL HARGUINDEGUY
Minister of the Interior in the first Argentina military junta, 1976-81

Childhood

'I come from an old cattle-ranching family. I went to school on our *estancia* with a private teacher along with the children of the farmhands. After four years they sent me to secondary school in Buenos Aires. The previous year the Argentine army had founded a new Military Institute, where young students could do their secondary studies at the same time as getting military instruction. The school was called Liceo General San Martín. Of the 280 kids who went that year, there were two future presidents — Alfonsín and Galtieri, two commanders-in-chief, ministers, brigadiers, admirals, generals, diplomats, surgeons, dentists.'

The Communist Threat

'We were being attacked, an attack that was just as dangerous as an attack from outside. If the Communist Party tried to take power in Britain and began to carry out attacks to annul democracy and the monarchy, if that group got to the stage when it overran the police, you too would send in the infantry battalions to keep your way of life. We intervened to save a way of life. Thanks to our intervention, Argentina remained a part of the free world. We didn't want another Cuba or Nicaragua in Argentina.

When a soldier is in combat, he thinks only of destroying the enemy, external or internal, in an undeclared war. In every war there are excesses of all kinds. Force cannot be measured. A bullet is a bullet. It kills or it doesn't kill. From the moment I sink a merchant ship with a torpedo; from the moment I bomb a city to rubble; from the moment I drop an atomic bomb on a city to make the enemy surrender unconditionally; from the moment that the resistance forces ambush the occupying forces, whether of left or right, they use any system or method and they don't take prisoners.'

The Armed Forces in Power

'We took power in 1976 because there was a political vacuum. Parliament was paralysed. I was a general in the first corps; many politicians came to see me, and I always said the same. "Mr Deputy, Senator, doctor, engineer, I'd like to hear you explain how you're going to replace the president by constitutional means, and yet you come here asking for a military coup — I don't need politicians for that, I have the guns!"

The replacement of a constitutional government by the armed forces was never an overnight decision of six generals. There has never been a coup that did not have the support of a large number of civilians, and their political leadership. There's always a situation of conflict beforehand, where rival groups of civilians pressurise the army to intervene.

The impact of power on the army is negative — it loses its professionalism. While it remains in the professional sphere, everyone falls in behind decisions taken by the high command. The armed forces are monolithic, vertical and totalitarian — when a commander gives an order, no-one argues, no-one votes. When the army enters politics, you get failures, divisions, internal fights, loss of prestige, and an enormous erosion. Generally it goes back to the barracks with much less power and internal cohesion to begin again and return to its proper legal function.

We suffered an enormous weakening in 1983, when the political failure of the last period of the government was combined with military defeat. We returned to the barracks ashamed, without prestige, defeated and divided. We even felt guilty for what had happened!'

cohesion by purging dissidents if necessary. Its continued survival has depended on its ability to give up power at the right time. Where armies have been totally destroyed by a revolution, as in Cuba or Nicaragua, it is partly because a military dictator has refused to preserve the army as an institution by giving up power. The resulting collapse of the military then paved the way for a revolutionary victory.

Despite the prevalent image of the Latin American military dictator as a barbarian in dark glasses, military regimes have varied enormously in both ideology and sophistication. In Peru and Panama, military leaders carried out reforms which gave out land to the poor and improved the lives of the workforce, while in Chile and Argentina they did the exact opposite. Generals Pinochet and Stroessner could have stepped out of the pages of Gabriel García Márquez's *Autumn of the Patriarch*, whereas military regimes in Brazil and Uruguay insisted on rotating the presidency to prevent any one officer acquiring absolute power. Increasingly, the military junta (committee) replaced the individual *caudillo*.

Peru 1968-75

The Peruvian military developed a much more reform-oriented strain of national security doctrine than other Latin American armies. They believed that the Peruvian elite was blocking reforms which were essential to the nation's economic progress, and were therefore creating the conditions for violent revolution. A 1963 document from the Peruvian Centre for Higher Military Studies commented:

> The sad and desperate truth is that in Peru, the real powers are not the Executive, the Legislative, the Judicial or the Electoral, but the large landowners, the exporters, the bankers and the American investor.

In 1968 General Juan Velasco seized power, promising sweeping reforms. Within months his government nationalised the property of the US transnational, International Petroleum Company, and began a radical land reform. These two measures marked the high point of military radicalism in Peru. Soon the government became engulfed in economic crisis and internal divisions, and just before Velasco's death in 1975, a conservative faction within the military seized power. However Velasco's reforms left a radically altered rural society, where the feudal powers of the hacienda owners had in many cases been destroyed for ever.

Brazil 1964-85

The Brazilian military seized power just as Brazil's attempt to industrialise through import substitution was running out of steam. By cutting real wages (by 35-40 per cent in the first four years of the government), opening the economy to foreign investors and transnational companies, and investing massively in state companies and economic infrastructure, they succeeded in re-galvanising the Brazilian economy. Yet although growth reduced dependency on commodity exports and developed a thriving manufactured exports sector, it failed to reduce inequality within Brazil. Furthermore, economic growth was only achieved at the cost of greatly increased control of the economy by transnational companies and an enormous foreign debt. The 1974 oil shock and the debt crisis of the 1980s severely undermined the economy and led to the military's long and orderly retreat from power. In 1985 a civilian president, José Sarney, took office.

Argentina 1976-83

In 1976, the Argentine army once again launched a coup to overthrow the chaotic regime of Isabel Perón, which was collapsing beneath an economic crisis and guerrilla war. Several years of cruel army repression ensued, during which thousands of people disappeared. The junta pursued a free-market economic model, encouraging imports to compete with inefficient local industries. The result was massive capital flight and the collapse of much of Argentine industry. In 1982 President Leopoldo Galtieri tried to fend off rising protest at the economic crisis by launching an invasion of the disputed Falklands/Malvinas islands. The military's defeat led to a humiliating retreat from power and the jailing of many of the junta's main leaders.

Chile 1973-90

In 1973 General Augusto Pinochet overthrew the elected left-wing government of Salvador Allende, ending an unbroken period of 51 years of civilian rule. The coup began a traumatic period of repression and persecution as the military moved to stamp out all voices of protest. Pinochet pursued an aggressively monetarist free market model, cutting subsidies and price controls, privatising state companies, allowing a flood of cheap imports which bankrupted local industries and encouraging different agro-exports to help reduce the country's dependence on copper.

Pinochet's rule began to unravel as street protests began once again in 1983. In 1988, he lost a plebiscite intended to consolidate his rule for a further eight years, and was forced to hold elections in December 1989, where his candidate was defeated by the opposition coalition.

A few countries in Latin America managed to buck the continental trend and avoid military dictatorships from the 1960s onwards. Foremost among them were Mexico, where the ruling Institutional Revolutionary Party (PRI) established control over the army in the early years of the Mexican Revolution, and Venezuela where after 1958 oil wealth enabled the Venezuelan elite to buy off a military which had previously been an almost permanent resident at the presidential palace.

Costa Rica has succeeded in ridding itself of its military altogether. After a brief civil war in 1948, Costa Rica's rival political parties agreed to abolish the army. Free of the military burden, Costa Rica now has a much higher standard of living than its Central American neighbours. However, thanks to US guns and training, the Costa Rican police force has recently started to look remarkably similar to a normal army! In Bolivia the revolution of 1952 also radically weakened the army, but within four years the government had agreed to re-establish the armed forces as a condition for a vital $25m loan from the International Monetary Fund. By 1964 the generals were back in power.

Retreat from the Palace

Just as the nature of military regimes has varied enormously between different Latin American countries, so has the way they handed over power to elected governments. In many cases, the outgoing military government tried to cover its retreat by passing legislation giving its officers immunity from prosecution over human rights violations. Success in achieving immunity depended on the strength of military unity during the withdrawal to the barracks and the pressure exerted by the civilian opposition. The military regimes in Brazil and Uruguay both managed an orderly exit, not only acquiring immunity for crimes committed in government, but retaining considerable political power. In some ways the civilian regimes in those countries are better described as post-military, rather than civilian or fully democratic.

In Chile, General Pinochet also tried to protect himself and his men from prosecution and spent his first months out of office in constant disputes with President Aylwin over the government's attempts to investigate past human rights abuses. A year after Aylwin's inauguration, the government-appointed 'National Commission for Truth and Reconciliation', released its report, documenting more than 2,000 killings by the security forces during the period of military rule. Pinochet responded in typical style, saying, 'the Chilean army certainly sees no reason to ask pardon for having fulfilled its patriotic duty'. During the post-Pinochet months Chile went through a cathartic process of self-discovery. Santiago was alive with bookshops and street vendors hawking the latest best-selling book of investigative journalism about human rights abuses under the old dictator.

The Argentine military's humiliation in the Falklands/Malvinas war gave the incoming Alfonsín government the chance to waive immunity, and in 1985 five military leaders including President Videla were found guilty and given long prison sentences. Alfonsín thus achieved a Latin American first — never before had officers of a defeated military dictatorship been brought to trial. But the civilian government stopped short of abolishing or radically restructuring the military, and by early 1987 the soldiers were up to their old tricks, as young officers threatened with human rights prosecutions mutinied during Easter Week. The government's resolve weakened; it brought a halt to further prosecutions and began to release those already found guilty. After a year in jail, General Harguindeguy could return to his ranch and his town flat over the Avenida Santa Fé. By the end of 1990 a new president, Peronist Carlos Menem, had freed the last of the imprisoned officers.

Given Latin America's history, it would be rash to predict that its experience of military government has come to an end. In 1990 alone there were military uprisings in Guatemala, Panama, and Argentina, although they all fell short of overthrowing the government. In any case, the military retain an extraordinary level of power and influence in many civilian-led countries, giving them a virtual power of veto over the decisions of government. In such circumstances, a simple distinction between civilian democracy and military dictatorship becomes extremely misleading.

In this century the US must take its share of the blame for militarising Latin American politics. All too often, Washington has preferred a pro-US military dictator to a non-aligned or left-wing elected civilian, and US agencies such as the Central Intelligence Agency have frequently been involved in helping the local military overthrow elected governments like that of Salvador Allende in Chile in 1973. In the 1990s Washington appears to have turned over a new leaf, favouring civilian governments as better guarantors of development and economic stability. It remains to be seen, however, whether this policy will continue indefinitely or whether the US may not again turn to Latin America's military in the name of regional stability.

The civilian regimes of the 1980s have survived the economic battering inflicted by the debt crisis far longer than many predicted. Yet by presiding over a period of recession and hunger, they have destroyed much of Latin America's hope that democracy would bring better times. Amid the growing disillusionment, the danger is that political instability could once again spark a round of military coups, and that the unmarked Ford Falcons may return to prowl the streets of Buenos Aires.

Into the Sixth Century

The 500th anniversary of Columbus' first arrival in the Americas falls on 12 October 1992. The quincentenary has provoked controversy on both sides of the Atlantic. The Spanish government has organised multi-million dollar celebrations around the theme 'the meeting of two worlds', which have been severely criticised by many Latin Americans as celebrating the beginnings of a process of cultural and physical extermination of native Americans, and of the economic exploitation of the continent. Below we reprint some reflections on the quincentenary by Latin Americans:

Eduardo Galeano, Uruguay

Since the end of the 15th century, Latin America has suffered endless plunder. They have stolen the gold, the silver, the copper, the oil, the rubber, but they've also stolen our memory. At least they tried to, and to a certain extent they have succeeded, but I have a deep faith in the ability of the collective memory to survive ...

The owners of power have tried to lock history away in the museums. They have embalmed it to prevent it becoming dangerous, so that it neither breathes nor laughs. I believe we have to help recover history's living breath. At the moment history is the prisoner of museums, of speeches about trivia, of the deceitful versions of official history. But, there is another underground history which the oppressed people of the earth have managed to keep alive, and that's what interests me because that is real. There they could be drawing the features of the true face of Latin America.

'We must recover the historical memory of Latin America', *América: La Patria Grande*, Mexico, September 1988

Augusto Roa Bastos, Paraguay

We still have to discover a world of unity in a community of nations. Columbus did not realise that he had discovered the New World. We know that this world exists as potential, and that we must help to build it. It does not matter how long it takes. The great enterprises of peace, liberty, democratic solidarity are forged over generations. As a new millenium is about to begin, Latin America faces in its entirety the interrupted process of its emancipation, the construction of a second independence in the structures of an effective pluralist democracy which will allow us to participate actively in a responsible and equal way in tomorrow's world. Between the utopian and the real, that is the challenge of history. Or, which is the same thing, the challenge of the future.

'El Controvertido V Centenario', *El País Internacional*, Madrid, 24 June, 1991

Ignacio Ellacuría, El Salvador

We do not want to fight over what happened five centuries ago, but rather to use that experience to say to them — above all to the North Americans, and partly also the Europeans, that their present treatment of Latin America and the Third World has not changed much over the last five centuries.

What has happened in these last five centuries is the domination of some peoples, some cultures, some languages and some religions. Therefore, to my way of thinking, our task in the fifth centenary, and in all those that follow, is to achieve a liberation.

'Quinto Centenario América Latina', *SPES*, Lima, January 1990

Father Ellacuría was Rector of the Central American University, San Salvador, until his murder by the Salvadorean army in November 1989

Elena Poniatowska, Mexico

In Latin America, millions and millions of people, the subjects of a dominant power which has taken over their natural resources, are together looking for a new road, that of unity. We must unite to avoid disappearing, to stop being exploited, to help each other, to develop on our own our enormous potential and resources and manufacture our own consumer goods.

And liberation is for everyone, we don't want to be peoples without memory, uniting doesn't invalidate us, it doesn't weaken each person's character. On the contrary, once we have sorted out our economy and technological backwardness, we can tend our garden, our common garden, the enormous continental garden which will then flourish.

Together we will weave our integration, the gigantic cloak over Bolívar's shoulders, the cloak over our own shoulders

'Memory and Identity', *América: La Patria Grande*, Mexico, April 1989

Further Reading

Chapter 1: The Curse of Wealth: The Commodity Trade

John Crabtree, Gavan Duffy and Jenny Pearce, *The Great Tin Crash: Bolivia and the World Tin Market*, London, Latin America Bureau, 1987

Eduardo Galeano, *Open Veins of Latin America*, New York, Monthly Review Press, 1973

Nick Rowling, *Commodities: How the World Was Taken to Market*, London, Free Association Books, 1987

Chapter 2: Promised Land: Land Ownership, Power and Conflict

Tom Barry, *Roots of Rebellion: Land and Hunger in Central America*, Boston, South End Press, 1987

Sue Branford and Oriel Glock, *The Last Frontier: Fighting Over Land in the Amazon*, London, Zed Books, 1985

Roger Burbach and Patricia Flynn, *Agribusiness in the Americas*, New York, Monthly Review Press, 1980

Joseph Collins, *Nicaragua: What Difference Could a Revolution Make?: Food and Farming in the New Nicaragua*, San Francisco, Institute for Food and Development Policy, 1985

Alan Gilbert, *Latin America*, London, Routledge, 1990

Chapter 3: A Land in Flames: The Environment

Adrian Cowell, *The Decade of Destruction*, London, Hodder & Stoughton, 1990

Susanna Hecht and Alexander Cockburn, *The Fate of the Forest: Developers, Destroyers and Defenders of the Amazon*, London, Penguin, 1990

Chico Mendes, *Fight for the Forest: Chico Mendes in His Own Words*, London, Latin America Bureau, 1989

Chapter 4: Mean Streets: Migration and Life in the City

Alan Gilbert, *Latin America*, London, Routledge, 1990

Carolina Maria de Jesus, *Beyond All Pity: The Diary of Carolina María de Jesus*, London, Earthscan Publications, 1990

Patrick McAuslan, *Urban Land and Shelter for the Poor*, London, Earthscan Publications, 1985

Peter Ward, *Mexico City*, London, Belhaven Press, 1990

Hernando de Soto, *The Other Path*, London, IB Tauris, 1989

Environment and Urbanization, biannual magazine, London, International Institute for Environment and Development

Chapter 5: Growing Pains: Industrialisation and the Debt Crisis

Rosemary Bromley and Ray Bromley, *South American Development:*

A Geographical Introduction, Cambridge, Cambridge University Press, 1988

Tessa Cubitt, *Latin American Society*, London, Longman, 1988

Susan George, *A Fate Worse than Debt*, London, Penguin, 1988

Jackie Roddick, *The Dance of the Millions: Latin America and the Debt Crisis, London*, Latin America Bureau, 1988

Chapter 6: Writing on the Wall: Culture, Identity and Politics

Oriana Baddeley and Valerie Fraser, *Drawing the Line: Art and Cultural Identity in Contemporary Latin America*, London, Verso, 1989

Gabriel García Márquez, *One Hundred Years of Solitude*, London, Picador, 1978

Alma Guillermoprieto, *Samba*, London, Bloomsbury, 1990

John King, *Magical Reels: A History of Cinema in Latin America*, London, Verso, 1990

William Rowe and Vivian Schelling, *Memory and Modernity: Popular Culture in Latin America*, London, Verso, 1991

Chapter 7: Party Pieces: Democracy and Politics

Tessa Cubitt, *Latin American Society*, London, Longman, 1988

Phil Gunson, Andrew Thompson and Greg Chamberlain, *The Dictionary of Contemporary Politics of South America*, London, Routledge, 1989

Phil Gunson, Andrew Thompson and Greg Chamberlain, *The Dictionary of Contemporary Politics of Central America and the Caribbean*, London, Routledge, 1991

George Pendle, *A History of Latin America*, London, Pelican, 1976

Chapter 8: The Left: Guerrillas and Social Movements

Omar Cabezas, *Fire from the Mountain: The Making of a Sandinista*, New York, Plume, 1985

Che Guevara, *Che Guevara and the Cuban Revolution: Writings and Speeches of Ernesto Che Guevara*, Sydney, Pathfinder, 1987

Phil Gunson, Andrew Thompson and Greg Chamberlain, *The Dictionary of Contemporary Politics of South America*, London, Routledge, 1989

Phil Gunson, Andrew Thompson and Greg Chamberlain, *The Dictionary of Contemporary Politics of Central America and the Caribbean*, London, Routledge, 1991

Hugh O'Shaughnessy, *Latin Americans*, London, BBC Books, 1988

Jenny Pearce, *Promised Land: Peasant Rebellion in Chalatenango, El Salvador*, London, Latin America Bureau, 1986

Report on the Americas, bimonthly magazine, New York, NACLA

Chapter 9: Women's Work: Gender and Politics

Audrey Bronstein, *Triple Struggle: Latin American Peasant Women*, London, WoW Campaigns, 1982

Elizabeth Jelin (ed), *Women and Social Change in Latin America*, London, Zed Books, 1990

June Nash and Helen Safa, *Women and Change in Latin America*,

New York, Bergin and Garvey, 1986
June Nash and Helen Safa, *Sex and Class in Latin America*, New York, Bergin and Garvey, 1980

Chapter 10: Race Against Time: Indigenous Peoples

Elisabeth Burgos-Debray (ed), *I, Rigoberta Menchú: An Indian Woman in Guatemala*, London, Verso, 1984
Bartolomé de las Casas, *In Defense of the Indians*, Illinois, De Kalb, 1974
Roxanne Dunbar Ortiz, *Indians of the Americas: Human Rights and Self-Determination*, London, Zed Books, 1984
David Treece, *Bound in Misery and Iron: The Impact of the Grande Carajas Programme on the Indians of Brazil*, London, Survival International, 1987
The Amerindians of South America, London, Minority Rights Group, 1987

Chapter 11: Thy Kingdom Come: The Church

Trevor Beeson and Jenny Pearce, *A Vision of Hope: The Churches and Change in Latin America*, London, Fount Paperbacks, 1984
Sara Diamond, *Spiritual Warfare: The Politics of the Christian Right*, London, Pluto Press, 1989
Penny Lernoux, *Cry of the People*, London, Penguin, 1982
David Martin, *Tongues of Fire: The Explosion of Protestantism in Latin America*, Oxford, Basil Blackwell, 1990

Chapter 12: Men at Arms: The Military

Ronaldo Munck, *Latin America: The Transition to Democracy*, London, Zed Books, 1989
George Philip, *The Military in South American Politics*, London, Croom Helm, 1985
Total War Against the Poor: Confidential Documents of the 17th Conference of American Armies, New York, Circus Publications, 1990

Index

65; industry and debt 72, 75; culture 85; politics 102, 104, 106, 108, 110, 115; left 119, 125, 128, 130; women 144, 147, 148; Indians 156, 159, 163, 165; church 174; army 188, 189, 190

colonisation 31, 32, 36, 38, 163, 167

Columbus, Christopher 4, 8, 100, 154, 157, 158, 167, 171, 172, 203

commodities — boom-bust cycles 10-11, 16-8; dependence 16, 70

exports 69, 70, 81, 108; prices 4, 16, 75, 76, 77

communal land ownership 22, 23, 25, 32, 158, 159, 162, 167

Communist Party 112, 113, 122, 123, 128, 129, 130, 147, 151

Conquest, Spanish 6, 8, 22, 23, 24, 37, 38, 85, 86, 87, 91, 92, 155, 157, 163, 174, 188

conquistadores 5, 23-4, 90, 92, 171

conscientización 175

Conservatives 106, 108, 110, 173, 174

contraceptives 140, 142, 143

Contras 34, 114, 130, 184, 186, 196

copper 6, 81, 103, 200, 203

Cortázar, Julio 97

Cortés, Hernán 154, 156, 171

Costa Rica 46, 50, 72, 80, 112, 142, 144, 148, 182, 188, 201

cotton 6, 7, 44, 45, 148

counter-insurgency 126, 131, 154, 161, 183, 196

Cristiani, Alfredo 111

Cuba — land 22, 33, 34; 57, 66, 96; politics 102, 103, 113; 125; women 138, 143, 144, 147; 173; army 188, 189, 198 Cuban revolution 33, 34, 84, 94, 95, 97, 112, 118, 122, 130, 131, 151, 174, 186, 199

dams 43, 45, 46-48, 50, 74

death squads 7, 31, 98, 105, 135, 178

debt — 73, 74, 77, 78, 79, 80; burden 46, 50; crisis 38, 68, 69, 76, 80, 103, 116, 181, 200; interest payments 68, 75; rescheduling 75, 104; swaps 50

deforestation 31, 38, 39, 42, 46, 47

de las Casas, Bartolomé 172

dictators 186, 188, 199

disappearances 150, 187, 195

Dominican Republic 78, 122, 172

Duarte, José Napoleon 111

Ecuador 24, 32, 50, 55, 72, 110, 148, 156, 159, 173, 190

EEC 47

EGP (Guatemala) 129

Ellacuría, Father Ignacio 195, 203

ELN (Colombia) 128, 175

El Salvador — commodities 7, 10, 15, 16; land 22, 31, 33; environment 43, 44; urbanisation 55, 56, 60; industry and debt 72; culture 91; politics 103, 105, 111, 112, 113, 115; left 120, 126, 128, 130, 131, 135; women 144, 146, 148, 149, 150; church 171, 178, 179, 180; army 191, 192, 196; 203

encomienda 22, 24, 158, 171

EPL (Colombia) 128

ERP (El Salvador) 129

Escobar, Pablo 19

Europe 6-8, 10, 11, 13, 16, 18, 56, 63, 68, 70, 77, 80, 81, 85, 92, 100, 115, 131, 142, 147, 151, 158, 160, 172, 174, 203

evangelicals (see also protestants) 174, 181, 184

exports 7, 16, 24, 73, 75, 76

extractive reserves 42, 167, 168

Falklands/Malvinas 99, 192, 200, 201

FAO 38

FAR (Guatemala) 129

FARC (Colombia) 128

Financial Times 19, 80, 81

FMLN (El Salvador) 105, 118, 120, 121, 128

folk Catholicism 160, 174

folk magic 89, 160

football 93, 94

foquismo 118, 122, 125, 126

foreign capital 24, 26, 29, 68, 73, 82, 200

Forest Peoples' Alliance (Brazil) 167

FPL (El Salvador) 126, 128

France 10, 47, 196

Frei, Eduardo 111

free trade 17, 72, 82, 200

Fuentes, Carlos 85, 94, 97

Fujimori, Alberto 84, 94, 113, 116

Galán, Luis Carlos 19

Galeano, Eduardo 203

Galtieri, General 198, 200

García, Alan 110

García Márquez, Gabriel 84, 85, 89, 97, 98, 107, 188, 199

Germany 10, 11, 70, 82, 195, 196

global warming 40

gold 4, 8, 9, 10, 36, 37, 43, 48, 49, 157, 172, 203

grain 8, 10, 13, 30, 70

Grande Carajas 36, 46, 48

Grant, President Ulysses S. 17, 82

Great Depression 4, 51, 69, 70, 108, 116

Grenada 196

Guatemala — land 23, 27, 33, 34; 45; 55, 56; 72; 86; 112, 113; left 123, 125, 129; women 142, 143, 148, 150; Indians 154, 159, 160, 161, 166, 168; church 170, 182, 184; army 190, 191, 202

guerrillas 31, 103, 105, 106, 112, 114, 115, 120-3, 125-130, 171, 174, 175, 186, 192, 200

Guevara, Che 93, 97, 118, 120, 122, 123, 125, 126

Guyana 38, 56

Guzman, Abimael 127, 130

haciendas 24-6, 31, 32, 171, 172, 200

Haya de la Torre, Víctor Raúl 112

Hispanics 59, 96

homosexuality 144

Honduras 12, 15, 55, 56, 57, 72, 134, 148, 159, 173

human rights 81, 94, 119, 131, 170, 170, 175, 178, 186, 193, 196, 201, 202

Ibañez, Carlos 108

imports 11, 66, 78, 81

— substitution 16, 17, 70-2, 81

Incas 5, 23, 90, 154, 156, 159, 165, 174, 188

independence 4, 10, 26, 69, 92, 102, 108, 121, 157,

158, 170, 172, 186, 188, 189
indigo 10, 16
Indians 145, 154, 160, 161, 171, highland 159, 163, 166, 167, 168 lowland 159, 162, 163, 167; — and, commodities 4, 5, 6, 8, 15, 16; land 22, 23, 24, 25, 27, 32, 33; environment 37, 40, 45, 47; urbanisation 59; culture 85, 86, 87, 88, 92, 100; politics 112; left 125
industrialisation 7, 17, 36, 37, 42, 51, 54, 68, 69, 70, 71, 72, 73, 81, 102, 108
informal sector 64-66, 78, 145
International Coffee Agreement 4, 17
International Monetary Fund 75, 76, 77-81, 103, 104, 116, 148, 201
Institutional Revolutionary Party (PRI) (Mexico) 81, 102, 106, 115, 116, 200
Israel 191, 196
Itaipú 36, 46

Japan 6, 11, 47, 69, 70, 77, 79, 81, 82, 131, 146
Jara, Victor 84
Jaramillo, Bernardo 105

Kayapo Indians 49, 50, 86, 154, 159, 168
Kennedy, President 33

labour 7, 16, 37, 81, 158, seasonal 28, women 141-8
land — communal 22; distribution 26, 27, 62; grants 24; invasions 60, 61, 119, 134, 135; ownership 7, 23, 24, 25, 147, 159; reform 22, 31, 32, 33, 34, 43, 44, 52, 62, 66, 147, 199; tenure 30
Latin America Free Trade Association 72
Liberals 106, 108, 110, 173
liberation theology 175, 194
Lima 54, 55, 58, 61, 65, 94, 98, 115, 161
literacy 143, 144, 152
Lispector, Clarice 99
Lula (Luis Inâcio da Silva) 115, 136
Lutzenberger, José 36, 41

M-19 (Colombia) 126, 128
machismo 139, 140, 144, 147
magical realism 89
maize 8, 16, 24, 26, 30, 39, 43, 159
malnutrition 78, 140
Mapuche 157
maquila 81
Mariátegui, José Carlos 130
Marxism 102, 111, 128, 194, 195, 196
Maya 37, 156, 159, 182
Medellín 58, 170, 175, 178
megaprojects 47, 74
Menem, Carlos Saúl 110, 202
Mendes, Chico 36, 41, 42, 43, 104, 167
Mexico — commodities 4, 7, 13, 14, 15, 16; land 22, 24, 26, 28-30, 31-4; environment 38, 40, 51; urbanisation 55; industry and debt 68, 70, 72, 74, 75, 77, 79-81; culture 82, 85, 87, 93, 95, 96, 99; politics 102, 106, 107, 112, 115; left 122, 133; women 145, 146, 147, 148; Indians 154, 159; church 170, 171, 172, 173; army 188, 200
Mexico City 51, 52, 54, 61, 64, 156
Mexican revolution 32, 34, 84, 92, 118, 121, 173, 191, 201

migration 51, 52, 55, 56, 64
military 6, 31, 105, 106, 110, 113, 115, 121, 131, 133, 135, 166; coups 22, 29, 33, 81, 94, 98, 102, 106, 196-8, 202; governments 45, 59, 61, 72, 93, 96, 103, 115, 116, 123, 150, 176, 187, 196, 201, 202; schools 186, 190, 191, 193, 198
mining 5-7, 12, 15, 16, 20, 24, 42, 45, 46-9, 87, 88, 148, 158, 167, 172
mita 6, 24, 158, 165
Montoneros (Argentina) 112, 121, 126
Mothers of the Disappeared 138, 150, 187
MRTA (Peru) 130
MST (Brazil) 119
multinationals 11-4, 26, 27, 30, 31, 44, 47, 50, 52, 65, 69, 70, 200

national security doctrine 186, 193, 195, 196, 199
nationalisation 13, 30
neoliberalism 81, 82
Neruda, Pablo 94
Nicaragua — commodities 15, 16; land 22, 33, 34; environment 43, 44, 45; industry and debt 72; culture 84, 93, 99; politics 106, 114, 115; left 118, 125, 135; women 140, 143, 148; Indians 159; church 171, 173, 180-2, 184; army 186, 195, 198
Nicaraguan revolution 34, 98, 112, 113, 118, 121, 127, 130, 131, 138, 151, 196, 199
nitrates 11
Noriega, General Manuel Antonio 191
North American Free Trade Area 68

oil 4, 5, 6, 9, 13-5, 37, 73, 163, 200, 203
OPEC 13, 73, 75
'option for the poor' 170, 178, 194
Orozco, José Clemente 92
ORPA (Guatemala) 129

Padilla, Heberto 84, 98
Panama 39, 40, 54, 72, 100, 110, 112, 148, 159, 173, 186, 191, 195, 199, 202
Paraguay 15, 36, 46, 55, 56, 57, 59, 61, 68, 72, 75, 82, 103, 109, 110, 138, 148, 172, 191
Paz, Octavio 94
PCN (El Salvador) 113
PCS (El Salvador) 129
PDVSA (Venezuela) 14
peasant farming 9, 16, 18, 19, 25-8, 31, 39, 43, 46, 65, 66, 133, 147, 160
Pemex 14
Pentecostals (see also evangelicals) 180-2, 184
Pérez, Carlos Andres 78
Perón, Evita 109, 140, 149
Perón, Isabel 200
Perón, Juan Domingo 93, 102, 109, 110, 112, 149
Peronists 116
Peru — commodities 10, 11, 13, 15, 18; land 23, 24, 26, 32, 34; environment 38, 50; urbanisation 55, 59, 65; industry and debt 72, 79, 82; culture 84; politics 105, 110, 112, 115, 126, 127; women 140, 142, 148; Indians 156, 159, 161, 166, 168; army 189, 199
pesticides 37, 43, 45

NEW BOOKS FROM THE LATIN AMERICA BUREAU

Columbus: His Enterprise — Hans Koning

Reveals the personality and motivation of a man who accidentally found a continent and changed the course of history.

"Makes fascinating reading... should be compulsory." Christopher Hill, *New York Review of Books*

"The book is an idea that has finally found its time." *Publishers Weekly*

1991(UK edition)   144 pages ISBN 0 906156 60 2   £5.75

Published in the USA by Monthly Review Press

Brazil: War on Children — Gilberto Dimenstein

First-hand reportage, interviews and statistics paint a powerful picture of life for Brazil's eight million street children.

"An outstanding piece of investigative journalism and required reading for those who think Brazil is experiencing an 'economic miracle'."
Planet News

1991   100 pages ISBN 0 906156 62 9   £5.75

Panama: Made in the USA — John Weeks and Phil Gunson

Explores the unanswered questions behind the invasion of December 1989 and the challenges facing the US-installed Endarra government.

"This is one of the finest investigations about American complicity in Latin America I have read. Essential reading..." John Pilger

"A succinct and informed analysis of the invasion, its background and its aftermath. Timely... and instructive." Noam Chomsky

1991   150 pages ISBN 0 906156 55 6   £5.75

Dominican Republic: Beyond the Lighthouse — James Ferguson

As the Dominican Republic prepares to celebrate the 1992 Columbus anniversary with the inauguration of a US$250m commemorative lighthouse, this book looks at a country where extreme poverty exists alongside a booming tourist industry.

February 1992   150 pages ISBN 0 906156 64 5   £6.75

Prices are for paperback editions by post from the Latin America Bureau, 1 Amwell Street, London EC1R 1UL. Complete list of LAB books available on request.

LAB books are distributed in North America by Monthly Review Press, 122 West 27 Street, New York, NY10001.

LAB is a UK subscription agent for NACLA Report on the Americas, the largest English language magazine on Latin America and the Caribbean. Write to LAB for details.

The Latin America Bureau is a small, independent, non-profit-making research organisation established in 1977. LAB is concerned with human rights and related social, political and economic issues in Central and South America and the Caribbean. We carry out research and publish books, publicise and lobby, and work with Latin American and Caribbean support groups. We also brief the media, run a small documentation centre and produce materials for teachers.